THE ROOTS OF VIOLENCE

Fr. Vincent P. Miceli, S.J.

The
ROOTS OF
VIOLENCE

Abridged edition

SOPHIA INSTITUTE PRESS
Manchester, New Hampshire

Sophia Institute Press
Box 5284, Manchester, NH 03108
1-800-888-9344
www.SophiaInstitute.com

Sophia Institute Press® is a registered trademark of Sophia Institute.

paperback ISBN 978-1-64413-898-4

ebook ISBN 978-1-64413-899-1

Library of Congress Control Number: 2023938904

First printing

To Fr. Joseph F. Costanzo, S.J.
By the goodness of God
Priest, Professor, Prophet of Truth
Brilliant Defender of Humanae Vitae
Profound Teacher of Constitutional law
Author, whose original works
Have enlightened and inspired
His students, confreres, readers,
This Work is dedicated
With affection and admiration
By the Author, his grateful disciple.

Then Jesus saith to him:
"Put up again thy sword into its place:
for all that take the sword shall
perish with the sword."

—Matthew 26:52

Contents

The Roots of Violence

INTRODUCTION

We are living in an era whose atmosphere is saturated with the flames of hatred. It is an age of violence whose tempo of disruption is so rapidly escalating that there is scarcely a city, anywhere in the world, where humans can be assured of normal, physical security. It is an age of irrational aggressivity. Pope St. John Paul II, a spiritual leader dedicated to peace, was first gunned down and nearly killed in Rome, and then attacked by a bayonet-wielding priest in Fatima, Portugal; in Washington, D.C., the newly elected president of the United States was felled by gunfire; in Cairo, a presidential states-man, winner of the Nobel Peace Prize for his successful efforts in attaining peace between Egypt and Israel in the inflamed Middle East, was assassinated. Within the totalitarian nations, the litany of the liquidated has risen to such astronomical figures that only God knows the exact number. Within the so-called Christian nations of the West, the myriad millions of helpless, innocent children murdered in their mothers' wombs boggles the imagination. The violence-explosion is so horrifying that it stupefies the minds of men all over the world. Indeed, hundreds of thousands have already constructed underground survival hideaways to escape what they see will arrive in the near future—the Age of Violence Unlimited.

The Roots of Violence

Future historians—provided nuclear war does not usher in doomsday and obliterate the future—will be sorely taxed to explain the unparalleled, international crescendo of savage assaults in all forms of intimidation, vandalism, kidnapping, hijacking, bodily brutality, and guerrilla massacres against persons and institutions. For the explosion of violence represents a demonic reality similar to a hydra-headed serpent. It is a persistent, ever-increasing plague with many sources and causes. Indeed, the apologists for the new barbarism are not only, nor even primarily, demoniacally sick individuals, but rather often intelligent, organized groups who have raised nihilistic anarchism to the status of a religion whose fundamental dogma seems to be "I kill, therefore I am."

Inspired and sustained by this metaphysic of murder, centers of organized revolution have mushroomed in every nation. They seem bent on demonstrating the truth of Oscar Wilde's aphorism: "Moderation is a fatal thing. Nothing succeeds like excess." Moreover, they enthusiastically strive to experience both the subject and object of Shakespeare's truism: "Violent delights have violent ends."

But perhaps some may think that I am being an irrational alarmist, that I am exaggerating the ferocity, the degradation, and the spreading crescendo of violent crime. Commenting on the fact that in ten days recently New York City recorded seventy-four homicides, Det. James Ray, who works in Harlem, said, "The sad fact is we have very little regard for human life here, and we seem to be getting less all the time." How explain the mark of Cain, the first fratricide, that scars our generation? Let me first cite here a very recent example of the revolting phenomenon of violence that has now added the dimension of humiliating and degrading victims by forcing them to perform actions which destroy the dignity, privacy, and mystery of their most intimate relationships. These horrible, disgusting crimes took place on Long Island, Nassau County, New

York, on May 29, 1982. One hundred innocent persons fell victim to a group of six gun-toting sadists. Here is the report of the crime as narrated by the *New York Daily News* for Sunday, May 30, 1982.

> Police arrested three gang members who, authorities said, had forced their way into a family party ... and later raided a restaurant ... terrorizing more than 100 people in a spree of robbery, rape, sexual abuse, gunplay, and beatings. The first of the violent Nassau County raids occurred at 12:30 a.m. when five or six thugs, all heavily armed and none masked, forced their way into the Plainview home of Thomas and Janet Reilly. The Reillys were giving a party for their children and their children's friends. In twenty minutes of terror, the gunmen herded the Reillys and their guests into one floor of the split-level house and ordered the twenty victims to undress and lie on the floor. While some intruders rifled [through] the victims' clothing and ransacked the house, others sexually abused several female guests....
>
> The second raid occurred at 1:30 a.m. in the Sea Crest Diner on Glen Cove Road, Old Westbury, about four miles from the Reilly home. Six to eight gunmen, one carrying a rifle, walked into the Sea Crest, announced a stickup, and herded workers, waitresses, and seventy-five patrons into one of three dining areas. Many couples among the patrons were forced to disrobe, lie on the floor, and have sex while one of their captors, a six-foot-two man armed with two pistols, watched and laughed. Two men were shot in the buttocks when they hesitated. One gunman forced a twenty-three-year old woman into another room, where he raped her in front of six or eight other victims. Other

robbers sexually abused several women after the gunmen had collected their cash and valuables. As the violence continued for forty-five minutes, several people arrived at the restaurant, parked their cars and walked in, only to become victims. The restaurant had no windows that would have permitted the newcomers to see what was going on. Nicholas Boulaukas, forty-six, the proprietor of the restaurant, was pistol-whipped. He was reported in stable condition in Nassau Hospital with fractured facial bones. Finally, the Sea Crest robbers left, carrying shopping bags full of loot. Officials estimated that the robbers took $100,000 in cash and jewels from the Reilly's house and the restaurant.[1]

It is said that "the first casualty of war is truth," as both sides begin to blare out their propaganda. Unfortunately, men do not yet realize that the first casualties of violence are both truth and security. For the majority of people take violence for granted, looking on it merely as an ugly fact of life. And politicians use violence as a propaganda ploy to solicit votes and thereby gain the prize of political power. Seldom, indeed, do public servants or academic savants attempt to plumb the metaphysical and theological roots of violence. Yet we are all well aware of the tremendous role of violence in the unfolding of human events. Hence, it is essential to know the truth about the nature and causes of violence. Hannah Arendt writes in her book *On Violence:*

> No one engaged in thought about history and politics can remain unaware of the enormous role violence has always played in human affairs, and it is, at first glance, rather surprising that violence has been singled out so seldom for

[1] *New York Daily News*, May 30, 1982.

special consideration. (In the last edition of the Encyclope-
dia of the Social Sciences, "violence" does not even rate an
entry.) This shows to what an extent violence"—and its arbitrariness—are taken for granted and therefore neglected;
no one questions or examines what is obvious to all. Those
who saw nothing but violence in human affairs, convinced
that they were "always haphazard, not serious, nor precise"
([Ernest] Renan) or that God was forever with the bigger
battalions, had nothing more to say about either violence
or history. Anybody looking for some kind of sense in the
records of the past was almost bound to see violence as a
marginal phenomenon. Whether it is [Karl von] Clausewitz
calling war "the continuation of politics by other means,"
or [Friedrich] Engels defining violence as the accelerator
of economic development, the emphasis is on political or
economic continuity, on the continuity of a process that
remains determined by what preceded violent action.[2]

Jean-Paul Sartre, atheistic existentialist philosopher, goes to
great lengths in glorifying violence when he writes that "irrepress-
ible violence … is man recreating himself," that it is through "mad
fury" that "the wretched of the earth" can "become men." Moreover, he confirms his faith in violence in these words: "Violence,
like Achilles' lance, can heal the wounds it has inflicted."[3] In his
book *Reflections on Violence*, George Sorel writes that "the problems
of violence still remain very obscure." Yet, he advocated nothing
more violent than the general strike as he tried to combine Marxism with Bergson's philosophy of life. Frantz Fanon, in his book

[2] Hannah Arendt, *On Violence* (New York: Harcourt Brace Jova-
     novich, 1970), 8–9.
[3] Arendt, *On Violence*, 12, 13, 20.

The Wretched of the Earth, also glorifies violence stating that "only violence pays."[4] And he speaks of the "creative madness" present in violent action. The report *Violence in America,* issued by the National Commission on the Causes and Prevention of Violence in June 1969, came to the conclusion that "force and violence are likely to be successful techniques of social control and persuasion when they have wide popular support."[5] The history that popular movements have successfully used violence to attain their ends proves this report to be prophetically accurate.

Then there exists the consensus among political theorists — of various and even opposite persuasions — that violence is nothing more than the most flagrant manifestation of power. C. Wright Mills writes that "all politics is a struggle for power; that the ultimate kind of power is violence."[6] This statement calls to mind Max Weber's definition of the state as "the rule of men over men based on the means of legitimate, that is allegedly legitimate, violence."[7] In his book *On Power,* Bertrand de Jouvenel alludes to one of the great effects of violence when he writes, "A man feels himself more of a man when he is imposing himself and making others the instruments of his will,"[8] which gives him "incomparable

[4]   Frantz Fanon, *The Wretched of the Earth* (New York: Grove Press, 1961), 47.

[5]   Hugh Davis Graham and Ted Robert Gurr, *Violence in America: Historical and Comparative Perspectives: A Report to the National Commission on the Causes and Prevention of Violence,* vol. 2 (Washington, D.C.: US Government Printing Office, 1969).

[6]   C. Wright Mills, *The Power Elite* (New York: Oxford University Press, 1956), 171.

[7]   Max Weber, *Politics as a Vocation* (Minneapolis, MN: Fortress Press, 1965), 25.

[8]   Bertrand de Jouvenel, *On Power: Its Nature and the History of Its Growth,* trans. J. F. Huntington (Boston: Beacon Press, 1962), 122.

pleasure." And Voltaire, pointing toward the violence that can arise from power, says, "Power consists in making others act as I choose."[9] Max Weber is also indicating the presence of violence in the abuse of power when he asserts that power is present whenever I have a chance "to assert my own will against the resistance of others." This statement also calls to mind Karl von Clausewitz's definition of war as "an act of violence to compel the opponent to do as we wish."[10]

Now all these definitions and descriptions of violence view violence only as a means to an end; they consider violence as an instrumental agent and cause. Violence is used to perfect man, to win a war, to dominate the wills of others, to defeat the exploiters and liberate the proletariat, to hasten the arrival of a social utopia, and so on and so forth. They do not delve into the metaphysical or theological nature of violence. Though they reveal much truth about violence as an instrumental cause, they do not enlighten man about the nature of violence. It is this fundamental aspect of violence that we must first identify, expose, and appreciate before we can ever hope to conquer the epidemic of violence which is corrupting the whole world.

In a 1981 cover story entitled "The Curse of Violent Crime," which addresses the soaring violence in the United States, *Time* Magazine has this to say:

> Day by day, America's all too familiar crime clock ticks faster and faster. Every twenty-four minutes, a murder is committed somewhere in the United States. Every ten

---

[9] De Jouvenel, *On Power*, 93.
[10] Karl von Clausewitz, *On War*, ed. and trans. Michael Howard and Peter Paret (Princeton, NJ: Princeton University Press, 1976), bk. 1, ch. 1, p. 75.

seconds a house is burglarized; every seven seconds a woman is raped. There is some truth in the aphorism of Charles Silberman, author of Criminal Violence, Criminal Justice, that "crime is as American as Jesse James." But there is also something new about the way the Americans are killing, robbing, raping, and assaulting one another. The curse of violent crime is rampant not just in the ghettos of depressed cities, where it always has been a malignant force to contend with, but everywhere in urban areas, in suburbs, and in peaceful countrysides. More significant, the crimes are becoming more brutal, more irrational, more random—and therefore all the more frightening.[11]

The tragic truth is that what is written of America here is also true of almost every nation in the world. The fear of violent crime, and the flood of violent crime, is paralyzing human society in the whole world.

For the truth is that violence is in the ascendency. It practically reigns and rules the lives of millions. "Violence is the father and king of everything,"[12] said the Greek Heraclitus, almost five centuries before Jesus Christ. And H. G. Wells wrote, "Life is born of violence. On the head of each of us weighs the ancestral curse of fifty million murders."[13] Then too Friedrich Hacker, in his book *Agression, Violence dans le monde moderne*, states, "Everywhere and always, the strong have triumphed over the weak; the law of the jungle is the fundamental law of life ... one murder every twenty

[11] "The Curse of Violent Crime," *Time* Magazine, March 23, 1981.
[12] Heraclitus, quoted in Paul Tournier, *The Violence Within*, trans. Edwin Hudson (London: SCM Press, 1978), 32.
[13] H. G. Wells, quoted in Tournier, *The Violence Within*, 32.

seconds during the last fifty years."[14] All these statements, and many more that could be added, have a kernel of truth in them, even though they may be exaggerated. We must sort out in them what is true and proper, and what is erroneous folly. We must show that violence is always evil; that it flares with uncontrolled anger and unleashed power; and that it obliterates reason and begets counterviolence as its harvest of increased evil. We hope to demonstrate that the modern world is drowning in violence, because it has thought it possible to substitute Mammon for God, Libido for Liberty, and the cacophony of the media — television, the secular press, exploding radios, as well narco-mysticism — for the voices of reason and revelation as the ideological guarantors of the happy life.

---

[14] Friedrich Hacker, M.D., *Agression, Violence dans le monde modern* (Paris: Calmann-Lévy, 1972), 115.

1

THE TAPROOT OF VIOLENCE

You are of your father the devil, and the desires of
your father you will do. He was a murderer from
the beginning, and he stood not in the truth ...
for he is a liar, and the father thereof.

—John 8:44

For the sake of clarity, it is most important that the reader understand the meaning of the word *violence* as it is used in this work.
Moreover, it is absolutely necessary for grasping the truth of the
nature of *violence* that he also become aware of the essential difference between *violence* and *power*. For acquiring and appreciating
the truth of a subject depends very much on the skill for seeing
and making the proper distinctions among the realities involved
in that subject. Then, too, we must decide whether, and in what
sense, *violence* can be distinguished from *force*. Moreover, we have
to take into consideration the physical and spiritual dimensions of
these three realities. We have to study the dynamic relations among
these realities, how they flow into or issue forth from one another.
Only thus can we achieve an accurate and profound picture of

human relations—in the fundamental areas of metaphysics and theology—regarding the circumstances of violent activity.

We begin with an etymological analysis of the word *violence*. *Violence* as a word is derived from the Latin noun *vis* meaning force, strength, power exercised more often in a physical manner but yet also in a spiritual manner. For example, *vis fluminis* indicates the power of a river, while *vis mentis* the power of the mind. But *violence* is a dynamic noun; it always conjures up forceful activity. Hence the Latin verb *violare*, from which *violence* is also derived, contains the root of *vis*, *vi*, and the infinitive root of the verb *facio*, *fare*, meaning to do, perform, make. Thus *violence* signifies to perform with force, to act aggressively so as to injure, ravish, outrage, or transgress the dignity and integrity of an innocent person in his physical and spiritual welfare. To be more specific, violence is often used to subdue, dominate, rob, rape, or kill the innocent, perhaps too even his family, friends, and properties.

When such attacks of violence are made against institutions, then the violence engendered takes on a more heinous aspect, because of a more social and religious aspect. For the Greeks, Romans, and Jews, and for us, their cultural and religious heirs, violence against sacred persons is called a sacrilege, against temples, a profanation; against the state, treason; against oaths, perjury. Such violent acts are seen as acts of irreligious contempt for the law, a dishonoring of the gods, barbaric attempts to overthrow religion, the holy empire, and its emperor gods. Though used today more often in its first, predominantly secular meaning, *violence* still retains its profane, sacrilegious dimension, especially when sacred persons, places, and things are victims of its onslaughts. And this onslaught on sacred beings is occurring more frequently today as violence becomes a worldwide phenomenon. Popes, ministers, rabbis, nuns, priests, temples, mosques, synagogues, and churches have been frequently and flagrantly assaulted within the last fifteen years. And there is no end in sight. It suffices to look at some of the ruins. The universities, once centers of secular and Christian wisdom, are now very often training grounds for militant revolutionaries. In the cities, mass confrontation has often degenerated into guerrilla warfare. In the churches, clergymen and clergywomen, seeking notoriety, proclaim the "new morality" of hedonism and engage in the destruction of property, even at times supplying other rebels with lethal weapons. In the media, under the rubric of liberty and reform, the role of traitors and violent protestors is romanticized. Thus factories, schools, theatres, civic halls, and chapels become launching pads for the most vulgar forms of violence streaking nakedly into the surrounding peaceful neighborhoods.

And now for an analysis of *power* and *force*. Power signifies the ability to do something, the strength to accomplish an undertaking often in the face of great obstacles. Power may be exercised in the field of physical or spiritual activity. We speak of mechanical energy as a certain amount of "horsepower." We speak of the pope having the "power of the keys," whereby he is able to exercise the supreme spiritual authority given to him by Christ, the Son of God. Power is usually understood to be morally neutral or indifferent. It does not carry within its concept a necessary connection with moral evil. In this, it differs essentially from violence. Thus a powerful person is not necessarily an evil person, but a violent person is almost always considered to be an evil person, always allowing, of course, for the violent mad man or woman who, because of insanity, cannot be held morally responsible for aggressive activity. Force likewise signifies strength, might, coercion. It, too, can be applied to physical or spiritual activity. A police force keeps order by legitimately using coercive measures. Demonic forces are bent on destroying man physically and spiritually. Force also tends to be used as a word in a morally neutral signification, thus essentially distinguishing it from violence, which is an unjust, an immoral use of force or power. It must be noted, however, that on the rare occasions when *force* and *power* are used in a morally pejorative sense, an adjective or phrase indicating the evil makes specific the abuse of force and power. For example, the military power of Nazism enslaved many free nations. The force of the serpent's arguments seduced Eve. With these distinctions clarified, we may now proceed to a more metaphysical and theological analysis of violence.

The Taproot of Violence

What is the taproot that is causing such growth in the delirium for violence rampant today? It is the attack against God, as demonstrated far and wide in *a hatred for the truth*. Behind the metaphysic of murder found in the slogan "I kill, therefore I am," lies the metaphysic of hatred of the created order, a hatred that is embodied in the slogan, "I will not serve, therefore I am." Refusal to serve God was the battle cry under which Satan rallied his revolutionaries among the angels to create a violent war against God and His faithful angels, as they stood trial in the vestibule of Heaven. Christ told His apostles, "I saw Satan like lightning falling from heaven."[15] Elsewhere in Scripture we read, "God spared not the angels that sinned, but delivered them, drawn down by infernal ropes to the lower hell."[16] Christ Himself testified that this "liar, and the father thereof ... was a murderer from the beginning,"[17] thus revealing the metaphysical-theological connection between hatred of the truth and the lust for violence. He warned the Pharisees that men who

[15]   Luke 10:18.
[16]   2 Pet. 2:4.
[17]   John 8:44.

reject God's plan for their salvation will become violent criminals by imitating Satan's wicked deeds.

As a matter of history, the religious leaders of the Jews were looking for a Messiah who would be a conquering hero, a military savior who would subject the Gentiles to the service of the Chosen People and thus usher in that worldly, materialistic utopia which the leaders had falsely fabricated from their misinterpretations of the Scriptures. When King Herod heard of the birth of the King of the Jews in Bethlehem, he sent soldiers to seek him out and kill Him. He saw in that royal Child a rival threatening his political power, so secularized had the notion of the Messiah become among the Jews. But God, ever faithful to the revelation He gave His prophets, sent His Son as a Suffering Servant to save all mankind through His humiliation and death on the Cross. Instead of a terrestrial kingdom of pleasure and power, the Son of God established a supernatural kingdom of sacrifice and sanctity. This plan of God, realized in history through the teachings, miracles, and death of such a humble Messiah, scandalized the Pharisees and the ruling high priests. They rejected Christ, fought against His kingdom, and plotted His death. If they could not have their own type of Messiah and kingdom, neither would they accept God's. To make sure the Jewish people would not accept Christ and enter this kingdom, they plotted the death of Christ and trapped the Romans into doing their dirty work for them. And then, as if this hatred of God's truth was not bad enough, in the presence of their Roman masters, whom they despised as tyrants, they justified their violence against God's Son and His kingdom by shouting out, in a frenzy of mob madness, this sacrilegious lie: "We have no king but Caesar."[18]

[18] John 19:15.

The Hatred of Truth

Falsity is the heart of immorality, and hatred of truth is the taproot of criminal violence. Now all Scripture testifies to this connection between the creatures' hatred for truth and the violent actions that flow from this hatred. Indeed, violence entered creation from the rebellion of Lucifer. This rebellion rose from the heart of pride. But the sin of pride is the offspring of the vice known as hatred of truth. And hatred of truth leads to the arrogant action whereby a creature attempts to rearrange God's hierarchy of beings and values into an order that the creature prefers to the plan of God. This attempt in itself is the violence of disorder that effects the chaos of falsity and immorality. For hatred of truth is really hatred of God, who creates all things wisely and governs them lovingly. Lucifer, the Morning Star, was instantly deformed into the Prince of Darkness because he attempted to live a lie. He wanted to de-throne God and become God himself. Here is Scripture's account of the violent event:

> How art thou fallen from heaven, O Lucifer, who didst rise in the morning? how art thou fallen to the earth, that didst wound the nations? And thou saidst in thy heart: "I will ascend into heaven, I will exalt my throne above the stars of God, I will sit in the mountain of the covenant, in the sides of the north. I will ascend above the height of the clouds, I will be like the most High." But yet thou shalt be brought down to hell, into the depth of the pit.[19]

And St. Peter relates the divine vengeance that hatred of truth drew down upon demons and evil men alike:

---

[19] Isa. 14:12-15.

For if God spared not the angels that sinned, but delivered them, drawn down by infernal ropes to the lower hell, unto torments, to be reserved unto judgment: And spared not the original world, but preserved Noah, the eighth person, the preacher of justice, bringing in the flood upon the world of the ungodly. And reducing the cities of the Sodomites, and of the Gomorrahites, into ashes, condemned them to be overthrown, making them an example to those that should after act wickedly.[20]

In the book of Revelation, St. John the Evangelist sees in a flashback vision the violence that broke out between Satan's demons and the holy angels:

And there was a great battle in heaven, Michael and his angels fought with the dragon, and the dragon fought and his angels: And they prevailed not, neither was their place found any more in heaven. And that great dragon was cast out, that old serpent, who is called the devil and Satan, who seduceth the whole world; and he was cast unto the earth, and his angels were thrown down with him…. "Woe to the earth, and to the sea, because the devil is come down unto you, having great wrath, knowing that he hath but a short time."[21]

Thus Satan, whom Christ calls "the father of lies," became the first violent, preeminent revolutionary. His lying pride has let loose upon all creation a hurricane of deeds of violence and blood whose escalating winds of wickedness are presently destroying the

[20] 2 Pet. 2:4–10.
[21] Rev. 12:7–9, 12.

nations of the globe, and attempting to extinguish the lights of love and holiness in the hearts and minds of all men who are seeking the truth given to man by God through reason and revelation. We can imagine the tremendous violence that must have burst forth in the war between the faithful angels and the demons. Being pure spirits, far more intelligent and powerful than men, that war in Heaven must certainly have dwarfed all the most violent wars in human history taken together. Holy Scripture relates that just one angel, passing over the sleeping army of the Assyrians who were besieging Jerusalem, killed in one night 185,000 soldiers (2 Kings 19:32-35).

Moreover, an indication of the power of the angels is suspected when one realizes the enormity of the act of violence that Satan and his demons planned to perpetrate in Heaven. They hoped to dethrone God and become gods with their own power and on their own terms. They attempted the impossible task of demoting the Creator and advancing themselves to almighty power and honors. Such was their hatred of God and the order of creation, that these demons would have destroyed both if they could. Indeed, in their attempted violence, Satan and his demons even violated their own natures, choosing for themselves a goal contrary to their natures and destiny. Their violence reduced them to being eternal failures hardened in iniquity. And when Satan and his devils were "cast unto the earth," Scripture tells us they continued their violence by becoming agents "who seduceth the whole world." "Woe to the earth, and to the sea," a voice from Heaven cries out in the vision seen by St. John in book of Revelation, "because the devil is come down unto you, having great wrath, knowing that he hath but a short time."[22] That short time is the last days, the time between

---

[22] Rev. 12:12.

the Ascension of Christ into glory and his Second Coming. St. Peter tells mankind how these demons are using this short time: "Be sober and watch: because your adversary the devil, as a roaring lion, goeth about seeking whom he may devour" (1 Pet. 5:8).

Violence in the Human Family

We have already seen how Satan, the Super-Rebel, introduced violence into the family of the angels. Now we want to investigate how he introduced violence into the family of mankind. But, in order to appreciate the tragic effects of human violence, it will be necessary to contemplate the wonderful plan God had for the family of man. It is only when we understand and are inspired by God's original plan to create the human family in the image and likeness of the Family of the Holy Trinity, that we can even begin to suspect on the one hand what the fall from grace reveals of Satan's violent hatred toward man, and, on the other hand, what our restoration in grace reveals of the Holy Trinity's infinite love for us.

Man certainly has the desire to share in the life and destiny of his fellow men. Not only is he made in the image and likeness of God as an individual person—possessed of a spiritual soul endowed with reason and free will—but man is also made in the image and likeness of God as a social person, as a family being, as a child and founder of a human family (Gen. 1:27–28). For man longs to burst the barriers of individuality and self-fullness. He longs to create a family of his own without, however, losing the dignity and uniqueness of his own personhood as he enjoys the full communion of a family. Man is made in the image and likeness of the Holy Trinity, of the Divine Family.

God is Father, not only because He loves us paternally as His creature children (such love does not penetrate into the innermost depths of the divine nature), but also because, from all eternity, He has fathered a Son equal to Himself. Being self-creative, the Father pours out His essence in an intimate second Person, in another Person who is the Substantial Wisdom and illimitable plenitude of the Father's being. Then again God is called Son, not merely because He became a Child of Mary, of man and of the human family, taking His human nature from man's heart and life. Once again such Sonship does not necessarily penetrate into the core of the Divine Being either. But the Son is the Son because, from all eternity, He is the Living Image of the Father, begotten not made. In the Son, the mystery of the Father is made manifest. The Son is the face that reflects the Father's face perfectly as in a mirror. The Son is the Substantial Spoken Word of an Omnipotent Father-Speaker. Here we have two countenances, two Persons in one God, distinct in all reality and truth, separated by their sacred, inexorable, unique dignity, yet one God.

But between the Father and Son lives another Divine Person from all eternity. This third Person makes possible the existence of the Father and Son as two separate Persons having one life, one essence unhampered by limitations of self-fullness or individuality that might isolate one Person from the other Persons. For in God is the Perfect Family of Divine Persons, three perfect Persons enjoying total self-possession, yet enjoying perfect family life in common. In the Family of the Holy Trinity, everything is open; there are no secrets, no closed doors among the Father, the Son, and the Holy Spirit. All truth, all love, all holiness is possessed perfectly by each Person and by the whole family. The Father and the Son are so open to each other that their mutual love breathes forth the perfect third Person, the Holy Spirit. From all eternity, the Holy Spirit is the gift of love between the Father and Son. And thus all three Divine Persons share a single, all-loving family life. They live so completely in each other that there is not a single pulse, not a breath, not a spark that is not mutual family truth and love. That is what is meant when we say God is Spirit. The Holy Spirit, the third Person of the Family of the Trinity, makes it possible for each Divine Person to find and possess Himself completely in the others. In the Spirit, the Father engenders the Clear Image of Himself, the Son in whom He is well-pleased. In the Spirit, Jesus receives divine truth and reflects it back fully and perfectly to the Father. "Philip, he that seeth me seeth the Father also."[23] In the Spirit, the Father pours out His essence, the Word, confident that in Jesus it will be invulnerable. In the Spirit, the Son receives the essence of His being from the Father, is His Word, and yet Lord of Himself.

Now man created in grace was meant to imitate both the personhood and the intimate family community of the Holy Trinity. Remaining individual persons, men and women were meant to enjoy the truth, love, fidelity, security, and holiness founded in a sacred personal existence that was to flourish in a family known as a community of saints. Man's triumph over sin would have benefitted all the generations that followed in their confirmation in grace. The human family, modeled on the Holy Trinity, was meant to be a created community of saints living in the grace of divine truth and holiness. But the violence of sin introduced by our first parents became the sin of all mankind just as their grace and holiness, had they remained faithful to God, would have become a legacy of family love in truth and holiness for all men. After the fall, the grace of holy personhood enjoyed in the grace of holy community and family was lost. That is why men live now at the expense of one another, rooted too deeply in themselves, contesting one another in animosity, competition, fear, suspicion,

---

[23] John 14:9.

and infidelity. The violence of sin introduced the violence of lying, crime, death. Eve complained to God, "The serpent deceived me." Adam explained, "The woman, whom thou gavest me to be my companion, gave me of the tree, and I did eat."[24] Thus began the disunity of sin, the endless chain reaction of excuse and counter-excuse, of accusation and counter-accusation within the human family that will endure until the end of time. The human family failed in its challenge of love to become like the Family of the Holy Trinity. Why? Because our first parents chose to believe the lies of Satan rather than the truth given to them by God: "For in what day soever thou shalt eat of it, thou shalt die the death.[25] Instead of living in truth, holiness, peace, and harmony, the human family is torn asunder by the violence of escalating immorality.

Within the very first human family, between the very first children of Adam and Eve, we read of the violence of fratricide. Both brothers, Cain and Abel, offered gifts as a sign of their reverence for the majesty of their Creator. But Cain offered God less than the best of his harvest; he offered God his "seconds," defective fruits. God rejected Cain's gifts. For whoever offers God "seconds," insults God. On the other hand, Abel, the shepherd, offered God the best of his flocks, and God loved Abel and accepted his gifts. Cain refused to face the reality of his sin and repent. Instead, burning with an all-consuming envy, a spiritual greed, and anger at his brother's advancement in God's love and favor, "Cain rose up against his brother Abel, and slew him."[26]

Perhaps those who have suffered violence most in the cause of truth have been the holy prophets of God, heralds of the gospel

[24] Gen. 3:13, 12.
[25] Gen. 2:17.
[26] Gen. 4:8.

known as apostles, missionaries, and martyrs. St. Paul, indicating the violence the apostles and all missionaries had to suffer for the truth, writes:

> For I think that God hath set forth us apostles, the last, as it were men appointed to death: we are made a spectacle to the world, and to angels, and to men. We are fools for Christ's sake, but you are wise in Christ; we are weak, but you are strong; you are honorable, but we without honor. Even unto this hour we both hunger and thirst, and are naked, and are buffeted, and have no fixed abode.... We are reviled, and we bless; we are persecuted, and we suffer it. We are blasphemed, and we entreat; we are made as the refuse of this world, the offscouring of all even until now.[27]

And again St. Paul writes, "For thy sake we are put to death all the day long. We are accounted as sheep for the slaughter."[28] The book of Exodus is replete with the violent miseries the Pharaohs inflicted on the Chosen People because of their obstinate, stubborn opposition to God's commands. In turn, the Pharaohs were ravaged by ten plagues and their armies drowned in the Red Sea. Elijah the prophet had to flee for his life from King Ahab and Jezebel because he upbraided them for having killed God's prophets and leading Israel into idolatry. Elijah complained to God thus: "They have destroyed thy altars, they have slain thy prophets with the sword, and I alone am left, and they seek my life to take it away"[29] Micah, the prophet, was struck in the face, jailed, and put on bread and water for having prophesied concerning the ruin

---

[27] 1 Cor. 4:9–13.
[28] Rom. 8:36.
[29] 1 Kings 19:14.

of the king of Israel who led his people into idolatry.[30] Zechariah, priest and prophet, was stoned to death by order of Joash, king of Jerusalem, because he upbraided princes and people for serving groves and idols.[31] Concerning respect and love for the truth, the book of Proverbs says, "He that trusteth to lies feedeth the winds" of violence. Lying lips hide hatred. "Lying lips are an abomination to the Lord, and "a false witness shall not be unpunished: and he that speaketh lies, shall perish."[32]

Jeremiah, the prophet, was first brutally beaten, put in the stocks, and made the laughingstock of the nations. Then he was stoned to death,[33] all because he revealed to the people the punishments God was sending to them for their infidelity. Daniel was twice thrown into the lion's den, once under Darius the Mede, because he had transgressed the king's edict by praying three times a day, and another time under Evilmerodach[34] because of a sedition of the people against him as God's herald of unpalatable truth.[35] The three youths, Shadrach, Meshach, and Abednego, were cast into a fiery furnace because they refused to fall down and idolatrously adore the golden statue erected by King Nebuchadnezzar. St. John the Baptist was beheaded because he upheld the moral law of God, when he told King Herod that it was unlawful for him to take his brother's wife. And Christ Himself, the Son of God, as He stood before Pilate waiting to be sent off to be crucified

---

[30] 1 Kings 22:16–27
[31] 2 Chron. 24:17–22.
[32] Prov. 10:4, 12:22; 19:9.
[33] According to a tradition in the early Church.
[34] Also rendered "Evil-Merodach."
[35] Daniel 14:26–42. Regarding the identity of the king, Fr. Miceli is relying on a tradition recorded in the Douay Rheims Bible. See https://www.drbo.org/chapter/32014.htm.

testified thus: "For this came I into the world; that I should give testimony to the truth."[36]

St. Paul, writing of the heroes of the truth and of the Faith, testifies to the violence they had to endure from the hands of those who hated the truth:

> And what shall I yet say? For the time would fail me to tell of Gedeon, Barac, Samson, Jephthe, David, Samuel, and the prophets: Who by faith conquered kingdoms, wrought justice, obtained promises, stopped the mouths of lions, quenched the violence of fire, escaped the edge of the sword, recovered strength from weakness, became valiant in battle, put to flight the armies of foreigners.... Others were racked, not accepting deliverance, that they might find a better resurrection. And others had trial of mockeries and stripes, moreover also of bands and prisons. They were stoned, they were cut asunder, they were tempted, they were put to death by the sword, they wandered about in sheepskins, in goatskins, being in want, distressed, afflicted: Of whom the world was not worthy; wandering in deserts, in mountains, and in dens, and in caves of the earth.[37]

Closer to our own age, we have the courageous defense of truth in the face of lying violence demonstrated by Sir Thomas More. Upon learning from the Duke of Norfolk that the Bishops of England in Convocation submitted to Henry VIII's threats and approved the royal lie that Queen Catherine was not his lawful wife, More resigned his post, removed the chain of his authority as Lord Chancellor of England, and addressed Norfolk thus:

---

[36] John 18:37.
[37] Heb. 11:32–38.

The King's Act of Supremacy whereby he makes himself the Supreme Head of the Church of England opposing the Pope isn't a Reformation. This is war against the Church. Our King, Norfolk, has declared war on the Pope—because the Pope will not declare that our Queen is not his wife....

Hear me out, Norfolk. You and your class have "given in," as you rightly call it, because the religion of this country means nothing to you one way or another.... The nobility of England, my lord, would have snored through the Sermon on the Mount.[38]

When Master Cromwell attempts to cajole More by legal traps and brutal threats into taking the oath acknowledging King Henry's supremacy over the Church of England, More replies,

Is it my place to say "good" to the State's sickness? Can I help my King by giving him lies when he asks for the truth? Will you help England by populating her with bars?... It is not for the Supremacy that you have sought my blood—but because I would not bend to the marriage.[39]

Just after his condemnation to death, More, in a final statement, sums up his case in defense of the truths for which he is about to violently executed:

Yes (I have something to say). To avoid this (arrival at a destiny which executes me as a traitor) I have taken every path my winding wits would find. Now that the Court has determined to condemn me, God knoweth how, I will discharge my mind.... Concerning my indictment and

[38] Robert Bolt, *A Man for All Seasons*, act 2, pp. 52, 71.
[39] Bolt, *A Man for All Seasons*, act 2, p. 89.

the King's title. The indictment is grounded on an Act of Parliament which is directly repugnant to the Law of God. The King in Parliament cannot bestow the Supremacy of the Church because it is a Spiritual Supremacy. And more to this the immunity of the Church is promised both in Magna Carta and in the King's own Coronation Oath.[40]

Master Cromwell unwittingly and succinctly exposed King Henry's violent animosity to the truth about the validity of his marriage in these words: "The king's a man of conscience and he wants either Sir Thomas More to bless his (new) marriage or Sir Thomas More destroyed."[41]

---

[40] Bolt, *A Man for All Seasons*, act 2, p. 92.
[41] Bolt, *A Man for All Seasons*, act 2, p. 69.

2

VIOLENCE AND PHILOSOPHERS

*The easiest way to get a reputation is to go outside the
fold, shout around for a few years as a violent atheist or a
dangerous radical, and then crawl back to the shelter.*

—Ernest Hemingway, from one of his Field Notebooks

We have already seen that, in the situation of the world today,
violence has become contagious. We now want to concentrate
on an analysis of this contagion. It is quite clear that what seems
to be meaningless violence is spreading throughout the whole
world. Indeed, men have become so habituated to the frequency
of violent events that they now act as if such events were normal
human behavior. But what is not realized is that the apparent
arbitrariness and haphazardness of violence can be, and ought to
be, seriously and precisely analyzed from the philosophical and
theological point of view. The need for a thorough-going treatise
on criminal aggressivity is testified to by the rising flood of objective evils perpetrated by individuals and organized groups who are
dedicated to violence as a way of attaining their objectives. Whereas
previously, some fifty or so years ago, when public violence broke

out, man and his societies shook as if caught in a deadly seismic quake. Today, violence is merely a press clip among an avalanche of other sensational events that appear in the media and forgotten quickly amid the public-opinion hurricanes regarding the latest political scandal. It needs to be restated that the fundamental cause of the escalating cyclone of violence is because man and his societies have broken their friendly connections with the God of revelation. Nations have chosen to plan and live out their temporal lives by creating new relations and references to the world and the lord of this world. Mankind seems to have taken on the role of God, identifying itself with God. This ascent into hubris has effected a profound devaluation of man's own person and a derailment from his social and personal destiny. Logically, such a position has brought about a vast disorientation among men and nations, so that mankind is no longer ruled by a hierarchy of permanent truths issuing from the natural law God established. Rather, it is divided by conflicting currents of subjectivism that are producing the violence of anarchism. At this point, it seems very profitable to consider St. Thomas Aquinas's analysis of violence.

St. Thomas and the Nature of Violence

St. Thomas starts with a truth taught by Christ to His apostles, that all evil issues forth from a wicked heart ruled by a bad will. "The things which come out from a man, they defile a man. For from within out of the heart of men proceed evil thoughts, adulteries, fornications, murders, thefts, covetousness, wickedness, deceit, lasciviousness, an evil eye, blasphemy, pride, foolishness. All these evil things come from within, and defile a man."[42] Then, in his discussion of violence, St. Thomas lists five elements that

[42] Mark 7:20–23.

constitute the nature of violence and describe its circumstances. (1) Violence is that which causes any being to act contrary to its nature and natural inclination. (2) The agent of violence is always extrinsic to that which is violated. (3) The natural inclination of a being is always prior to the violence it suffers, and its natural rights are presupposed by the act of violence. Here, a brief explanation is perhaps helpful. The agent of violence attacks the victim from outside, brutally, ignoring the victim's right to a peaceful and secure existence. The violent criminal forcefully imposes upon the victim actions repugnant to the victim's natural desires and goals. Although man's prior natural goodness and destiny make the violation of them possible in a world saturated with temptations and sinners, this possibility must not be interpreted as a permission from God, nor, from reasonable persons or lawful societies, that this possibility be actuated. On the contrary, God, reasonable persons, and just societies establish strict punishments for criminals who exercise their lust for violence. In fact, this warped penchant for violence emphasizes that man, as an agent, cannot—strictly speaking—create anything. It also reveals, unfortunately, that man is too often the efficient cause of the chaos of wickedness. For man, at best, is the cause of becoming, never the cause of being. Thus, it is precisely existing natures—with their intrinsic inclinations and rights—that render the violent act possible by the criminal. (4) The intensity of the violence is proportionate to the severity to which the victim's natural inclination is thwarted, and his ability to work for his natural goal is blocked. For example, murder is a more heinous crime than mere robbery. For murder completely extinguishes man's natural inclinations for the good and his capacity to attain his destiny in time. Whereas mere robbery violates man's natural right to property, frustrates temporarily his economic good, but does not extinguish irrevocably the victim's capacity, possibility, or natural inclination to regain his material goods, even as he moves to prosecute the criminal and restore private and public justice. (5) Evil is always related to violence and vice versa.[43]

In this connection, it is well to recall that power and force must not be confused with violence, for power and force—physical or spiritual—are morally neutral in themselves; or, as the scholastics say, "morally indifferent." That is, in themselves, neither good nor bad. They become evil—that is, they degenerate into violence—when adhered to for evil purposes or employed under evil conditions, e.g., in acts of aggression. Even when force is used in a just war, as in the Second World War against Nazism, it can degenerate into criminally unjust violence. This took place when the Allies, following a decision approved by Winston Churchill in England, decided to apply saturation bombing against the enemy. This meant the deliberate, wanton killing of innocent men, women, and children—clearly noncombatants—in order to break the morale of the Germans.

In summary, then, violence is an attempt by an external agent to constrain innocent victims to perform actions contrary to their natural inclinations and against their legitimate goals. Although these victims—with their natural rights—constitute the ontological condition without which violence would be impossible, nevertheless the criminal is responsible for his free, deliberate use of this condition to perform acts of aggression. Then, too, the intensity of the violence, and magnitude of the evil effects produced, are proportionate to the severity by which the victims are rendered incapable of attaining their legitimate goods and goals. Thus, violence can be understood as the rebellious creature's attempt to rearrange, redefine—indeed, recreate—other beings, directing them

---

[43] St. Thomas Aquinas, *Summa Theologica*, II-II, q. 66, art. 8.

away from their divinely appointed natural and supernatural ends toward an evil and arbitrarily selected purpose for the convenience, pleasure, and even self-glorification of the violent, criminal agent.

Nietzsche and Violence

Perhaps the modern philosopher who can lead us to understand the growing violent metaphysical, ethical, theological, and political nihilism of our day is none other than Friedrich Nietzsche, that prophet of doom. For he can be called, in all truth, the philosopher of anguish and violence. In fact, he is the prophet who foresaw and foretold the coming beast of international violence. He realized that modern man no longer fostered a communion of friendship with the God of Christianity as his creature and image. This rebellion for Nietzsche was tantamount to man's assassination of the God of revelation and his seizure for himself of the role of being his own god. But this self-aggrandizement into divinity was also a decision that opted for a life of violence. We here produce Nietzsche's famous prophecy found in his book *Joyful Wisdom*, a theme he later developed in *Thus Spake Zarathustra*:

> Have you ever heard of the madman who, on a bright morning, lighted a lantern and ran to the marketplace calling out unceasingly, "I seek God! I seek God!" And, as there were many people standing about who did not believe in God, he caused a great deal of amusement. "Why? Is he lost?" said one. "Has he strayed away like a child?" said another. "Or does he keep himself hidden? Is he afraid of us? Has he taken a sea voyage? Has he emigrated?" the people cried out laughingly, all in a hubbub. The insane man jumped into their midst and transfixed them with his glance. "Where is God gone?" he called out. "I mean to tell you! We have

killed him—you and I! We are all his murderers! But how have we done it? How were we able to drink up the sea? Who gave us the sponge to wipe away the whole horizon? What did we do when we loosened this earth from its sun? Whither does it now move? Whither do we move? Away from all suns? Do we not dash on unceasingly? Backwards, sideways, forwards, in all directions? Is there still an above and below? Do we not stray, as through infinite nothingness? Does not empty space breathe upon us? Has it not become colder? Does not night come on continually, darker and darker? Shall we not have to light lanterns in the morning? Do we not hear the noise of the gravediggers who are burying God? Do we smell the divine putrefaction? For even Gods putrefy! God is dead! God remains dead! And we have killed him! How shall we console ourselves, the most murderous of all murderers? The holiest and mightiest that the world has hitherto possessed, has bled to death under our knife. Who will wipe the blood from us? With what water could we cleanse ourselves? What lustrums, what sacred games shall we have to devise? Is not the magnitude of this deed too great for us? Shall we not ourselves have to become Gods, merely to seem worthy of it? There never was a greater event, and, on account of it, all who are born after us belong to a higher history than any history hitherto!"[44]

In book 5 of *Joyful Wisdom*,[45] written four years later, Nietzsche expounded further on this awesome, tragic event:

---

[44] Friedrich Nietzsche, *Joyful Wisdom*, 95, 96, quoted in Walter Kaufmann, *The Portable Nietzsche*.

[45] Also known as *The Gay Science* or *The Joyous Science*.

The most important of more recent events—that "God is dead," that the belief in the Christian God has become unworthy of belief—already begins to cast its first shadows over Europe.... In the main, however, one must say that the event itself is far too great, too remote, too much beyond peoples' power of apprehension, for one to suppose that so much as the report of it could have reached them; not to speak of many who already knew what had taken place, and what must all collapse now that this belief had been undermined. Because so much was built upon it, so much rested on it, and had become one with it: for example, our entire European morality. This lengthy, vast, and uninterrupted process of crumbling, destruction, ruin, and overthrow that is now imminent: who has realized it sufficiently today to stand up as the teacher and herald, as the prophet of gloom and eclipse, the like of which had probably never taken place on earth before?[46]

Nietzsche's prophecy is infinitely tragic, because he states that apostate Christians themselves have killed God. This accounts for the sacred dread that he experiences over the oncoming cataclysmic wars he sees advancing on Europe and the whole world. For him, violent nihilism is linked inevitably to the decomposition of Christianity. Nietzsche then went on to become "the man of refusal" against Christ, Christianity, Christian morality, and Christian philosophy. More than that, he proclaimed a revolution against Christianity, whose final consummation would produce the neo-pagan, "Godless self-God": the Superman. The Superman's greatest accomplishment would be the transvaluation of

[46] Kaufmann, *The Portable Nietzsche*, 447, 448.

all Christian values. His greatest commandment would create a society of slaves ruled ruthlessly by Superman. "The time has come," wrote Nietzsche, "to oppose morality with immorality, to call what priests call good, evil; and what they call evil, good. The time has come for the transvaluation of all values."[47]

This prophet of modernity, of revolutionary society and radical thought, became the champion of extremes. Again he wrote, "We moralists do not even need to lie ... We would come into power even without the truth ... The magic that fights for us is the magic of extremism."[48] Nietzsche, who accepted with pride his designation as "an aristocratic radical," was used by Karl Marx to further the violent struggle between the classes. For Marx, the proletariat became the "human Gods"; they were to overthrow the bourgeois lords and exploiters through class warfare. Thus, Marx and his followers today have created citadels in such countries as Russia, China, Cuba, the Eastern Satellites,[49] and Nicaragua as camps for the training of armies of proletarian terrorists. These centers of organized revolution, which are creating professional terrorists, radiate to the whole world the call for violence and revolution. This call is beamed everywhere, twenty-four hours a day. For these centers and their agents of hatred throughout the world work effectively and ceaselessly—yet secretly, like the unseen, silent law of gravity—to pull down and destroy every civil and religious community that strives for social justice, freedom, and peace.

Now both Nietzsche and Marx foresaw the public victory of the violent, extreme dimension of their thinking. This assurance gave them both the experience of triumphant power. There is a

[47] Nietzsche, *Thus Spake Zarathustra*, 144.
[48] Karl Jaspers, *Nietzsche and Christianity*, 94.
[49] Eastern European nations aligned with the former Soviet Union.

hypnotizing fascination in their fanaticisms. Their chaotic excesses, their iron wills, their high- voltage writings have attracted millions over the last hundred years—and still attract millions today—to fly with suicidal enthusiasm and madness into their incandescent ideologies. Nietzsche was forever knocking down things and taking wild delight in their fall:

> O My Brothers, am I cruel? But I say, "What is falling we should still push. Everything today falls and decays: Who would check it? But I—I even want to push it. Do you know the voluptuous delight that rolls stones into deep depths? These human beings of today—Look at them! How they roll into my depths! I am a prelude of better players. O My Brothers! A precedent! Follow my precedent! And he whom you cannot teach to fly, teach to fall, faster!... To this mankind of today I will not be a light, nor be called a light. Those I will blind! Put out their eyes, O Flash of my Wisdom!"[50]

Karl Marx founded Communist ethics on his pseudoscience of historical materialism and the dynamism of class warfare. Vladimir Lenin added a violent emotional fanaticism as another source of Communist morality by following the radical, violent immoralism of Sergei Nechayev. Eugene Lyons, reviewing five decades of violent Communist immorality in his book *Workers' Paradise Lost*, writes, "Lenin, it is important to recall, had found Sergei Nechayev—the apostle of violent, absolute immoralism—even before he found Marx. In 1868, Nechayev wrote his celebrated *Catechism of a Revolutionist,* in which he renounced all norms of civilized behavior and prescribed every imaginable form of violence and depravity in pursuit of the ideal. It is as fanatical and hate-breathing a document

[50]   Nietzsche, *Thus Spake Zarathustra,* 321.

as the human brain has ever produced. "The revolutionist," he wrote, "knows only one science, the science of destruction, which does not stop at lying, robbery, betrayal, and torture of friends, or murder of one's own family." His central dictum, that "everything that contributes to the triumph of the revolution is morally good,"[51] has been echoed by Lenin and his disciples to this day, indeed by figures in every Communist pronouncement on morality. Max Eastman writes that "the confluence of these two streams of thought (Nechayev and Marx) is one of the greatest disasters that ever befell mankind."[52]

Unable to create, even in embryo form, its dream of a classless utopia, Communist humanism—in irrational rage, and with unutterable brutality—has set about sacrificing the perfection and happiness of more than one-third of the world's population to the impossible (and, even, ever-receding) future happiness of mankind supposedly to be found in that mirage of a Socialist classless society. For more than seventy years now it has, and continues even today, to inflict unimaginable physical and psychological torture on its slaves, exterminating millions for the sake of the messianic mirage that keeps receding into an impossible future. During those many years, it has been plowing under living generations of normal human persons for the sake of the absolutely abstract generations of possible supermen to be formed some day from the uncertain womb of history. Eugene Lyons, a disillusioned devotee of the Marxist ideology, writes of this maniacal, cruel social engineering thus:

> By 1934, when I departed from Russia, nothing was left of the high mood of dedication, traces of which I had still

[51] Eugene Lyons, *Workers' Paradise Lost*, 376–377.
[52] Lyons, *Workers' Paradise Lost*, 377.

found among the Communists six years earlier. The very vocabulary of idealism had been outlawed. "Equality" was lampooned as bourgeois romanticism. Excessive concern for the needs and sensibilities of ordinary people was punished as "rotten liberalism." Terror was no longer explained away as a sad necessity. It was used starkly and glorified as "human engineering." Means had blotted out ends and have held this priority since.[53]

We are living in the days of Nietzsche and Marx's "better players" at violence, who, ecstatic with "the voluptuous delight which rolls humans into deep depths," keep pushing society to the brink of social chaos and suicide. William Butler Yeats, in his poem "The Second Coming," reveals the murderous zeal of Nietzsche and Marx's modern offspring:

> Things fall apart; the center cannot hold
> Mere anarchy is loosed upon the world,
> The blood-dimmed tide is loosed, and everywhere
> The ceremony of innocence is drowned;
> The best lack all conviction, while the worst
> Are full of passionate intensity.
> Surely some revelation is at hand;
> Surely the Second Coming is at hand.[54]

Another author and poet, viewing the modern scene of universal confusion, writes as a prophet of tragedies present and tragedies to come from the hurricanes of violence formed in the blazing hatreds of evil men and societies. Placing himself in a spaceship

---

[53] Lyons, *Workers' Paradise Lost*, 380.
[54] William Butler Yeats, "The Second Coming."

with the astronauts and looking back across the vast expanses of space at that sapphire jewel, the Earth—spinning in the heavens, bright with ocean blues, flecked with snowy clouds, ruddy with crimson sands, yet but a revolving speck in a vast ocean of limitless galaxies—Scott McCallum laments the daily, close-up, rising suicidal violence erupting from the volcanoes of hatred that threaten to incinerate both the entire human race and the jewel-Earth, which is seen as a brilliant gem only from the moon and the far-off heavens. The poet writes:

> We took out God, killed Him, proclaimed Him dead;
> And God will do just that, stay dead.
> Let's take a leaf from Nebuchadnezzar's outdoor cinema
> The writing's on the wall; I told you so already;
> It's called the Apocalypse, where man kills all mankind.

> From the original atom we've progressed
> Through hydrogen to cobalt.
> With all the clever Plumbers that there are around,
> Cobalt by now must be a back number.
> Anyhow, one of these days, somebody's going to press the
>   button,
> Drop the test tube,
> Somehow, somewhere set off a chain reaction,
> And so to bed.
> And if you care to thumb through that old number, the
>   Apocalypse,
> You'll find the stage directions for the Four Horsemen
> All strangely reminiscent of radioactive fallout;
> While some of the stage effects described on land and sea
> Are but the full-scale application
> Of our experimental junketings around the atolls.

No, don't have any doubts; the spectral steeds stand saddled
And the old chap with the egg timer stands whetting his
   scythe,
And goes to mow a meadow.
Mind you, if your accounts tot up,
There's no abnormal need for trepidation.
Since that far-off dawn referred to,
The world has ended every day for every man who died.
This way we just take off together.

Goodbye, Goodbye, Beloved World.
I loved you dearly.[55]

Shakespeare, with a poet's profound, prophetic vision, demon-strates in the tragic destiny of *Macbeth* that, when hatred of the just, legitimate order of reality is incarnated in irrational, ambitious, voluntaristic attempts to change that order of justice and truth, such greedy lust for power and prestige commits bloody, criminal deeds, which bring about that wicked nothingness known as sin. For the working of this mystery of iniquity, which aims at destroy-ing the ruler who holds power in law, only succeeds in destroying those criminals who would change the truth of reality by the use of violence. In this revolt against reality, Lady Macbeth is destroyed by madness; Lord Macbeth dies by the sword. Lord Macbeth, in a profound soliloquy, sensed the tragic finale of his violence, as he nurtured the temptation to rearrange the order of kingship in the kingdom of Scotland to his own and his wife's aggrandizement:

This supernatural soliciting
... cannot be good ...

[55] Scott McCallum, "Goodbye Beloved World."

If good, why do I yield to that suggestion
Whose horrid image doth unfix my hair,
And make my seated heart knock at my ribs,
Against the use of nature? Present fears
Are less than horrible imaginings:
My thought, whose murder yet is but fantastical,
Shakes so my single state of man, that function
Is smothered in surmise; and nothing is
But what is not.[56]

Bad Will the Bond between Falsity and Violence

From the thoughts developed so far, it becomes clear that violence involves man in a special type of metaphysics whose first principle is "To be is to be willed or to be is the effect of a creature's free decision." The real is what a creature wants it to be. Truth is what men want truth to be. We have here the philosophical and theological arrogance of violence known as subjectivism, i.e., a personal hatred of existing truth acting irrationally and rebelliously to create new truth. But that world of new truth is a world of fantasies, of lies fabricated in the pride of creatures who seek a world that satisfies their lusts. Now, because voluntaristic, irrational intentionality nurtures violence it is intrinsically evil, even as a thought, before the external act of violence is committed. For there is a willful commitment to the evil deed even before the act is committed, thereby orienting the whole person to adhere to sin. For example, Eve sinned before she took a bite out of the apple. For she took the word of Satan, the Father of Lies, over the word of God, who is Truth itself. She sinned when she decided that Satan's version of reality was the version she wanted to experience—to become

---

[56]   William Shakespeare, *Macbeth.*

God-like on Satan's terms, which she made her own. All this despite God's having warned from the very beginning, "For in what day soever thou shalt eat of it, thou shalt die the death" (Gen. 2:17). And so Eve chose the violence of death, rather than the joy and peace that would have necessarily followed from her fidelity to God. This prideful voluntarism is the mother of criminal violence, for it attempts to establish as law the creature's whims over the objective natural law that God established in the whole of creation and stamped on the consciences of all men through the two spiritual lights of reason and revelation.

3

The Lie as Interpersonal Violence

They have spoken vain things every one to his neighbor:
with deceitful lips, and with a double heart have they
spoken. May the Lord destroy all deceitful lips.

—Psalm 11[12]:3–4

The lie is the father of violence. It is the word, act, sign of cunning, or silence that makes use of wiles to deceive whoever has a right to know the truth. Consider the position of the listener who, in simplicity and ingenuousness, is eagerly expecting the truth. Then, consider the attitude of the liar who—full of subtlety, audacity and, at times, cruel cynicism—misleads his neighbor into the quicksand of falsity. The use of the lie reveals the liar as a person of evil intentions.

He who tells lies as a way of getting ahead lacks a love of truth. Now, truth is an objective social good meant to be shared by all mankind through the activity—pleasant or, even at times, not so pleasant—of communication. "The truth," Christ tells us, "shall make you free."[57] And this freedom is the freedom of the children of

---

[57] John 8:32.

God, who is Truth itself. What the liar lacks is not only frankness, honesty, and uprightness in his shady pronouncements, but also a love of his neighbor, whom he deliberately defrauds of a needed good—the truth—which is necessary for binding the community of mankind in a closer communion of justice and trust. The liar is a self-centered dissimulator, who cunningly manipulates his fellowmen for his own evil purposes. He or she cannot be trusted. And herein lies the psychological violence that is the evil fruit of violence. The clue to the mentality of the liar, in his hatred of truth, is his hatred of God. And this hatred of God floods over into hatred of those whom God loves, the innumerable millions for whom His divine Son died. At other times, the hatred of the liar begins with hatred of his fellowmen. and then inevitably expands to hatred of God. But, in both cases, the liar's animosity is usually cloaked under the facade of friendship. Shakespeare condemned this tactic of the liar's cunning when he wrote, "O serpent heart, hid with a flowering face!"[58]

What does the lie do to interpersonal relations? It becomes the self-poisoning of the "I" of the liar and, at the same time, the spiritual abductor of the "thou" of the deceived. When the deceived realizes that he has been taken advantage of, while his defenses were down and he remained open in good faith to receive the truth, a variety of hostile reactions blaze up into the relationship. Immediately the healthy, interpersonal indwelling of persons in communion and community begins to disintegrate. Intellectual harmony is shattered as storms of distrust beget the turbulence of aggravation. Suspicion of all that the liar says and does now reigns supreme. Hesitations, reservations, and a state of cold suspense are predominant in the now shaky interpersonal encounter.

[58] *Romeo and Juliet*, act 3, scene 2.

Resentment, which is the poisoning of the self and society, is the fruit of the perversion of the truth.

Simultaneous with the flight of the intellect from confidence and faith in the liar, who is recognized as acting as an agent of Satan, the emotions and passions of lovers of truth explode. God Himself is represented by the Psalmist as being upset by the infernal activity of hypocrites who have made themselves a medium of the devil. Thus, on the liar, the anger of both Heaven and earth descend. The Psalmist writes of the Lord who says, "He that speaketh unjust things did not prosper before my eyes."[59] Displeasure, dislike, ill-humor, and hate blaze forth from humans caught in the web of the deceiver. For grievous lies stir up rancor, the desire for justice, and, at times, even for revenge. The fear that one deception will beget a chain reaction of lies paralyzes dialogue and normal social relations. The very bonds of peace, that "tranquility of order" advocated by St. Augustine, are snapped. Estrangement, antagonism, and cold aloofness produce a heartless confrontation. Often enough, fear, that parent of cruelty, enters this sinister enmity. Malice rears its ugly head. There often follows the outbreak of splenetic temper against the crooked statements which dishonest persons propagate. Then, too, if the lie is expressed with the intention of ruining one's reputation, the battle of litigation is enjoined. Thus, the accuser and the accused square off in a court showdown that announces to the world their mutual and implacable hatred. As the Rev. George Herbert has observed, "Lawsuits consume time, and money, and rest, and friends."[60] And we add that lawsuits, which are increasing

---

[59] Ps. 100[101]:7.

[60] Rev. George Herbert, quoted in *Roget's International Thesaurus*, 658. Rev. Herbert also observed, "The worst of law is, that one suit breeds twenty."

as a social plague in this Age of Alienation, are consuming entire professions that were established to serve the common good.

We are living in the Age of the Persistent Lie. The art of disinformation has advanced spectacularly. This has been partly due, in a material way, to the magnificent improvement and refinement of the means of communication—radio, TV, satellites in space, and new telephone techniques. But the instruments created by man's technocratic genius are morally neutral, neither good nor bad, though they are certainly physical benefits in man's normal life. The scourge of the lie arises from the heart of the wicked, who know how to abuse our marvelous media to propagate instantly—all over the globe—their distortions of truth. False words are not only evil in themselves, but they corrupt with evil the souls of millions of unaware listeners. For often those who pervert truth through the media do so acting as agents of parodies, creators of caricatures that lead men to the most biased and heartless decisions against God and their countrymen. Let us study a few demonstrations of this ruthless deception.

Satan and Eve

Satan, the serpent in the Garden of Eden, is also the dragon of the book of Revelation. Before his rebellion against God, he was Lucifer, the brightest of all in the choirs of angels. But he fell in love with his own brilliance. And this trial proved to be the occasion of his downfall. He rejected God in a preferential act of love for his own self-glorification." "I will not serve!" And, and the prophet Isaiah reports, "I will exalt my throne above the stars of God.... I will be like the most High."[61] This was his battle cry against his Creator.

---

[61] Isa. 14:13–14; see 14:12–20.

Now, his brilliance must have attracted an army of admirers among the angelic hosts. For Scripture records that, in his fall from grace, Satan dragged down with himself "the third part of the stars of heaven"[62] In succumbing through pride in his own glory, Satan attempted to live the lie of an admiration and importance for him, as if he were equal in being to God. He thus became the First Liar in all creation, which is why Christ calls him "the Father of Lies." Moreover, since he introduced supernatural death for himself and the millions of the angels he seduced, Satan became the First Murderer of all intelligent creatures, which is also why Christ calls him "a murderer from the beginning."[63]

What then must be the mentality of the fallen Prince of Darkness? A study of his interpersonal relations with Eve will reveal that reality. The author of Genesis writes, "Now the serpent was more subtle than any of the beasts of the earth which the Lord God had made."[64] Satan is a virtuoso in the art of cunningness. He immediately demonstrates his expertise in his conversation with Eve. He conceals his evil intentions as he proceeds to act the exegete, concerned about Eve getting the right understanding of God's command not to eat that fruit. Eve had revealed that God had forbidden anyone to eat of the fruit of that tree under pain of death. But Satan works to seduce Eve into error, and from error to catch her in his web of wickedness. He denies the meaning of God's command and insinuates it is unjust: "No, you shall not die the death. For God doth know that in what day soever you shall eat thereof, your eyes shall be opened: and you shall be as Gods,

---

[62] Rev. 12:4.
[63] John 8:44.
[64] Gen. 3:1.

knowing good and evil."[65] The nasty insinuation is that God is a tyrant, keeping His creatures' eyes shut, and so blinded to an act of eating that would lead them to become divine. This wily lie conceals from Eve the truth that she will know good and evil by sinning and thus becoming evil, something God, who is holiness itself, could never become.

There it is again, the same satanic temptation: "You shall be as God." It was this arrogant ambition of Satan's—to become like God on his own terms, rather than on God's—that led to his fall. Pride is the essential vice in the mentality of Satan. Pride is the vice he instills into Eve and Adam to seduce them into sin, for disobedience is always a form of pride. Satan still regards himself in the Garden as God, even while being a demon destined for Hell. For he is giving our first parents instructions on how to become like God. The fruit once eaten, our first parents in reality become not God-like, but apes of Satan in their Fall, knowing good and evil by choosing to become evil through their sin of rebellion, a rebellion that imitated the rebellion of Satan himself.

Holy Scripture clearly indicates the deadly consequences of pride: "The beginning of the pride of man, is to fall off from God: Because his heart is departed from him that made him: for pride is the beginning of all sin" (Sir. 10:14–15). In the seduction of man from God into sin, we discover the vindictive obsession of Satan's mentality. The Father of Lies is the Hater of Mankind, cloaked in the mantle of the friendly exegete anxious to explain God's commands. He knows full well that he is the harbinger of death into human history. We fully understand now why Christ has defined Satan as the Father of Lies. But to quote Leon Cristiani in his book *Evidence of Satan in the Modern World*: "And yet even

---

[65] Gen. 3:4–5.

this epithet is, for us, only one aspect of the total truth. *Satan is not merely guilty of homicide, but of deicide!"*[9]

Christ and Satan

Satan recognized Jesus as his greatest enemy. At the end of Christ's forty days of fast and abstinence from all food and drink, the cunning tempter approached the physically hungry Christ. What perfect timing for provoking an affirmative response from a religious person on the verge of vertigo, isolated in the wilderness with wild animals. The tempter's "If thou be the Son of God" manifests, once again, his obsession with becoming God himself (Matt. 4:3). We are also reminded of the trick used to bring down our first parents: "Eat . . . and you shall be as Gods."[66] Once again, the hellish obscurity aimed at seducing the innocent, at poisoning the simplicity of fidelity and trust in God. This clever ambiguity is more nefarious than any blatant lie: "Command these stones to become loaves of bread" (Matt. 4:3). But the enticement away from God is rebutted immediately: "Not in bread alone doth man live, but in every word [the bread of truth] that proceedeth from the mouth of God," Jesus firmly replies.[67]

But the insane pride of Satan persists. He takes Christ to the pinnacle of the temple. There the tempter has Christ look down upon the crowd below. What an opportunity to begin your mission, in a spectacular descent into the temple courtyard announcing your arrival as the Messiah! Again, the madness for divine honors seizes Satan: "If thou be the Son of God, cast thyself down, for it is written: 'He hath given his angels charge over thee, and in their hands shall they bear thee up, lest perhaps thou dash thy foot

---

[66]   Gen. 3:5.
[67]   Matt. 4:4.

against a stone.' "[68] Satan can certainly quote Scripture to tempt worshipers of God to succumb—in a lust for notoriety—to the fantastic desire for the extraordinary. He is the master at creating delusions. Again, Christ sees through the deception. "Thou shalt not tempt the Lord thy God."[69] No discussion, no parrying, but a curt, straight rejection.

But the lust to be God drives Satan to his greatest act of arrogance. From a mountain peak, the tempter displays the whole vast glory of this world. As Lord of this world, he invites Christ to possess all these kingdoms: "All these will I give thee, if falling down thou wilt adore me."[70] Tremendous temptation! Again, the enticement to betray God. Once again, the satanic ambition to be like God, to seduce worshipers away from adoring God, to adoring God's rebellious creature, himself. This time Christ abruptly ends the tempter's wily games: "Begone, Satan: for it is written, 'The Lord thy God shalt thou adore, and him only shalt thou serve.' "[71] The devil left, but St. Luke adds, "for a time."

Satan's fantastic project to seduce souls away from God, and draw them to adoration of himself, failed miserably in his showdown with Christ. Yet history, that implacable witness, reveals that in religion Satan has, in a large measure, succeeded; and that, even today, is succeeding beyond his wildest dreams in replacing God as the object of worship among men. True, at times, this worship may not be directed explicitly to him in person. But he stands behind every cult, every idolatrous religion. Moreover, the Church of Satan, which does directly and explicitly worship him,

---

[68] Matt. 4:6.
[69] Matt. 4:7.
[70] Matt. 4:9.
[71] Matt. 4:10.

has escalated from a small beginning in California to functioning in twelve countries of once-Catholic Europe. Then, too, modern man has created shrines to his own gods of human pride—Science, Progress, Technology, Matter, Sex, Wealth, Secular Humanism—to name but a few self-divinizing philosophies. These false gods also testify to Satan's triumphs in his hatred of God and man.

Christ and the Pharisees

The envy of the devil pursues Christ into His mission. The struggle to the death with Satan is inevitable. Christ knows that Satan is the personal power who radically wills evil, totally adheres to evil: evil for evil's sake, evil per se. But Jesus has come specifically to bear witness to the truth against the kingdom of darkness ruled over by this Master of Deception. He has come to break the devil's complete enslavement of fallen man. He has come to destroy the power of one who defies God, who would tear this universe from God's hands, who would even dethrone God. Unable to touch God, Satan is determined to seduce the world into apostasy and self-destruction. In the Pharisees, he finds willing allies. These religious leaders of the people create, with Satan's cooperation, a darkness among the people which rejects the light coming from God in His incarnate Son.

Why did the Pharisees reject Christ as the Messiah, as the Suffering Servant of the Lord? Because God's plan of salvation did not agree with their plan. They demanded, preached, and looked forward to having a Messiah who would be a great military leader, a king who would destroy the Gentiles and create an earthly utopia—with the Chosen People in command over all the other nations of the globe. In other words, they rejected the truth of God's plan. They too were bitten with the temptation to be like God, determining their own style of Messiah, and rejecting God's. So they struck at the heart of Christ, arousing doubt and hatred in the hearts of the masses. "Is not this the son of David?" the amazed crowds cried out, as they witnessed Christ curing a possessed man who was blind and dumb, and who immediately saw and spoke.[72] The Pharisees were quick to poison the atmosphere with an unspeakable blasphemy: "This man casteth not out the devils but by Beelzebub the prince of the devils."[73] In answer to this demonic lie, Jesus flings forth His challenge: "He that is not with me, is against me: and he that gathereth not with me, scattereth."[74] Satan himself could hardly have blasphemed more contemptuously against the Holy Spirit, through whom Christ performed all His marvelous works. He must have been delighted with hateful joy to hear the Pharisees, in their rejection of Christ, accuse the God-Man of being a subordinate of his.

Once again for Satan, and this time also for the Pharisees, the lust for being like God inflated their egos. The proud tempter is again on the attack against Christ, this time through the arrogant religious leaders of the Chosen People who, on one occasion, attempted to stone Christ, and, having failed, still plotted His execution. To attain their wicked goal, the Pharisees willingly became Satan's accomplices when they coerced the Roman leaders to commit their sin of deicide. It appeared that, finally, Satan had risen above God, whom he had executed. The Pharisees, "sons of Satan," as Christ identified them (see John 8:44), cooperated in the greatest act of violence in the history of angels and of men—the Crucifixion of the Son of God incarnate as a blasphemer and criminal.

What does it really mean to be an agent of violence? It means to commit an act of violence not only against a person, place, or

[72] Matt. 12:23.
[73] Matt. 12:24.
[74] Matt. 12:30.

thing, but also to attack eternal truth and justice. To stand in hateful animosity not only to the eternal moral code, but also to the author of that code, the living and holy God, in imitating Satan's age-old attack: the creature's senseless, but profoundly exciting and fascinating attempt to dethrone, degrade, and destroy his Creator. Human violence is also directed against the sacred, God-given life in man, and it works itself out in the degradation and destruction of natural life.

If we wish to know how violence manifests its presence among us today, we must try, on the one hand, to discern the great lies of the times, and, on the other, the progress made in the art of killing men. The more unrelentingly an age is addicted to falsehood, the more the life of man and the being of all sacred things are held in contempt—indeed, exposed to the threat of murder and destruction. For the person who takes time out to reflect seriously on moral and religious matters, it is impossible to question that addictive falsehood and escalating homicide are both effective instruments of Satan in his campaign to dominate persons, families, cities, nations—indeed the whole world—in slavery to his lying, murderous kingdom. Violence, like all immorality, does not remain in the solitary cell of the individual conscience, but, like a runaway cancer, swiftly spreads to form a diseased community known as the *Corpus Mysticum Diabolicum*, the Mystical Body of Satan. This community is composed of criminals who have chosen to become accomplices with Satan in the professions of lying and terrorism. They willingly submit to satanic suggestions and live by demonic hatred, blasphemy, and the lust to destroy all that is true and holy. Satan and his evil hordes are present everywhere, working to obliterate God's presence in the hearts of men by establishing centers that propagate major falsehoods and train terrorists to execute massacres of the innocent.

The Greatest Violence of Our Day: The Lie of Atheism

The greatest lie that has led to worldwide violence is the lie that "God does not exist." This lie is engulfing whole nations, growing more brazen and arrogant today. For millions today, atheism is a way of life. Modern science, which seeks to be self-sufficient unto itself, creates a climate and mentality favorable to atheism. Scientism is very much alive today. For modern scientists reject the contemplative mentality and replace it with the belief in positivism, the attitude of effective explanation. Hence, it experiences no need for God. Thus, the scientist does not contemplate the wisdom of God; instead he creates the meaning of the universe. He has created scientific, godless humanism. Thus, science strips the world of its sacred character; in it the scientist finds, not God, but himself. In the realm of the social sciences, Pierre-Joseph Proudhon protests against believers, "He who speaks to me of God wants either my money or my life."[75]

Marx bases his atheism on his conception of work. For him, man is his own God, making himself human through his conquest of nature. Religion is the "opium of the people."[76] Marx holds that, through the denial of God, man liberates himself from a projected, illusory phantom. "Religion is but the illusory sun which circles around man—unless he becomes his own sun. Atheism thus appears as man's demand for absolute freedom."[77] "I choose to be free," writes Francis Jeanson. "I shall choose to exist not in relation to God, but in relation with my brothers who share my

---

[75] Hannah Arendt, *On Violence*, 26.
[76] Karl Marx, "Toward the Critique of Hegel's Philosophy of Right," in *Marx & Engels: Basic Writings*, ed. Lewis S. Feuer (New York: Doubleday Anchor Books, 1959), 262–263.
[77] Marx, "Toward the Critique of Hegel's Philosophy of Right," in *Marx & Engels: Basic Writings*, 262–263.

predicament, even though their predicament may be worse than my own."[78] Nietzsche's phrase sums up this independence of God well: "Perhaps man will be able to raise himself up from the moment he is no longer engulfed in God."[79]

Every man must make a fundamental choice between faith or skepticism. The atheist is a skeptic and refuses all meaning, except what he puts on reality. He who refuses faith of any kind adheres to the sole, true atheism. In the realm of morality, Dostoevsky writes, "If God didn't exist, everything would be possible."[80] And Sartre interprets this correctly: "This is the very starting point of (atheistic) existentialism. Indeed, everything is permissible if God does not exist, and, as a result, man is forlorn, because neither within him nor without does he find anything to cling to. He can't start making excuses for himself."[81] Atheism consists in repudiating every responsibility before God. The only responsibility it accepts is before the abstraction of history. Sin is not committed before God, but before history. Humanity must look to its own destiny. The supreme lie of Marx is that truth is not natural, not metaphysical, and—above all—not supernatural. For him, truth is economic, political, dialectical, and historical, because the political—in his mind—is the noblest dimension of human existence.

Atheists vaunt themselves and ridicule all believers in God. Philosophers like Jean-Paul Sartre not only say God doesn't exist, but they also claim that the very idea of God contains a contradiction, so that God is really an impossible nonentity. Here we have

[78] Francis Jeanson, *La foi d'un incroyant*, 114, 123.
[79] Friedrich Nietzsche, *Thus Spake Zarathustra*, 188.
[80] Feodor Dostoevsky, *The Devils* (New York: Penguin Classics, 1954), 126.
[81] Jean-Paul Sartre, *Existentialism and Humanism*, 33–34.

the worst intersubjective relationship of animosity and hate. The creature rejects and stands in judgment over his Creator. This is the most ungrateful and culpable of lies. It is also the most heinous of insults against the Tripersonal God of power, wisdom, and holiness. This is the God called by St. John the Evangelist: "God is love."[82] This psychological violence, consisting in the alienation of man against his Maker, has led to the physical violence in which millions upon millions have been slaughtered in two major world wars. Moreover, the lie of rampant atheism has prepared the present "Cold War" atmosphere, in which spying, intrigue, suspicion, terrorism, arms-racing, and some forty-five mini-wars—of so-called liberation—are speeding mankind toward a cataclysmic third world war, this time a war fought with horrendous chemical, bacteriological, and atomic weapons.

There are at least two trends to this lie about God. Theoretical atheism spawns the kindred lies of materialism, scientism, secular humanism, and certain forms of existentialism. These "isms" spread false philosophies about man, his world, his history, and his destiny. They elevate man as his own "God." But man, once divinized, begins to devour his fellowmen, imposing on nations various forms of totalitarian tyrannies: Nazism, Fascism, Communism, Laicism, Secular Humanism, to mention but a few. Then there is the lived lie of practical atheism. In this style of life, man does not so much verbally deny God as simply ignore Him. Man gives God lip service, but his heart is given to Mammon. Thus this type of atheist has his heart preoccupied with business, politics, worldly affairs, trade, scientific research, the pursuit of riches, pleasures, notoriety for their own sakes. He no longer finds any place for God in his life. His religion is mere religiosity, a sacred social veneer.

---

[82] 1 John 4:8.

Theoretical atheism has captured the souls of the high and the mighty in circles of power and authority in secular, academic and cultural societies. There is a clandestine collective agreement, a sort of atheistic kinship, among godless governments, indeed especially in the United Nations, to see that God is frozen out as a nonbeing, a nonperson from all social and public affairs of men.

How did this monstrous lie come about? Leon Cristiani in his book *Evidence of Satan in the Modern World* explains. It took about three hundred years for modern atheism to evolve into its present forms. To begin with, the *Libertins* of the seventeenth century wrote books that diluted the Christian idea of God. They were French agnostics. Following them, the "philosophers" of France — in the so-called Age of Enlightenment of the eighteenth century — ridiculed Christianity, supernatural truth, and morality in their writings, which had tremendous influence then and have even greater influence today. There then followed the "Freethinkers" and "Secular Humanists" of the present times. They have liberated "man-come-of-age" from all divine trappings — religious dogmas, morals, miracles, and the Church. Their pronouncements come down from the high chairs of academia, from the podiums of radio and TV studios, from the halls of the U.S. Congress and from the pulpits of man-established churches.

And what have been the results of ages of all these false teachings? Well, God is not mocked. What things men sow, those they reap. When men sow lies, they reap violence.[83] The Lord has vomited these godless generations out of His mouth into cauldrons of horrible wars. God has abandoned them to their own raging passions, so that they perform unspeakable crimes, engage in unnatural vices, and suffer excruciating diseases. Why? Because the

---

[83] See Gal. 6:7, 8.

post-Christian pagan nations have become lieutenants of the Father of Lies. Indeed, they have become his mediums, de-Christianizing the world while satanizing it as the reigning kingdom in the hearts of millions: a kingdom of darkness, wickedness, and despair.

4

Modern Violence

We do not have a choice between purity and violence, but between different kinds of violence. Inasmuch as we are incarnate beings, violence is our lot. Life, discussion, and political choice occur only against a background of violence.... It is allowable to sacrifice those who, according to the logic of their situation, are a threat and to promote those who offer a promise of humanity. That is what Marxism does when it creates its politics on the basis of analysis of the situation of the proletariat.

—Maurice Merleau-Ponty, *Humanism and Terror: An Essay on the Communist Problem*

The reality of epochal violence is the cause of national and world-wide anxiety. The fear of violence has chilled the hearts of millions. In fact, this fear has produced the international siege society. Events of violence flash forth every moment in multicolored gore from TV screens, newspaper photos, blazing jackets of novels, sleaze magazines, and pornographic ads for X-rated movies. Moreover, for several years now, seminars on the problem of modern violence have been held at the University of Pamplona in Spain, the University of Paris, cultural centers in Rome and Florence, and schools of philosophy and law at the University of Rome. As individuals, we cannot escape the epochal violence that engulfs us. Much less can we stem the tide of escalating violence. Moreover, we admit in this study that mere thought alone, or even profound reflection, will not eradicate violence.

Yet a beginning must be made in this process of uprooting violence by analyzing the nature of this evil, taking apart its mechanisms, criticizing its justifications, and unmasking its roseate promises. Unless we do this, we run the risk of falling into the deception of accepting violence for a reality that it is not, and thus even succumbing to the seduction of its fascination. In this chapter, we hope to study violence in a phenomenological manner and thus arrive at *how* modern violence attained such a universal, dramatic importance. Moreover, this same method will help us to understand *why* violence has taken on such a new aspect, namely the character of being considered a good and efficient means—almost a salvific sacrament—for guaranteeing mankind a just, political, economic, moral, and dignified maturity.[84]

Ancient and Modern Violence

How does ancient violence differ from the violence of our day? Today violence permeates every strata of human activity. It rages in international relations; it explodes in merciless guerrilla warfare, political terrorism, ideological and religious persecution, private banditry, on the plane of internal family relations, as well as in kidnappings, lynchings, organized crime, frequent surprise bombings,

[84] Many of the themes treated here are inspired by an excellent study of modern violence by the Italian philosopher Sergio Cotta, in his book *Perche' la Violenza?* [Why violence?], ed. L. U. Japadre (L'Aquila, Italy: L. U. Japadre, 1978).

the hijacking of airplanes, and the arbitrary, medical massacre of millions of innocent persons. Modern violence is cradled in the antinomy of our present day style of living, above all in industrialized countries where persons are treated as things, problems, collectivized, intellectualized, artificialized, naturalized, torn to pieces between a mad rush for the necessities of life—almost always artificially aroused by blaring ads—and immersed in productive activism that begets an escalating lust for entertainment, power, and happiness. Modern violence even permeates our style of speaking and communicating. We suffer it in the amplified, inhuman booming of loudspeakers at receptions and political gatherings, in demonstrations, in entertainment halls where acid-rock rhythms, psychedelic lights, and sexual gyrations are vibrating pandemoniously off-pitch, off-time, and off-hinges; and also from intolerable noises roaring up from smog-polluted streets. Indeed, such violence is also found in the continual use of words and images that are deliberately chosen to be obscene, sacrilegious, cruel, degrading, and which are brutally imposed on anyone regardless of his or her sensitivity, modesty, or dignity. Speech has become a weapon of violence, war, and hostility. Violent speech has transformed polite, civil dialogue into a war of noise and words where victory is sought at any cost in every confrontation, where asperity is fomented in every discussion between persons and classes of people who would normally relate to each other peacefully. In big cities, the eyes and minds of the citizens suffer violence from the wild graffiti smeared over buildings, transportation vehicles, national statues, and sacred places. The only message the graffiti announce is that we live in an age of irreverence, vandalism, and nihilism.

In the situation described above, the private and public conscience are overwhelmed with the escalation of violence. They can only oppose this violence with futile words and useless sermons.

And when they are defeated by this violence, they do not realize that they themselves become carriers of this violence. For they are afflicted with two flaws that prevent them from evaluating modern violence accurately. In the first place, they see today's violence as being the same as the violence of past ages. For them, violence is as old as man and has accompanied him throughout the ages. In the past, violence produced brutal tyrants, inhuman effects, torture, even genocide. Perhaps ancient tyrants like Nebuchadnezzar or Nero might be considered less violent than, say, Adolf Hitler or Joseph Stalin, but only because they had less efficient instruments of torture and death than modern technology has supplied our up-to-date killers. This view completely disregards how history, civility, culture, and law moderated and controlled violence in the past. Here is the first flaw in the modern appraisal of today's violence. For violence today rushes dramatically towards the destruction of all life, in a blind disregard for the massive suffering it inflicts on the whole world. Modern man must see that the violence of today finds its moments of joy, exaltation, and delirium in its utter contemptuous oblivion of man's dignity.

The second fault of modern man, in assessing the nature of today's violence, is that he is convinced that his laws, civility, refinement, and progress—intellectual, scientific, political—are still capable of vanquishing violence. For modern man, who is convinced he has "come of age," also thinks he has advanced far beyond the cruelty of the primitives, the barbarians, the "cavemen," and the ignorance of the "dark ages," and entered the ages of light. Confidence in this mentality was strengthened in the Age of Enlightenment. The illuminati and positivists, led by such wise men as Voltaire, Henri de Saint-Simon, Auguste Comte, Herbert Spencer, Jean-Jacques Rousseau, and a host of others—especially the Encyclopedists—felt secure at having tamed the violent nature of man.[85] But, of course, this was a grave self-deception. Violence has never been vanquished; it merely put on the mask of "good manners"; it acted under the aura of politeness and deference to law. When it functioned sanctimoniously, as in the case of the Reign of Terror, violence was supposedly protecting citizens, and never mind its ghastly harvest of bloody human heads reaped under the blade of the guillotine. Yet, because modern man has adhered to this illusion tenaciously, the explosion of modern violence astonishes him. He sees it as a passing novelty, not realizing that it has become institutionalized. Thus his fraudulent pose, fragile from the beginning, is now unmasked and shattered. Modern man must now escape from the illusions of the past and take action with a clear, cold-blooded mind against a violence that refuses to change its course but is determined to level all before the hurricane of its onslaughts.

Is There Something New about Modern Violence?

There certainly is. There are two aspects of its newness. First, the way in which violence is perceived. Today, it is seen as being diffused everywhere; it is spatially omnipresent, for man himself is enjoying planetary space in a contiguous and undivided manner. For everything today is contiguous and intercommunicating. There are no longer any unknown places in whose mystery man may avoid fearful brutality and attain, in perfect harmony and peace, the island of happiness. Neither hope nor a roseate imagination can any longer feed on these fantasies. In our atmosphere of intense communication, messages of violence arrive and are circulated from every quarter of the globe. This new audio-visual language dominates the masses and dramatizes the news as a form

[85] *Perche' la Violenza?*, 9.

of violence itself. For such news strikes immediately, and leaves no time for reflection. Moreover, it fills souls with the acrid, and at times masochistic, taste for excitement. The thrills of violence are enjoyed habitually and considered to be daily psychological fare. Indeed, carefree and undisciplined youths act out in raw reality much of the violence they see in movies or read about in murder-thrillers.

Secondly, in the measure in which human space is contracted, manipulated, or masked by such violent news, not only is the dream of perfect happiness obliterated, but man's very peaceful conduct loses its meaning. For whom is there today who has the refinement to want to know that, in a particular country, no rulers or judges have been massacred, no hostages taken, no trains blown up, no incest discovered being practiced on a large scale? This is good news and it is buried in silence. But paradoxically, because it is unreported, it ends up seeming to be conduct without motivation. While violence, by exception, ends up seeming to be the norm of human conduct. Now, only an enormously shattering act of violence seems to be considered exceptional. And even that event is gotten used to quickly and forgotten speedily. Thus, a human consciousness is created and diffused in which violence is universalized, enjoying an escalation much like the wildfire spread of an endemic, uncontrollable disease. In their activities, there is no human group, no nation, no continent that does not find itself immersed in violence. And, without doubt, it is this realization of the omnipresence of violence that fosters the consciousness which — even for us here, "among ourselves" — there exists nothing but violence.

Then there is the perception of the concentration of violence in time. We live in a contracted space-time situation, so that previous and contemporary time compenetrate each other through reciprocal "feedback." Thus, in the constant reporting of violence from every time and part of the world, our times present themselves as an age saturated with violence. The immediate speed of the news, which favors violent events, presses down upon the masses with such overwhelming force that any moment of serene reflection is not only emarginated but actually squelched. Thus, violence in its globality has a greater complex duration, prevailing beyond discontinuous time or the single events in which it is activated. Then there is the extension of the field of violence. There is such a quantity of violent facts reported that the precise meaning of violence itself is lost. The forest of violence is lost among the innumerable trees of violence.

Thus, every discrimination is considered to be violent situations. Parents who correct their children responsibly are viewed as violent; and schools that exercise normal discipline are accused of violence. One need not multiply examples; there is a multitude from which to choose. Thus violence, once restricted to evil human acts, is now applied to normal social situations, customs, and codes of conduct. Violence has now become an end in itself; it is founded on the arbitrary will to power, the very absence of all rational norms of behavior. Proudhon could write, "Property is theft."[86] Thus, in our times, violence has been raised to the altar of exaltation. By the end of the nineteenth century, this evaluation of violence was unknown. In fact, it was considered an evil, the radical evil, springing from "hubris," irrationality, and arrogance that considered itself to be beyond every law and all accountability for the peace and just harmony of society.

But this proper appraisal of violence has been sharply rejected. Engels could write, "It is necessary to educate the masses

---

[86] *Perche' la Violenza?*, 19.

systematically on this ... concept of violent revolution."[87] There is an echo of this thinking in the work produced in French, *L'Union de lutte des intellectuels revolutionnaires* (The Union for the Battle of Intellectual Revolutionaries), where we read of "incitement to violence," "fanaticism," "the death penalty," and "the physical destruction" of the slaves of capitalism.[88] This work was published in the 1930s. And was it not Mao Tse-tung who affirmed that "power grows out of the barrel of a gun"? Moreover, Sartre, in his preface to Fanon's *Damnes de la terre* (The Damned [Wretched] of the Earth) wrote, "The weapon of the fighter is his humanity."[89] Merleau-Ponty brings these expressions to their ultimate boldness: "History is terror, because it is fraught with contingency.... Our world is a world of violence because we are incarnated."[90] Again, according to the graphic expression of Sartre, "Violence is the spear of Achilles, which wounds and at the same time heals."[91] Merleau-Ponty again addresses violence thus: "We say all law is violence ... that the human condition may be such that it has no happy solution."[92] Raymond Aron, critiquing the morality taught by Christ says, "Sanctity has no place in the life of collectivities. Politics is, in essence, immoral; it forms a pact with the powers of hell, because it is a struggle for power, and power leads to violence over which the State has a legitimate monopoly.... There is more than rivalry here among the gods; there is an implacable struggle."[93]

---

[87] Engels, *The State and Revolution* [*Stato e Rivoluzione*] (Roma, 1917), 24.
[88] *Perche' la Violenza?*, 22.
[89] Maurice Merleau-Ponty, *Humanisme et Terreur* [Humanism and Terror] (Paris, 1974), 98, 118.
[90] Merleau-Ponty, *Humanisme et Terreur*, 13.
[91] *Perche' la Violenza?*, 23.
[92] Merleau-Ponty, xxxvi, xxxviii.
[93] Quoted in *Humanisme et Terreur*, xli.

According to Marx, for man to rediscover himself, "to be born of himself," he must use violence as the salvific instrument that will destroy every institution, every superstructure—political, ethical, cultural, economic, or religious—which has kept him in slavery through their exploitation of him. Thus the human universe, collectivized by violence, logically and rigorously calls for violent revolution. In a world of struggle, of a human history which is essentially violent, there is no margin of indifferent action that classical thought accords to individuals, for every action unfolds and we are responsible for its consequences. For Marxism, this is the inexorable fact of class struggle.[94] Violence must level all men, much as an earthquake levels all structures and leaves a ravished land for a new beginning in reconstruction. But there is this difference: violence "as an earthquake" is an act of God, involving no responsible action on man's part, whereas Marxist violence is calculatedly wicked and hateful. It is deliberately provoked and planned as a "liberation," a mad hope of attaining the concrete, active realization of the absolute value of man. Marxism holds that it does not invent violence, but found it already institutionalized in Western liberalism; its violence is "progressive," tending to its own suspension. Western violence, on the other hand, is "regressive," tending toward self-perpetuation.[95] Now, it is this very positive concept of revolution and violence as a hope, "the hope of revolution"—to use the expression of Vittorio Mathieu, and on which recently a theology of revolution has been founded—that legitimizes and exalts violence as the only road to man's maturity.[96]

---

94   *Humanisme et Terreur*, 33.
95   *Humanisme et Terreur*, 1, 2.
96   Vittorio Mathieu, *La Speranza Nella Rivoluzione* [The Hope in Revolution] (Milano, 1972), 11–12.

The Roots of Violence

Violence and Force

We must now make a distinction between violence and force. Unfortunately, this distinction has almost entirely been forgotten in our age of philosophical darkness. But distinguish we must, if we would understand violence and force as distinct realities. For today, every use of force is identified as violence. As far back as *The Republic* of Plato, we find Socrates handling the thought of Thrasymachus and Callicles, Sophists whose praises of force were contradictory until this genius of intellectual midwifery led them to confront force with the quite different reality of violence. In the end, the two questioners of Socrates arrived at this truthful conclusion: the domination that force exerts arises from a law of nature; the domination of violence attacks the law of nature.

Perhaps the best way to grasp the nature of violence is to oppose it to that human experience that is most removed from it—the experience of charity. St. Paul relates that "charity is patient, is kind ... not provoked to anger, thinketh no evil ... beareth all things ... hopeth all things.[97] These descriptions demonstrate the vast, impassable distance between violence and charity. If charity is the thesis, then violence is the antithesis in this complete antinomy. There can be no compromise, no equivocation, and no synthesis between these two realities.

Let us move on to explore the proximate genus and specific difference between violence and force. Despite that force is often confused and identified with violence, nevertheless, force does not appear to be reduced entirely to violence. There is, first of all, the extrinsic difference between them. Violence concretizes itself in a physical attack upon the bodies of humans. For violence creates physical damage, wounds, and, at times, inflicts death itself. Hence,

[97] 1 Cor. 13:4-7.

it arouses and feeds on fear and a spirit of rejection, disrespect, and contempt for its victims. Its physical character appears, at first sight, as a valid criterion for discriminating violence from force. For force is not exclusively physical, nor does it function exclusively against the bodies of others. For the noun *force*—apart from its metaphorical use, e.g., force of reason, or its artistic expression, e.g., the force of destiny—can be used in a perfectly correct manner to designate a human action that is neither physical, nor physically applied upon the bodies of others, but can be seen as a force on the spirit of others. The force of persuasion is one such example. The force of the spirit resists the violence of enslavement or torture.

But this analysis, good up to this point, is yet inadequate. Why? Because it does not take into account another vast area of human conduct. Certainly, it would seem, spiritual force is in no way violent. But there is a physical force that can, in a certain exterior manner, be considered violent. When policemen must rescue hostages from criminals holding them in a siege condition, physical force will often be necessary in the liberation action. But no one in his right mind would dream of calling this rescue action, whatever its physical costs, violence. Thus, the absence or presence of physical action does not adequately define the nature of force. Moreover, this very example demonstrates that it is a totally arbitrary decision, quite contrary to reality, to restrict violence only to the realm of physical action.

The reason is that there are nonphysical actions that cause physical damage to others. For example, when one, using false arguments, suggestions, or even lies, causes another—through these psychological means—to suffer physical harm. Shakespeare dramatically demonstrates such fatal consequences in his play *Othello*. Iago poisons the mind of Othello with the evil suggestion that Desdemona, his beautiful wife, has been unfaithful to him.

This lie drives the Moor of Venice into a jealous rage that leads him to murder his innocent wife. Iago then kills his own wife, Emilia, for revealing his lie to Othello, after the Moor has murdered his calumniated wife. Finally, Othello, in unsupportable grief over his tragically useless murder, kills himself.[98] There are other non-physical violent acts leading to physical harm: preventing people from congregating freely or expressing their thoughts in speech or writing; restraining them to house arrest without reasonable cause; and threatening them with blackmail or other dire punishment for exercising legitimate rights. Max Scheler, demonstrating an act of nonphysical violence, writes of "an emotional infection," or of "the crime of plagiarism." Certainly such actions are somewhat different from physical violence, but to exclude them from the class of violence would be to fall into the error of begging the question. Thus, if there is a difference between violence and force, the aspect of physicality cannot be the distinguishing mark. The difference must be established on another, more fundamental, plane. For there exists such a reality as psychological violence.

Now, the institutional criterion of violence takes its origin from the agent of violence. For it is a commonly accepted truth, even in scientific quarters, that the act of the assassin is an act of violence, while the act of the executioner is not. The kidnapping of an innocent person is an act of violence, but the arrest and detention of a criminal is not. From these examples and circumstances, we can arrive at the following distinction. Force is exercised when the act inflicted is accountable, directly or indirectly, to a responsible institution or validly constituted authorities. Violence is exercised when the act inflicted is not accountable to a responsible institution or

---

[98] Shakespeare, *Othello: The Moor of Venice*, act 5, scene 2.

validly constituted authorities, but to a private, unauthorized, and illegal source. Accountability to the institution or its authorized agents constitutes the valid criterion for discriminating between two acts that are inflicted—the one being force, the other violence. And it is good to remember that the institutional criterion does not have a relation only to the State. Consider the classic case of a band of robbers. While their external activities constitute acts of violence, the internal action of the *capo*, or leader of this illegal organization, and command over his followers, is recognized as an institutional authority. For evil and violence can be and are today institutionalized. St. Augustine supplies this example in his *The City of God*.[99] Force, therefore, is exercised in the public domain; violence in the private.

But not even this distinction is totally satisfactory in specifying exactly the difference between force and violence. Especially because violence is today given a topsy-turvy, head-over-heels significance. For the anarchist, the liberationist, and the radical, the act of violence is itself identified with the action of institutions, not only when they inflict sanctions, but simply because they establish laws, directives, and hierarchies. On the other hand, the actions of individuals who oppose institutions are considered actions that reject violence, or even as expressions of spiritual force of high moral character. Witness the actions of the Berrigan brothers,[100] both convicted of criminal activities several times. Yet, they are held in high moral esteem, even in their own religious orders. But apart from this extreme antithesis—for which every form of institution with power constitutes violence—it is difficult to dismiss the impression that some regimes are violent by their very

---

[99] St. Augustine, *The City of God*, ch. 4, p. 4.
[100] Fr. Daniel Berrigan, S.J., and Fr. Philip Berrigan, S.S.J.

institutional structure. For example, despotic regimes such as the Nazi, the Fascist, and Communist States are violent by their very institutional structure. For it is not by chance, but by calculated and carefully planned domination, that they rule through fear and terror, as Baron de Montesquieu has, with lucid foresight, indicated.[1011] On the same line of thought some scholars of our times, such as Hannah Arendt, Zbigniew Brzezinski, Carl J. Friedrich, Franz Neumann, etc., have discovered in violence and terror the fundamental characteristics of the totalitarian system. It is evident that in these cases the institutional criterion cannot validly exclude the violence of their activities.[102]

But the inadequacy of this criterion appears in its full light if we examine the case of the so-called "legitimate defense." In this case, two private parties confront each other. One is exercising violence, the other is responding with an activity that no reasonable person would dream of defining as violence. Now, for those of normal intelligence, this difference does not arise heedlessly from the action of self-defense's being founded in the natural law and accepted as an article of morality demanded by justice. For the common understanding in such cases is far more lucid than the tortured doctrines of the intellectual. The normal mind sees immediately the entirely different natures of the two acts; it grasps the different significance of these acts; it appreciates the wholly opposed relational structure of these acts. Briefly, then, the criterion of the institution—as an adequate means for defining the difference between force and violence—appears too formal and extrinsic to escape the frequent contradictions of the complex circumstances of reality.

[101] *Perche' la Violenza?*, 30.
[102] *Perche' la Violenza?*, 62.

The Criterion of Relationship to Values

The inadequacy of the distinctions already examined seems to have reached a felicitous summit in this next distinction. This criterion clarifies the limits—and gives the true meaning—of the previous criteria; for it subordinates and critically reveals their insufficiency. For violence can be physical and spiritual and noninstitutional (private) or institutional (public), as we have discovered from our previous phenomenological analysis. For what prevented our defining violence adequately previously was our failure to give its conscious relationship to value. For man, the agent of violence and force, lives in a dynamic stream of relations. He is a wreath of roots. A physical act is violent, not because it is physical, but because—when it is performed—it is performed through greed, deception, egoism, anger, the lust to dominate, or from any motive despoiled of a true value. If such are its moving forces, the act is violent, even if it is a spiritual act, like the act of lying. And the same can be said of public, institutional acts.

Conversely, force can be spiritual or physical, public or private, for that which makes possible the distinction of force from violence is its relationship to true codified values. The reason why physical force—with which one defends his own life and property or that of others, and by which one captures or punishes criminals—is not violence, is because such acts are motivated by and reside in excellent values, e.g., life, liberty, justice, charity, etc.

This criterion of referral to values explains the reason of our treatment of the other two criteria and the depth of truth hidden within them. Thus, when one calls certain human conduct violent—whether it be spiritual, institutional, or juridical—one does this not because these circumstances possess, in themselves, the capacity for discriminating between violence and force; but because one assumes, with a more or less conscious generic judgment, that there is implied in such conduct a referral, or at least a predisposition to, true values. This is the final and, therefore, the fundamental criterion. In this sense, the judgment of Walter Benjamin seems to me to be rather paradigmatic: "An acting cause becomes violence, in the pregnant sense of the word, only when it cuts into moral relationships. The sphere of these relationships is defined by the concepts of 'right' and 'justice.' "[103] In this sense, the criterion of relationship to the value of justice establishes a link of means to end. If the end is not a value but a disvalue, the means will be identified as violence.

But not even this criterion of a relationship to value seems to give an adequate distinction between force and violence. Why? First of all, because, with respect to reasons that deal with values, there are two aspects that we must consider. First, if there is a parity of conception regarding the plurality of values, it becomes impossible to arrive at an assessment—in a univocal manner—of the acts exercised in the conduct of violence. In fact, what is violence in respect to a given value, such as liberty, can appear as force with respect to another value, such as equality, and vice versa. To escape this equivocation, one must admit that values must be organized in a hierarchical table. But even this action is insufficient, for it only reveals the second aspect of the problem. If one has a subjectivistic or relativistic conception of values, whether singularly or in a hierarchical system, it again becomes impossible to stabilize—in an univocal manner—what is and what is not violence. In fact, an act that an individual or collective subject considers legitimate, that is, nonviolent, because it is in accord with their own conception of values (liberty, equality, justice), and because it is in harmony with their own hierarchy of values will, in contrast, often appear

[103] *Perche' la Violenza?*, 64.

to be illegitimate, that is, violent to one who has a different understanding of these same values and their hierarchy.

In order to escape from this vicious circle, it is not enough to make clear that there is here a relationship with recognized values in themselves and their hierarchy, because, in doing so, one returns to the institutional criterion already seen to be insufficient to determine the clear difference between force and violence. In fact, recognized values are those that have already been in some manner institutionalized, either in a juridical-formal or an historical-sociological manner. Moreover, this recognition always remains partial, limited, and transient. In a word, the criterion of relationship to values can be adequate only if it references universally recognized values, independent of their factual institutionalized form, because they are ontologically founded in themselves and in their hierarchy. Only thus can one rescue true values from chaotic plurality, from subjectivism and the relativism of the opposing values arising from these sources. But the truth there exists an ontological foundation for true values is not very popular today.

Secondly, the reference to values, even in the case where they may be ontologically founded, is not sufficient to remove every doubt about the violence of an act. It is certainly easy to distinguish the kidnapping of a person for ransom, from the capture of an adversary as a hostage for a just cause. Fundamentally, the relational criterion in the first case indicates an act of violence, while an act of force in the second. But the relational criterion to a true value no longer functions if the hostage, though taken in an objectively just cause, is a neutral, innocent party or a baby of two months. One could, it is true, maintain that declaring oneself neutral in a just cause is to line up on the side of injustice, thus ceasing to be neutral, and that even a baby is, objectively, found to be in the enemy camp. But, in both of these cases, one would display an irrational extension of the notion of responsibility, contrary to the common understanding of people for whom, indeed, kidnappings in general are typical manifestations of violence. For this reason, total war and total revolution are considered violent events. For they blindly strike out at everyone and everything—enemies, neutrals, innocents, noncombatants—because they accuse and involve the whole of humanity in a dark, collective responsibility in the name of an insane pretext to establish justice.

The fact remains, however, that, in order to defend a true value, there are different methods of doing so. There is a profound difference between a petition to Congress and a break-in there, even if both methods are addressed to the same value that motivates the actions. A just cause does not justify an evil, violent means. Walter Benjamin observes that, even if the criterion of reference to a value is working, "the question remains open whether violence in general, as a principle or as a means for just ends, is a moral good. But, to decide this question, one needs a more penetrating criterion, a distinction within the sphere of means without regard for the ends which they serve."[104]

Because the external parameters of criteria so far investigated have not provided us satisfactory reasons to distinguish clearly between force and violence, we are led to seek another route to that distinction: i.e., analyzing the interior nature of the acts of force and violence. We do this in order to see whether is possible to find structural differences between violence and force whereby we can finally arrive at a valid, incontrovertible criterion for that distinction. As we have indicated earlier in this work, *violence* is derived from the verb *violare*; this immediately makes clear its negative element. From this connection, rape is called violence by another name. In

---

[104] *Perche' la Violenza?*, 66.

the French language, there is the greatest evidence of this connection. Rape is called *viol*, the root of *viol-ence*. Under this semantic
profile, violence appears to be a function of contempt. It removes
all preciousness from a person, situation, institution, etc. While
a person degrades the respect and dignity of another, he or she
is performing the violence that rejects respect for others. On the
other hand, whoever acts with respect for others does not commit
violence. Moreover, showing respect is not an easy or spontane-
ous behavior. Over and above a true and proper philosophical
understanding of man, respect calls for self-control, acceptance
of the other in the full knowledge of our reciprocal rationality.
When respect is exercised in concrete reality, it calls for a force,
a tension in which the linguistic use of this word, commonly accepted, emphasizes the element of physical and spiritual force.
One often hears the expression "He imposes respect." And even
more illuminating is the French formula *Il force le respect*, i.e., "He
compels or commands respect," or "I impose *upon myself* respect
for others." Under this consideration, respect calls forth the idea
of force, while disrespect calls forth the idea of violence. The connection is even more interesting when we reverse the terms of the
relationship. Force sustains—or can sustain—respect, even to the
point of producing admiration. Violence, on the contrary, arouses
resentment, even to the point of producing hatred and contempt.
In this connection, the analyses of Scheler are most illuminating.[105]

The connections that bind violence and force symmetrically
to disrespect and respect, two styles of human behavior so distant
from each other, offer us a very valid structural difference for
these two activities. If force can sustain a respect, which is never
manifest in actions of violence which only arouse fear, rebellion,

[105] *Perche' la Violenza?*, 67.

and reluctant submission, that means that their difference is to be found in their manner of existence, in the way both behaviors develop or unfold. In their profound roots, therefore, the difference between force and violence is founded on the structure of their actions. Let us now try to individualize these structures.

A useful point of departure is afforded us from the very natural definition that mechanics gives us for force. For mechanics, force is whatever can modify the state of inertia or motion in a rectilinear and uniform body. Transferred to the plane of human activity, this definition demands immediately a sub-distinction, because, as is evident, one can also modify a situation, relationship, movement, etc., in two very different ways. One, through conviction; two, through imposition or compulsion. But it would be superficial to believe that this is enough to distinguish the two phenomena under examination. In the first case from which violence is clearly excluded, one is certainly correct to speak of force, e.g., the force of reasoning, example, personality, or sentiment. But force here is used only in a metaphorical sense. For reasoning convinces, not because it is strong, but because it is true, logical, and rigorous, just as a good example calls forth imitation because it is good, courageous, and efficacious. In concrete reality, therefore, both force and violence fall into the area of actions of imposition and compulsion. They are both "activities-against," insofar as they exercise themselves on whomever is not in agreement. With such activity, we enter the field of "pression" in the word of Bergson, i.e., the field of pressure. In other words, we enter into a field where there is not an agreement of intentions or will. Yet, both of us are in the field of the one who is weighing, critically analyzing, the field of the *pesanteur* (gravity), to use Simone Weil's symbolic term.[106] Are we, therefore, in a state

---

[106] *Perche' la Violenza?*, 68.

of darkness that excludes a true human relationship? I would say No! Why? Because the pressure does not, again, imply a valuation, while the one weighing, in the Weilian sense, allows the negation of a relationship to a true value. To have reduced force and violence to a proximate genus of "activity-against," does not authorize us to ignore their specific structural difference. To orient ourselves in this field, it will be useful to, once again, consider the common linguistic usage of words. It is habitual to speak of an "explosion of violence," a "violent effort," or to say that "violence is blind," or that a person is "blinded by violence," and so forth. Now, on the other hand, it would not be possible, in the same contexts, to use the word *force* this way. These linguistic indications permit us to individuate certain structural dimensions of the act of violence already intuited by the common use of people. First, there is the immediacy or directness of violence, for such an act manifests itself all of a sudden—like something which unexpectedly liberates itself impetuously—exploding or breaking loose without there being some stability between the will and the act of violence, for no time is allowed for reflection or meditation. Second, there is the discontinuity of violence, because the violent act does not extend itself into a mediate, and therefore, normal activity, but is destined to exhaust itself in its very explosion, except for another rebirth in another situation. Third, the disproportion of its goal, because being immediate the violent act—though related to a goal—is not so in a reflective or reasonable way but in a blinded one, so that often it is equivocal about the direction it should take. Fourth, the nondurability of the act of violence, for it exhausts itself in its rapidity, more or less, without ever acquiring a consistent durability. Fifth, the unexpectedness of violence. This arises both from its origin and exhaustion, as well as from its direction and results. Strictly coherent among themselves, these are the principal dimensions that determine the act of violence. Moreover, this is the common understanding of violence as found in the constant and concrete experience of all men. And the common understanding of violence always harmonizes with the figure—or agent—of violence. For the violent person is habitually understood as being impulsive, inconstant, incoherent, passionate, and upon whom no one can place his trust—not only, as is obvious, for one's good but even for one's evil. Even considering this case, lucidity and constancy are very productive. In truth, the violent person is totally different from the strong man who exudes trust. In any case, once again we must reveal the immediate and precise knowledge concerning the differences that separate violence from force.

So far, our observations have considered violence as an act of an individual. But they are valid even in a collective situation. The most typical collective act of violence is perpetrated by the crowd or mob, or mass of people rioting in the streets. Understood in a psycho-sociological sense, and not merely in a numerical quantitative one, this extremely unsteady form of collective aggregation constitutes a unitary collective agent through what Scheler calls "affective contagion."[107] Through this contagion the individual is integrated into the crowd, raised above his psychosomatic condition of being a mere individual, and dispossessed of his spiritual personality. Now, the acts of the violent crowd reveal the same diseased symptoms as do the individual acts of violence. Like the latter, they are sudden, discontinuous, nondurable, disproportioned, and unexpected as to their violent goal. On the other hand, the specific affective contagion that brings the crowd together is due to the violent impact of a violent emotion. It is the passionate fruit of an imposed pressure, of a domination exercised over a certain

[107] *Perche' la Violenza?*, 70.

84

number of individuals because of an event—real or imaginary—that always has the capacity to inspire emotion. An impassioned leader of a special cause often arouses the masses to delirious violence. Whoever succumbs to this domination is reduced to a usable object, manipulated by the one—or group—who is dominating the masses. Such persons undergo the experience of being violently depersonalized. On the other hand, the mob thus collected makes its own the violence it has created and experienced, and unloads it by spreading violence everywhere on everyone, reducing others to becoming objects of the enraged mob. It is within this vicious circle, brought about by the depersonalization of the mob and the depersonalizing of all its victims, that violence is born and triumphs.

We need not expound endlessly on this analysis of violence, which has been treated more thoroughly in the studies of such writers as Gustave Le Bon, Scipio Sighele, Sigmund Freud, Scheler, and that final analysis of Sartre on *Gruppo in fusione*, the Fusion Group. Nobody doubts that the masses are seen to be agents of violence in the same measure as individuals. For the mobs are commonly called "blind, blinded, unchained." The similarity is so great that the mob can be seen as the collective analogue of the violent. The mob is the violent individual writ large. On the other hand, it would be very incongruous to speak of "a forceful mob." Moreover, everyone recognizes the difference between a "forceful nation" and "a violent nation."

So far we have discussed the act of violence done by individuals or collectives as agents of that violence, and we have clearly demonstrated that both act with delirious passion. Indeed, it is passion itself which gives them their typical tone and style of acting, distinguishing them in their manner of acting—immediate, sudden, shocking, discontinuous, unexpected, and unchained in fury. Even here, common language allows us to establish the difference between force and violence. If we use the expression "force of soul," which resists and rejects uncontrolled passion, we find that it likewise rejects violence. This is a manifestation and good effect of "force of soul." Moreover, the most frequent source of violence is properly a passion that one has undergone and suffered in his own person or his loved ones—a passion that is beyond reason, out of control, autocratic, intemperate, and subject to no form of moderation. Violence is joined to passionateness, to delirious excitability, under a double aspect. First, insofar as violence begets more violence. And, second, insofar as passionateness creates an habitual violent style of living. For wherever there is violence, there is also present delirious passion.

From the horizon of passionateness, therefore, there is revealed with clear prominence the structural, unitary, and fundamental character of violence, which are condemned by the various phenomenological aspects we have already indicated, especially the absence of rationality and moderation known as intemperance in the extreme. For what is the common element at the root of the suddenness, discontinuity, nondurability, unexpectedness, and delirious excitability of all violence, if it is not the lack of temperance and moderation? On the other hand, passion suffered in one's own person in a spirit of self-sufficiency will not accept any external moderating influence, and thus abandons itself to its own instinctive madness. Opposed to this attitude, moderation appears to be a typical characteristic of force. For force goes into action at specified times of emergency and with the rhythm of moderation, thus becoming even a criterion of temperance and moderation itself.

It seems, however, that we can distinguish *within* the genus of "activity-against," i.e., force as a regularity vs. violence as intemperance. Under this perspective, the specific difference between them is constituted by their different internal structure, and this difference is not deduced from the questionable external criteria and parameters. The rediscovery, under the exterior, imaginary facet of violence, of a constructive unitary structure — its intemperance and absence of moderation — permits us to arrive at the existential significance of a violent phenomenon. It is the depersonalizing cycle in which we find ourselves trapped, whenever we perform or undergo violence. This is the first aspect of violence to be considered, the point of departure for reflection rather than the terminal for our arrival. In fact, within the horizon of violence, depersonalization is made precise by the dispossession of the self, a self which stands in itself and possesses itself. For *persona est sui juris* — that is, a person who belongs to himself or is his own — he takes responsibility for actions that he himself has generated. A person enjoys substantial reality when he or she is conscious of himself or herself. Thus, whoever becomes a victim of violence is reduced to being an object; he or she is reified, no longer an agent in control of his own conscious actions, no longer able to act intelligently and freely. Instead, he or she loses the very consciousness of their personhood, having been reduced — as has been observed by the penetrating brilliance of Simone Weil — to a "naked vegetative egoism, an egoism without an I."[108] But, reciprocally, whoever violently imposes himself upon another abandons himself to violence and, arriving at extreme excess, dispossesses himself of his own personhood. Then, in the words of Kierkegaard, "he surrenders himself to animality,"[109] and, according to Scheler, "falls away from his own spirituality." As is evident, the cycle of

---

[108] *Perche' la Violenza?*, 71.

[109] Søren Kierkegaard, *La Folla* [The Mob: A Diary] (Brescia, Italy, 1963), no. 2853.

dispossessing one's personhood presses down upon the violent person punctually, and intensifies his cycle of depersonalization.[110] In this evil cycle, reciprocal recognition of the dignity of persons is obliterated, disfigured by violence; people no longer recognize each other. In other words, there is lost and obliterated the normal moderation that recognizes all men are equal and endowed with spiritual dignity.

What is the existential significance of this process? It is quite clear that there is canceled any possibility of personal communication. For friendly and trustworthy communication is possible only when one is favorably disposed and willing to share common concerns in the moderation of mutual respect. Without this friendly attitude, communication remains unilateral and inane, because it never escapes the spiritual straitjacket of a closed, hardened mind and heart. It never can arrive at the rapport of mutual comprehension. True, there exists an abyss between the chitchat of a gossiper and the dialogue with a true friend. For an inveterate gossip-artist speaks only of himself or herself. Others serve the gossip-monger as objects of support for his or her narcissistic love. The gossiper rules out the discovery of a common ground for reciprocal communication. On the contrary, that complete and authentic form of social rapport, which is dialogue in mutual friendship, necessarily is founded on mutual charity and moderation. Now it is such charity and moderation that is abandoned in violence. For its very intemperance succeeds in preventing, from its very foundation, any realistic possibility for the development of friendly dialogue. Violence constitutes the most explicit and radical rupture of communion in community. Indeed, it cannot even be called unilateral communication because it communicates nothing. It

[110] *Perche' la Violenza?*, 73.

merely dominates in a brutal, cruel manner. Unfortunately, it is no way as innocuous as silly chitchat.

But even this is not enough of an explanation. For a more profound explanation of the question is possible. Cancellation of reciprocal recognition, rupture of communion in community, negation of disciplined temperance are also, and above all, indications that there is also lost any consciousness of the ontological relationship of harmonious and peaceful coexistence through whose social dynamism all persons discover their whole being, and develop their persons. Not only is the friendly I-thou relationship ruptured between human persons, but violence strikes at the very nature of Supreme Being, who has established between Himself and every individual person an I-thou, a being-with that is the divine foundation of all love and community. Perhaps Gabriel Marcel has best expressed this truth most felicitously: "Ego-centrism is always a cause of blindness."[111] For him, only insofar as persons are open to others, insofar as they exist for all others and all others exist for them in the mutual activity of welcoming, serving, surrendering, and loving each other, can the I and thou coexist as co-presence in communication and community. The man of violence is caught in the bondage of self-idolatry. For he is irrevocably unavailable to others, refuses to be at their disposal, and uses techniques of degradation, i.e., violence, lying, imprisonment, deportation, blackmail, subversion, propaganda, and disloyalty to create worldwide fear and confusion.

Conscious that his relationship and availability to and for others constitutes the foundation of his existence, the person who rejects violence understands his own individuality, not a fantasy

---

[111] Gabriel Marcel, *Man against Mass Society* (London: Harvill Press, 1952). The entire book treats this theme.

individuality. For his own personal individuality is founded in his I-thou relationship, a being-with which conquers the hidden and killing tendency of narcissism. The person is then ready to live his life in coexistence harmoniously with others. He thus creates a loyal intermingling of human vines, each one of whom cares for the other. Now, violence brutally breaks this harmonious intermingling, rejecting the dimension of otherness and thus dissolving coexistence in a dictatorial fashion.

We see then, clearly, the lack of commitment the violent man has toward his fellowmen for whatever is good. The violence to which he habitually abandons himself, denying inter-subjective communion, keeps him locked within himself. He becomes a displaced person, falling away from the spiritual consciousness of his being toward resentment, vindictiveness, hatred, existence without meaning, and social suicide that could even end in physical suicide—so as to escape the absurdity of all reality. On the other hand, it is a fact that the man of force promotes trust, because he is available to others, moderate in action, open to friendly dialogue, and anxious to live harmoniously in communion within the community. In conclusion, then, looked at in its very structure, violence reveals its totally clear specific character and its existential significance. We can therefore define violence thus: violence is an activity-against that is intemperate, irrational, resentful, self-idolatrous, inimical to dialogue and coexistence, and overwhelmingly arrogant in its *libido domandi*, i.e., its lust for domination. The habitual value judgment that condemns violence is founded on this existential structure of pure negativity. Thus, we have arrived in the clear field of being weighers, critics, thinkers, and presenters of violence in the Weilian sense. Violence is a dark rejection, a refusal to care for anyone, an irrational imprisonment of oneself in the chosen cell of hardened hatred, and an absolute surrender to animality. We see here that not every metaphysics of being is indeed identified with deductive philosophizing. But, often to get at the truth of a reality, we must proceed from an analysis of human experience, examining all the riches of its manifestations, to arrive at the roots of this reality. Thus, from a phenomenological analysis of the experience of violence, we have arrived at an ontological interpretation of its meaning and being.

In summary, here—in a tabular scheme—are the major phenomenological differences between violence and force.

Characteristics of Violence	Characteristics of Force
Violence is:	*Force is:*
Private, unauthorized action	Lawful, public action
Disrespectful of persons	Respectful of persons
Intemperate in action	Temperate in action
Arouses resentment, hatred	Arouses admiration, love
Against dialogue, unsocial	For dialogue, social
Imposes blind compulsion	Imposes lawful compulsion
Domination of others	At the service of others
Acts without reflection	Acts thoughtfully
Always activity against	Activity for justice
Rejects accountability	Accepts accountability
Cares only for itself	Cares for all

The Roots of Violence

Characteristics of Violence	Characteristics of Force
Physical destroyer	Physical preserver
Spiritually corrupt	Spiritually inspiring
Motivated by hatred	Motivated by common good
Producer of mad mobs	Preserver of communities
Despiser of lawful values	Defender of lawful values
Degrader of its victims	Restorer of victims
Manipulator of propaganda	Faithful to truth
Agent of instability	Agent for security, peace
Poser as a messiah	Servant of human rights

Because violence and force are actions of man, who is an inexhaustible mystery, the phenomenological aspects of these actions are also inexhaustible. We could go on analyzing these human actions *ad infinitum*. But the above, enumerated characteristics should indicate that violence leads to the pulverization of man and society, whereas force to the preservation and improvement the same.

5

THE VIOLENCE OF LUST

*Now the works of the flesh are manifest, which are fornication,
uncleanness, immodesty, luxury, idolatry, witchcrafts, enmities,
contentions, emulations, wraths, quarrels, dissensions, sects, envies,
murders, drunkenness, revelings, and such like, . . . I have foretold to
you, that they who do such things shall not obtain the kingdom of God.*

—Galatians 5:19-21

Somewhere St. Augustine has written: *Peccatum poena peccati,* that is, "Sin is the punishment of sin." To form a variation on that truth we can say, *Violentia poena violentiae,* that is "Violence is the punishment of violence." And to go a step further, we can add: "Lust is the punishment of lust."

In what does the violence of lust or *luxuria* consist? Lust is the inordinate craving for, or indulgence of, the carnal pleasure that is experienced in the whole body, but especially in the human organs of generation. We have already established hatred of truth, otherwise known as pride, as the taproot of all violence. Now we hope to show that lust, as a capital sin which spawns many other vices, is, in reality, another evil root of violence originating from that common mother of all vices. St. Thomas Aquinas enumerates the ugly "daughters of lust" as follows: "blindness of mind, thoughtlessness, inconstancy, rashness, self-love, hatred of God, love of this world, and abhorrence or despair of a future world."[112] These are the "ugly daughters" that besmirch the lecher himself or herself. But there are also the more despicable and damaging acts of violence that lust perpetrates against human persons, families, and society.

The psychological and social violence of lust is founded on the lived lie that human beings are incapable of attaining real communion in an interpersonal relationship of love and friendship. Others are seen not as intelligent, lovable persons made in the image and likeness of God, and with whom one is called to imitate the three, august Divine Persons of the Family of the Holy Trinity, i.e., in mutual, loving self-donation that shares truth and holiness in spiritual friendship. No, others are seen as sex objects to be seduced, dominated, and used for venereal pleasure. Others are not persons with an inviolable life of their own: founded on physical and spiritual integrity; standing on their own as spiritual substances which are not reducible to anything else; endowed with intelligence and freedom; and destined for the Beatific Vision in the family of God. Lust sees others as mere bodies: beautiful, alluring, pluckable, and enjoyable.

Lust has no friends; it is not interested in persons. Lust is concerned merely with the gratification of its own concupiscence—not in the perfection of man's whole nature, but only in the appeasement of an animal appetite that it is unwilling or unable to control. Lust reduces its partners to being mere objects, sexual problems possessed for a time and solved and used for sexual gratification. The human

---

[112] St. Thomas Aquinas, *Summa Theologica*, II–II, q. 153, a. 5.

partners in a lustful relationship become depersonalized instruments available for casual, carnal service. Lust dominates its participants as useful, momentary property. Lust is perhaps the worst form of self-love, extending to the contempt of God and man.[113]

It is worthwhile to consider some of the characteristics of lust. Lust imposes on its victims the brutality and tyranny of an unchained libido. Lust is cruel, full of envy; it is impatient and seductively self-seeking. Lust thinks of nothing but evil, for it is full of dominating pride. It never acts with an open heart or mind, but always and only with open genitalia. Lust is joyless and without charm, for it is obscene and, in its wantonness, leads millions to ruin and death. The lusts and greed of the body scandalize and kill the life of the soul. The victim of licentiousness runs in madness from one lustful experience to a new, self-emptying surrender to sex, seeking in a futile, endless "cruise" ever receding thrills that can only end in despair and disaster. Lust never attains peace, for it is never stated in its voluptuousness of feeling; it is always on the prowl for new and indiscriminate victims, whether these victims are humans, animals, or mere things used to stimulate and satisfy a parched flesh. Lust turns to perversions when the natural use of the flesh ceases to satisfy its insatiable, delirious, animal impulses and fantasies. Lust degrades the flesh, as well as the personhood, of its human partners. In the name of a false freedom, which is really licentiousness, lust has become the prevailing and persistent perversity of our age. It has today loosed a whirlwind of unharnessed libido, and sent it roaring with escalating violence through a world that has become a "synagogue of Satan" (Rev. 2:9), a sewer of "trashed" humanity.[114]

---

[113] Henry Fairlie, *The Seven Deadly Sins Today*, 175–190.
[114] Fairlie, *The Seven Deadly Sins Today*, 175–190.

The Roots of Violence

Some Forms of Lustful Violence

There are many forms of lustful activity. Here we analyze some of them, indicating their violence against man and society. Wherever one turns—on television, or in movies, newspapers, magazines, and long civic, even national, parades—one is astonished at the homosexual epidemic that is engulfing the whole world. Over four thousand years ago, Sodom and Gomorrah had become Sodomite cities. The word *sodomy*—meaning men practicing sex with men—is derived from that city's sexual corruption. And these cities were full of violence. The Old Testament graphically relates how the men of Sodom attempted to sexually molest the angelic messengers, who took the form of men in fulfilling their mission to warn Lot to flee with his family before God's wrath consumed both cities in fire and brimstone. Lot offered his daughters instead, but his angelic guests thankfully preempted any sexual abuse (Gen. 19:8–11).

Not too long ago in San Diego, the press reported the "trash can murders" of twenty-four homosexuals—performed in a sadistic fashion. These clearly indicate that the malice of sodomy consists in the perverted affection towards the same sex, in the attraction and performance for the unnatural method of sexual gratification. Even between consenting homosexuals, whether they be men or lesbian women, the basic violence arises from the mutual depersonalization, the degrading reduction of each other from being spiritual beings to being treated as mere sex objects or instruments. There cannot be any true spiritual love, or even carnal love worthy of man; there cannot be any communion or intelligent interpersonal community between persons who are merely manipulating one another's bodies for their self-centered carnal pleasure.

True carnal love is always subordinated to the recognition and affirmation of the human person's value. This spiritual, intellectual affirmation moves the will to love the beloved with the moral love of friendship. Lovers then love each other as persons who are their own masters *(sui juris)*—inalienable, untransferable *(alteri incommunieabiles)*, non-substitutable subjects—and who then willingly renounce their autonomy and inalienability in the ecstasy of total self-donation to each other in a permanent union of spiritual friendship. True lovers give the gift of themselves to the beloved as persons, and find a fuller existence in this communion. In the case of "betrothed love," which finds its fulfillment in marriage, sensual love subordinates and integrates itself with the spiritual love of the persons that gives primacy of value to the persons, not their bodies. Only when it is directed toward the integral person is love true love.

But in the perversions of homosexuality and lesbianism, erotic love—or the sexual value of the partners—is identified with their bodies as objects for mutual sexual exploitation. Here, each partner momentarily belongs to the other as an instrument of use, and both strive to derive pleasure from allowing each other to manipulate their bodies sexually. Such activity is utterly incompatible with the full spiritual love to be found in betrothal.

Indeed, an erotic love centered solely on the body creates conditions for a conflict of interests, which eventually explode into violence. Egoism, especially that of the senses and emotions, driven by a rapacious will, is the mother of violence in sexual affairs. Since lust is fed on the cravings of lust, it never takes time out to explore or develop any relationship to the full. In his book, *The Seven Deadly Sins Today*, Henry Fairlie explains this inconstancy of lust:

> It [lust] will whip itself [perhaps an appropriate term in the context] to try anything that will revive its jaded feelings. It is tired of fellatio. Then it will try its hand [hardly the

appropriate phrase in the context] at a little sodomy. Weary of only one partner, it will advance to group sex. Unsure at last of its own sexuality, it will have recourse to bisexuality. Wearied and bored by the flesh, it will call for chains and leather jackets. Who knows when, abandoning the last shred of its humanity, it will turn to bestiality?[115]

In order to increase the delirium of its sexual ecstasy, the partners in erotic sex very often create a new and hideous relationship. One takes the role of the sadist and whips or tortures a submissive partner, using brutality and cruelty to attain a more exquisite sexual orgasm. The other partner accepts the role of masochist, seeking his refined pleasure from being dominated, mistreated, and hurt physically. Often this preference for punishment and torture leads to murder. We have here, created by erotic madness, the most violent form of relationship—the slave-master degradation of human persons.

Lately, homosexuals and lesbians have assumed a high public image. They have taken to the streets to demonstrate in the thousands, challenging normal society to grant their perverted way of sexual life the acceptance that is given to heterosexual life. They are confronting the churches, the government, and the law to put their stamp of moral approval on a sexual lifestyle to which they claim they have a right. They have invaded schools, hospitals, nursery homes, daycare centers; they have even become foster parents raising children committed to their care. To attain these ends, they often have recourse to force and violence. Moreover, they have discovered the power of the ballot, and, in San Francisco, have succeeded in electing a mayor favorable to their designs. Their

[115] Fairlie, *The Seven Deadly Sins Today*, 175–190.

political power is growing at an alarming speed. Hence, they are a threat to children, families, societies, and nations by their unnatural, sterile, and violent lifestyle.

St. Thomas Aquinas defines lust as a capital vice thus:

> A capital vice is one that has a very desirable end, so that through desire for that end a man proceeds to commit many sins, all of which are said to arise from that vice as from a principal vice. Now the end of lust is venereal pleasure, which is very great. Wherefore this pleasure is very desirable as regards the sensitive appetite, both on account of the intensity of the pleasure and because such like concupiscence is connatural to man. Therefore, it is evident that lust is a capital sin.[116]

Some of the many sins that arise from lust are fornication, sex between unmarried persons; seduction, the venereal act whereby a virgin or married woman is violated; rape, the violent sexual assault upon another person; adultery, sexual intercourse with another man or woman in contravention of the marriage contract, whether through the impulse of one's own lust, or with the consent of the other party; and incest, unlawful intercourse with persons related by consanguinity or affinity. In all these sins of lust, and in any other species of this sin, the violence that is common to them is the degradation of a spiritual person to the level of a sex object. This spiritual and psychological violence often involves physical violence, as in the case of rape, where another's physical and moral integrity is brutally violated—and often the rape ends in the murder of the victim. Moreover, in cases of incest, children unable to endure the sexual molestation of relatives often seek escape in suicide.

[116] St. Thomas, *Summa Theologica*, II–II, q. 153, a. 4.

The Roots of Violence

Today, there is another form of hideous lust that I might call the commercialization of sex. It is perpetrated on society through the kidnapping of children in the hundreds of thousands. They are then used in hard-core pornographic movies. Once used for profit in the millions, these children are never heard of again, and most likely are destroyed to prevent them from ever giving evidence in court against this satanic racket. We have here the physical violence of kidnapping, violence of theft against parents, degradation of the children, and the corruption of society that is exposed to these lewd films.

In a May 13, 1983 article in the *New York Times*, "Studies Find Sexual Abuse of Children Is Widespread," Glenn Collins writes,

New research on child molestation shows that each offender may be responsible for abusing unexpectedly large numbers of children, and that child molestation is more widespread and a more violent crime than was formerly supposed....

"The dimensions of the abuse are staggering," said Dr. A. Nicholas Groth, director of the sex offender program at the Connecticut Correctional Institute in Somers, who has studied one thousand child molesters over the last sixteen years. "If we saw these same numbers of children suddenly developing some kind of illness, we'd think we had a major epidemic on our hands," he said....

National statistics on the actual number of children molested are only estimates, since research has shown that most incidents are unreported. But a new study of sexual offenders shows that each was responsible for completing—or attempting—an average of sixty-eight child molestations. This was three times the average number of rapes of adult women attempted by those offenders studied....

"It used to be supposed that child molestation was a primarily passive crime," said Dr. Gene G. Abel, director of the Sexual Behavior Clinic of the New York State Psychiatric Institute at Columbia-Presbyterian Medical Center in Manhattan. "However, 50 percent of all child molestation may involve violence," he said. A recent study of police and emergency room records of child molestation by Dr. William Marshall and his colleagues at Queens University in Kingston, Ontario, reported that forty percent of the cases of sexual abuse involved force or violent acts....

"The largest group of victimizers are caretakers—parents, babysitters, and those to whom we entrust children" ... said Dr. Groth.... The Federal Bureau of Investigation estimates that only one in five of all sexual assaults are reported....

The cause of child molestation is much debated. Dr. Groth said, "There has usually been trauma or victimization during the offender's formative years." Of the imprisoned offenders he has studied, 80 percent of them were themselves sexually abused as children.[117]

Promiscuous sex burns and dries up human persons—and inevitably human relationships. For lust is also the mother of hypocrisy. Because the lustful person lacks the virtue of reverence, that fundamental attitude which makes persons see and adhere to spiritual values. The lustful person is impertinent, rooted in pride, self-love, and concupiscence. Interested solely in the pursuit of pleasure—the practice of seduction and voyeurism—lustful

---

[117] Glenn Collins, "Studies Find Sexual Abuse of Children is Widespread," *New York Times*, May 13, 1982.

persons become the false fronts they have so cleverly developed. This hypocrisy, being a living lie, empties them of all concern for truth and any fidelity to their neighbors. Perpetually agitated by ego-spasm, lustful persons, in the end, lust after lust in an existence that is a form of dying, a dying which has displaced religion with carefree sex as the opium of the people.[118]

Another insidious lie, which the advocates of carefree sex have promulgated and succeeded in having the public and the courts accept, is the shibboleth that what consenting, lustful partners do in private is nobody's business but their own. But what is the catastrophic reality arising from this lying propaganda? Actually, what persons do in private has tremendous repercussions on society at large. What families do in the privacy of their homes affects not only their own behavior, but also what they expect from others and will tolerate as the morality of their children and the nation. After all, the morality they teach their children goes out with the children into society.

Then, too, we have a frightful example in our day of how private lust flows over into public mores. For ages, homosexual partners, who in private practiced sodomy as consenting adults, now have moved into public, seeking to have their sexual lifestyle legalized and accepted. They are now allowed to enter into legally accepted "homosexual marriages," a reality that was an abomination in the West for thousands of years. Moreover, to show how that shibboleth is not strictly applied, society does intervene if two consenting adults are found molesting their children in the privacy of their home. It is sheer nonsense and dangerous to preach that lust is merely a private affair. Morally diseased adults, practicing in private all forms of lust, are more dangerous to the health and survival of

[118] Fairlie, *The Seven Deadly Sins Today*, 175–190.

nations than persons physically afflicted with contagious diseases that could lead to epidemics.

Then, too, lustful moral diseases often lead to physical diseases. This has been demonstrated fearfully in our day in the rise of AIDS, the dreadful, once incurable disease, which springs from unnatural and frequent sexual misbehavior. The truth is that all humans are social animals and their private moral mores necessarily flow over into public life, often changing the manners and discipline of society at large. It may take a while for rampant, widely accepted lust to destroy a civilization, but it will inevitably ruin any civilization of high cultural or religious caliber. St. Paul graphically relates, in his Letter to the Romans, how the widespread, accepted, lustful perversity rampant in the Roman Empire brought that empire to ruin and annihilation (see 1:18-32).

Right reason and moral theology condemn what they call sexual anesthesia—the death of the sexual faculties—in which one cannot satisfy their sexual cravings because they've been burnt out from excessive abuse. It also condemns sexual hyperesthesia, which consists in a morbidly intense sexual excitability—usually fed by pornographic novels, magazines, peep shows, conversations, and movies. Finally, taking its sexual values from the revealed Word of God, truly Catholic and Christian moral theology strongly censures, as does God, sexual paresthesia: that is, that style of sexual activity that is affected not so much by venereal matters as by objects altogether foreign to sex life. Forms of that perversion have already been alluded to, namely, sadism, masochism, and homosexuality. There remains the activity of fetishism, that is, the arousing of sexual passion by things which, in themselves, have no relation to sex and are not represented by the imagination as having any reference to any person. Fetishism, for example, would arouse sexual passion from one's sight or imagination; the touch of a hand, hair, or garment; or from a show or anything.[119]

It is important to note that such lustful passions, and especially homosexuality, are condemned in the Bible. In Genesis 18 and 19,

> the Lord said: "The cry of Sodom and Gomorrah is multiplied, and their sin is become exceedingly grievous." ... And [the angels] said to Lot: "Hast thou here any of thine? son in law, or sons, or daughters, all that are thine bring them out of this city: for we will destroy this place, because their cry is grown loud before the Lord, who hath sent us to destroy them." ...
>
> And the Lord rained upon Sodom and Gomorrah brimstone and fire from the Lord out of heaven. And he destroyed these cities, and all the country about, all the inhabitants of the cities, and all things that spring from the earth. [120]

In the book of Leviticus we read:

> The Lord spoke to Moses, saying: "Speak to the children of Israel, and thou shalt say to them: ... Thou shalt not lie with mankind as with womankind, because it is an abomination. Thou shalt not copulate with any beast, neither shalt thou be defiled with it. A woman shall not lie down to a beast, nor copulate with it: because it is a heinous crime. ... Beware then, lest in like manner, it vomit you also out, if you do the like things, as it vomited out the nation that was before you."[121]

[119] Rev. Herbert Jone, O.F.M. Cap. *Moral Theology*, 168–169.
[120] Gen. 18:20; 19:12–13, 24–25.
[121] Lev. 18:1–2, 22–23, 28.

Again in Leviticus we read, "If any one lie with a man as with a woman, both have committed an abomination, let them be put to death: their blood be upon them." And in the same chapter further on we read, "Walk not after the laws of the nations, which I will cast out before you. For they have done all these things, and therefore I abhorred them."[122]

And, as noted, in Romans St. Paul condemned men who, "leaving the natural use of the women, have burned in their lusts one towards another, men with men working that which is filthy and receiving in themselves the recompense which was due to their error.... Who, having known the justice of God, did not understand that they who do such things, are worthy of death; and not only they that do them, but they also that consent to them that do them."[123]

Pornography and Violence

Pornography is material that is predominantly sexually explicit and intended primarily for the purpose of sexual arousal. It leads almost inevitably to an increase in aggressive conduct toward its victims, but especially toward women and children. Sexually violent fare is sweeping the country. It has become eye-grabbing fare for producers, programmers, and advertisers. Often inserted into violent media offerings, it has saturated, and is continuing to saturate, the minds and souls of millions. For pornography is the literature of sexual deviance. Each type of sexual deviance is clinically called a *paraphilia*. Each of these sixty different specialized paraphilias—psychiatric disorders such as voyeurism, fetishism, pedophilia, homosexuality, and sadomasochism—has its own style

---

[122] Lev. 20:13, 23.
[123] Rom. 1:27, 31.

of literature: at least one, and sometimes more, specialty magazines backed up by films, videotapes, and trade newsletters.

Some of the material involves sadomasochistic themes, with whips, chains, and other devices of torture. Other materials involve the repeated theme of a man making sexual advances to a woman, being rebuffed, and then raping the woman. In the course of the rape, the woman becomes ecstatically aroused over the forced sexual activity. Then there are the "slasher films," which serve up suggestive nudity coupled with extreme violence such as disfigurement or murder.[124]

From the 1986 "Meese Report," we learn how technology is making pornography easily available to the whole world and every family:

> Broadcast TV has become sexually explicit with frequent themes of adultery, fornication, prostitution, sexual deviation, and sexual abuse. There is a significant amount of material that qualifies as sexual violence.... Some seventeen hundred new sexually explicit videocassettes were released in 1985.... Dial-a-porn is a totally new form of pornographic communication. The acts described on these phone calls include lesbian sexual activity, sadomasochistic abuse, sex acts with children, sodomy, rape, incest, excretory functions, bestiality.... The volume of calls is immense. Some companies can handle fifty thousand callers per hour without any caller getting a busy signal! During one day in May 1983, eight hundred thousand calls were placed to one sexually explicit recorded message service....

[124] [U.S.] *Attorney General's Commission on Pornography: Final Report*, vol. 1 (Washington, DC: U.S. Department of Justice, 1986). Edwin Meese led the Commission.

In California, dial-a-porn providers earn $1.26 per call, while the telephone company earns seventy-four cents.[125]

The Violence from Pedophiles

There are several hundred thousand pedophiles nationwide prowling around seeking to sexually molest children. These marauding victimizers prey on children of all ages, and, at times, on adults as well. They seek weak, vulnerable victims—aiming to begin a "cruelty relationship" giving them control over their human prey, which leads to the coercion, punishment, humiliation, and, at times, murder of their victims. Serial killers are active in this category. One is reminded of Charles Manson or John Wayne Gacy, and also incestuous fathers. Ironically, a recent California study estimated that 95 percent of arrested child molesters do not go to prison. Of thirty thousand child molesters in California in 1979, only 160 were jailed or hospitalized. Now pedophiles have created numerous national and international organizations. They collect and exchange information from children's addresses and write pseudo-scientific articles supporting sex with children.[126]

These include organizations such as the North American Man/Boy Love Association (NAMBLA), the Rene Guyon Society, the Lewis Carroll Collector's Guild, the Pedophile Information Exchange (PIE), the Childhood Sensuality Circle (CSC), PAN and a variety of other smaller European groups. What are the doings of such organizations? The North American Man/Boy Love Association (NAMBLA) was formed in Boston in 1978 to promote pedophilia as a lifestyle, defend men accused of sex crimes involving

---

[125] *Attorney General's Commission on Pornography: Final Report*, vol. 1.
[126] David Alexander Scott, *Pornography: Its Effects on Family, Community, and Culture*, 13.

boys, and lobby against age-of-consent laws for sexual activities. They believe that the age of consent should be lowered to four. Although they claim to have twenty thousand members, observers estimate the actual membership to be fewer than five hundred. The Rene Guyon Society, with a motto of "sex before age eight, or else it's too late," has lobbied at state and federal levels for changes in laws relating to children and sex. They also circulate a newsletter, provide a speakers bureau, and have a summer camping program for the daughters of members. The society, based in Southern California, has a membership variably estimated to be between 670 and five thousand. The CSC, based in San Diego, characterizes itself as a lay research organization, and has a nine-point statement of purpose concerning the sexual rights of children. One must realize that, like collectors of murder "memorabilia," successful child molesters don't advertise. These groups, then, are high-profile shock troops. Their basic purpose is political: to distract the public and blur the broader issues of child sexual molestation and deviance. They are the highly visible tip of a much more complex and threatening iceberg. Now, the traditional or conventional family as socially normative is inimical to pedophiles. They support efforts to redefine the family, and call for separation of the procreative and affective/supportive aspects of human sexuality in general and family relationships in particular. The demise of the conventional family is the goal of the pedophile movement. In an article in *NAMBLA News* on "Men/Boy Love and Feminism," David Thorstad describes the "new" family that would replace the old. In it, "the child himself should have the right to decide with whom to live, whether a lesbian mother or a gay father, the 'natural' parents, a boy-lover or someone else."[127]

[127] Scott, *Pornography*, 13–14.

What has been discovered about the background of such sex offenders? Two-thirds of convicted sex offenders had a criminal record.[128] Pornography viewing became an addiction with them before they acted out their fantasies in actual sexual assaults. Gordon Russell, a psychologist at the University of Lethbridge in Alberta, Canada, found that violence viewing led to an increase in—and enhancement of—hostility in fans viewing sports.[129] In a similar manner, constant exposure to pornography produces an enhanced interest in deviant sexuality. For this reason, scores of adolescents and children, many of them runaways, are killed by pimps who prey on and exploit the hundreds of thousands of young runaways and young prostitutes. In her book *Rape and Marriage*, Diana Russell reports the results of her long-term study of sexual abuse of females, in particular the relationship between male interest in pornography and deviant sexual behavior, and its effects on the subsequent abuse of women. In her study of 930 victims of rape and other sexual abuse, Russell found that the depiction and dissemination of "rape-myth" type pornography was a significant element in reducing inhibitions to use violence even in marital relationships, and habituating both males and females to the idea of rape as well as to the acceptance of sexual deviance as normal behavior. Repeated exposure to rape-myth imagery contributed significantly to her subjects' reports of dissatisfaction in their sexual relationships with their spouses.[130] In like manner, adult pornography is used to initiate children into sex, and constant viewing of pornography habituates them to deviant, even violent sex. Dangerous offenders—i.e., child molesters, incestuous fathers,

---

[128] Scott, *Pornography*, 14.
[129] Scott, *Pornography*, 5.
[130] Scott, *Pornography*, 7.

serial killers, and rapists—develop a fondness for deviant material and incorporate it into their preparatory stimulation before seeking out a victim, whether it is a child to molest, a woman to rape, or an adolescent boy to assault.[131]

The Current Research on Pornography

The Meese Report gives us some findings about pornography from the most recent research on that subject.

1. Exposure to nonviolent, noncoercive "soft-core," consenting sex pornography desensitizes, leads to callousness, and can sometimes trigger emotionally violent behavior.

2. "Hard-core," deviant depictions—including graphic violence without sexual consent, soft-core depictions of consensual sex between heterosexual couples, and even "neutral," sex education materials—all, in different ways, desensitize and habituate the viewer.

3. Pornography affects the most dangerous sex offender as well as the normal person, and it interferes with interpersonal relationships and personal moral development in *everyone* who uses it, not only in the disturbed and demented.

4. The negative effects of pornography harm normal persons and their marriages, as well as individuals with a wide variety of personality disorders.

5. Both normal and disturbed people not only become "desensitized" to soft-core materials, they also develop a fondness for more deviant materials. Both incorporate them into sexual practices, and begin to fantasize

[131] Scott, *Pornography*, 9

about—and even endorse—the use of force in their sexual relationships.

6. Both normal and emotionally disturbed individuals become "habituated" to pornographic materials. They require increasingly deviant and bizarre images to re-establish their original pre-habituation level of sexual arousal.

7. For the increasingly addicted normal consumer of pornography, habituation is overcome: (a) by engaging in increasingly unusual and bizarre sex acts which often lead to dissatisfaction within marriage; and (b) seeking out a greater variety of sexual partners, including prostitutes, outside of marriage. Both sets of behavior are soon perceived to be quite normal. This perception evolves into the belief that these materials do not harm others, even children.

8. The bottom-line effect of long-term exposure to pornographic materials has been: (a) an increasing callousness and insensitivity towards others, and (b) a more gradual, malignantly regressive "primitivization" of emotional relationships that cuts across all social strata.

9. Sex offending, particularly for the dangerous offender, is compulsive and addictive. His mechanisms for reducing anxiety have become sexualized. Repetitive sexual molestation has become compulsive. The sex offender's anxiety-reducing fix is sex with a child or an adolescent, rather than drugs, alcohol, or nicotine.

10. His need for a child—many different children, or the same child—is just as frequent and urgent as the addict's need for chemical substances. The sex offender must offend repeatedly to maintain his psychic stability. Failure

to satisfy this need can presage emotional breakdown, suicidal ideation, and even suicidal behavior—not only the offender, but sometimes his adolescent victims as well.

11. An increasingly visible and steadily growing class of more than two million sexually deviant adults—rapists, pedophiles, "hebephiles," incestuous fathers, sexual sadists, habitual felons, and customers of teenage prostitutes seeking "little girls" (and boys), year in, year out—are sexually victimizing a like number of children and youth.

12. The actual number of assaults is more than two million due to the repeat offending against the same victim by incestuous fathers, homosexual and heterosexual pedophiles, and the customers of child and adolescent prostitutes. Relatively few of these incidents are reported to the authorities.[132]

Some Witnesses from the Meese Report

Linda S.: The incest started at the age of eight. I did not understand any of it. My dad would try to convince me that it was okay. He would find magazines with articles and/or pictures that would show fathers and daughters.... He would say that if it was published in magazines, it had to be all right because magazines could not publish lies.

Former prostitute: We were all introduced to prostitution through pornography. There were no exceptions in our group, and we were all under eighteen. Pornography was

[132] Scott, *Pornography*, 3–4.

our textbook. We learned the tricks of the trade by men exposing us to pornography and us trying to mimic what we saw.

Another man: I understand pornography to be a force in creating violence in the gay community. I was battered by my ex-lover who used pornography. The pornography, straight and gay, I had been exposed to helped convince me that I had to accept his violence, and helped keep me in that destructive relationship.

A letter to the Commission: A mother and father in South Oklahoma City forced their four daughters, ages ten to seventeen, to engage in family sex while pornographic pictures were being filmed. This mother drove the girls to dates with men, where she would watch while the girls had sex, then she would collect fees of thirty to fifty dollars.

Another witness: The day came when I invited a small neighborhood boy into my apartment, molested him, and then killed him in fear of being caught. Over the next few years, I kidnapped, sexually abused, and murdered four other boys. Pornography wasn't the only negative influence in my life, but its effects on me were devastating. I lost all sense of decency and respect for humanity and life.

A former Playboy bunny: I was extremely suicidal and sought psychiatric help for the eight years I lived in a sexually promiscuous fashion. In Los Angeles, my roommate, who was a bunny, had slashed her wrists because she was so suicidal.... I felt empty and worthless. Out of despair, I attempted suicide on numerous occasions.

The Roots of Violence

A young victim of a sex ring: I became involved in bondage. I was shown pornography and was bound in various ways and photographed.

A mother on her son: My son, Troy Dunaway, was murdered on August 6, 1981, by the greed and avarice of the publishers of *Hustler Magazine*. My son read the article "Orgasm of Death," set up the sexual experiment depicted therein, followed the explicit instructions of the article, and ended up dead. He would still be alive today were he not enticed and incited into this action by *Hustler Magazine*'s "How to Do."

Born-again Brenda MacKillop writes of herself: I am a former Playboy bunny ... I was extremely suicidal and sought psychiatric help for eight years while I lived in a sexually promiscuous fashion. There was no help for me until I changed my lifestyle to be a follower of Jesus Christ and obeyed the biblical truths regarding no premarital sex.... I implore the Attorney General's Commission to see the connection between sexual promiscuity, venereal diseases, abortion, divorce, homosexuality, sexual abuse of children, suicide, drug abuse, rape, and prostitution to pornography. Come back to God, America, before it is too late.... What a distorted image of sexuality this pornography gave me! For pornography portrays sex as impersonal and insatiable. It depicts everything from orgies, to sadism, to incest, to bestiality. I never questioned the morality of becoming a Playboy bunny because the magazine was accepted at home. I found that premarital sex with single men led me to affairs with married men. I looked on men as power objects and got on casting couches in an attempt to become a movie star. I experienced everything from date rape, to physical abuse, to group sex, and finally to fantasizing homosexuality as I read Playboy magazine. The "Playboy Philosophy" gave me no warning as to the emotional, physical, and spiritual devastation that accompanied supposed sexual liberation. In reality, it was an addiction to sexual perversion.[133]

The argument is made by devotees of sexual promiscuity — and even by some ballyhooed, dissident Catholic theologians — that some people are born physically and psychologically oriented sexually to persons of the same sex. Thus, they cannot help being homosexual or lesbian. From the moment of birth, they were destined — fatalistically determined by nature or the author of nature — to such a sexual lifestyle. Thus, there can be no guilt or responsibility imposed on them for their sexual actions. Leaving aside the blasphemy this doctrine hurls against God, scientific research itself explodes this falsehood:

Most evidence suggests that all sexual deviations and their variations are learned behavior. There is no good evidence suggesting genetic transmission of sexual pathology. In fact, Stanley Rachman at the Maudsley Hospital in London has repeatedly conditioned young males into sexual deviations (fetishes), using standard conditioning procedures.... Many sexual deviations occur (or are learned) through the process of masturbatory conditioning. Vivid sexual memories and fantasies are masturbated to which, at the moment of climax, further reinforces their linkage in the brain and leads

[133] *Attorney General's Commission on Pornography: Final Report*, vol. 2 (Washington, DC: U.S. Dept. of Justice, 1986).

in time to the increased probability of their being acted out in real-life behavior.[134]

No person is conceived or born as a thief, murderer, alcoholic, homosexual, or sexual pervert. True, we are all born with a fallen human nature due to original sin, with intellect darkened and will weakened. But this condition does not yet indicate any personal sin, just its possibility or even probability. For habitual styles of sinful life begin—and are developed—by repeated personal acts of learned behavior. There is no genetic transmission of a fatalistic orientation to sinful habits. If one does not resist temptation, if one does not avoid the occasions of sin, if one fosters fantasies of sinful actions, then one has freely committed himself or herself to a sinful style of life leading to violence. Dr. Victor Cline, professor of psychology at the University of Utah, testified to this truth:

> Put more simply, a certain percentage of adolescents—whose first sexual experiences are triggered by pornography of violent sex—will develop a fetish, a conditioning that will associate violence with sex. We are training rapists and murderers with pornography.... Pornography is the theory; rape and violent sex is the practice. There is a real link between pornography and crime, child abuse, and violence.[135]

There is also a real link between sexual violence and Satan. We give here a case study that took place in the Middle Ages, though there are many similar cases happening today, because sexual violence and ritual satanic sacrifice of animals and humans is on the rise today. Christopher Nugent relates it in his book *Masks of Satan*:

---

[134] *Attorney General's Commission on Pornography: Final Report*, vol. 2.
[135] *Attorney General's Commission on Pornography: Final Report*, vol. 2.

Gilles de Rais (1404–1440) was one of the greatest and wealthiest noblemen of France, a warrior who had distinguished himself in the Hundred Years War and ridden side by side with St. Joan of Arc. He was also a pervert, a sadist, a demonist, and one of the greatest mass murderers of history. After the execution of Joan of Arc in 1431 … he surrounded himself with a pack of sophisticated but unscrupulous sorcerers like the Italian Francesco Prelati, who reportedly made a pact with the devil. Sorcery may have whetted Gilles's appetite for the forbidden.… By 1432, he was having his retainers round up children in the environs, whom he compelled to submit to his unspeakable pleasures. These were children, generally boys, between the ages of six and twelve. Gilles, assisted by his evil companions, fondled and ravished both the living and the dead bodies of the children and severed parts thereof, often trying to time the seed of life and the shrieks of death, and sometimes even staging a bizarre necrophilic beauty contest. A holocaust was made of the remnants. This continued for some eight years until Gilles, by then suspect, overreached himself and violated a church, and was thereupon brought to swift and final justice. By then, he had butchered and defiled more than one hundred, some have even said eight hundred, children.[136]

When a person goes down the path of a lustful lifestyle, he or she delivers himself or herself into the violent hands of Satan. The sexual perverts of the sadistic mass murders in Houston and Chicago are but the modern counterparts of Gilles. The common

[136] Christopher Nugent, *Masks of Satan*, 55–56.

root of their violent lives is the attraction and decision to pluck the forbidden fruit in the pleasure coming from activities of sexual sins and perversion. How do teenagers—Gilles's crimes began in his twenties—get involved in a lifestyle so horrible, frightful, and sanguinary that produces such diabolical enormities? It is the mystery of iniquity, in which man decides to rebel against the laws God established for his rational conduct, choosing to live according to his own whims in complete surrender to his irrational, evil allurements in the ecstasy of satisfying his runaway passions.

6

THE VIOLENCE OF ENVY

By the envy of the devil, death came into the world.

—Wisdom 2:24

Envy is sorrow at another's good fortune. It is a sin that is hardly ever admitted, much less confessed. Because the envious person sees his neighbor's good as his own evil, his neighbor's promotion as his own downfall. That is why envy begets in man a nasty, grim, petty, and jealous attitude. There is a viciousness in the grief over another's good fortune, good reputation, or good position and prestige. Moreover, the envious person is racked by fear that his more fortunate neighbor may do him harm. Hence, there is no joy, security, serenity, peace, or beauty in the contorted, anxious face of the envious. François de La Rochefoucauld depicts the nearest advance to happiness that an envious person can experience, even though it is an unnatural happiness: "Few are able to suppress in themselves a secret satisfaction at the misfortune of their friends."[137] And, of course, we can add that few are able to suppress a secret

---

[137] Quoted in Fairlie, *The Seven Deadly Sins Today*, 61.

envy at the success of their friends. Aristotle states, "Men are envious of such as are like them in genus, in knowledge, in stature, in habit, or reputation."[138] For the envious sorrow over the success or good of others. St. Thomas Aquinas writes, "A man is envious only of those he wishes to rival or surpass in reputation. But this does not apply to people who are removed from one another. For no man, unless he is out of his mind, endeavors to rival or surpass in reputation those who are far above him. Thus a commoner does not envy a king, nor does the king envy the commoner whom he is above. Wherefore, a man envies not those who are far removed from him, whether in place, time, or station, but those who are near him and whom he strives to rival or surpass."[139]

We have here an interpersonal relationship of resentment, hostility, and rivalry: hence, the psychology of violence in persons who feel that they are trapped like rats and must gnaw away ceaselessly at their own psyche, until they are convinced they have surpassed the challenge of the other. They hope, thereby, to escape the straitjacket of inferiority that envy has imposed upon them. The poet Horace relates, "Sicilian tyrants never invested a greater torment than envy."[140] And Sir Francis Bacon tells us, "Envy, which is proud weakness and deserves to be despised, has no holidays."[141] Then there is the statement of the great bard, William Shakespeare: "Envy is the green sickness."[142] For the envious person keeps his wounds green. Thus, the first violence that envy inflicts is upon the envious person himself. For the only gratification of the envious is endless self-torment, endless

---

[138] Aristotle, *Rhetoric*, 11:10.
[139] St. Thomas Aquinas, *Summa Theologica*, I–II, q. 36, a. 1.
[140] Quoted in *Roget's International Thesaurus*, 627.
[141] Ibid.
[142] Ibid.

self-mortification driven on by the motor of spiritual avarice. William Camden writes, "The envious man shall never want woe."[143] And Onasander observes, "Envy is a pain of mind that successful men cause their neighbors."[144] But, of course, this is not quite accurate from a philosophical point of view. For successful men are not the cause but the occasion by which jealous persons—in love with themselves—allow the green-eyed monster of envy to arise from their hearts. For envy is self-inflicted torture, leading eventually to private and public violence. Indeed, James M. Barrie focuses on this truth, when he writes, "Envy is the most corroding of the vices, and also the greatest power in any land."[145]

The Violence of Envy in Holy Scripture

And this brings us to the violence that envy inflicts upon others. For envy is a source of discord, a sower of suspicion, strife, and distrust between neighbors, friends, brothers, sisters, and—above all—spouses. For the envious are inordinately tempted to aspire after fame, reputation, and the credit of a good name on earth. And they believe they will attain these goods by downgrading their fellowmen through contention, calumny, gossip, murmuring, and spreading destructive rumors against their supposed rivals. The fangs of the envious tear at the good name of others, and their poison erodes their characters while defusing their virtues. The envious person is the character assassin par excellence. And when envy cannot goad others into a *loss* of self-respect, it will proceed to physical violence to destroy its spiritually invincible rivals.

143 Ibid.
144 Ibid.
145 Ibid.

It was the grotesquely secular greed and spiteful envy that led to the first murder in human history, a fratricide in the very first family of the human race. What were the circumstances of that crime? Cain killed his brother Abel, not for land or cattle—material greed—but because Abel attained a position of preferential love in the presence of God, to whom he had sacrificed the best of his flocks. Cain, on the other hand, had given God in sacrifice his seconds. Now he who gives God his seconds, gives him nothing. Rather he insults God. Spiritual envy allied to spiritual greed and gluttony is infinitely more heinous a sin than mere carnal or material greed. Enraged at his brother's ascendancy in God's favor, and at his own downfall in that respect, Cain murdered Abel out of spiteful envy.[146] The Spanish poet and philosopher, Miguel de Unamuno, addresses this subject in his book *The Tragic Sense of Life in Men and Nations*: "If the so-called problem of life, the basic problem of food, were ever solved, the earth would be turned into a hell, as the struggle for spiritual survival (and superiority) would become even more intense."[147] The curse of envy, more than any other sin, has the capacity to create a hell on earth. For it provokes men to avarice and spiritual gluttony in a fierce, often violent, attempt to outstrip rivals—by fair or foul means—in the accumulation of riches and honors in this life.

Holy Scripture testifies often to the violence of envy. Job laments, "Anger indeed killeth the foolish, and envy slayeth the little one."[148] Isaiah reveals that envy calls down the wrath of God: "Lord, let thy hand be exalted.... Let the envious people see, and

---

[146] Gen. 4:1–16.

[147] Miguel de Unamuno, *The Tragic Sense of Life in Men and Nations* (Princeton, NJ: Princeton University Press, 1972), 62.

[148] Job 5:2.

be confounded: and let fire devour thy enemies"[149] St. Matthew exposes the motive of the Pharisees in their plot to kill Christ: "Pilate said: 'Whom will you that I release to you, Barabbas, or Jesus that is called Christ?' For he knew that for envy they had delivered him."[150] St. Mark testifies to the same motive for the crime of deicide perpetrated by the chief priests and Pharisees of the Jews: "Pilate answered them, and said: 'Will you that I release to you the king of the Jews?' For he knew that the chief priests had delivered him up out of envy."[151]

In the Old Testament, we witness the cold, cruel violence of Joseph's brothers, who hated and envied him because of his God-given talent to interpret dreams and because of their father's preferential love for this youngest of his children. One day they saw him in the distance, coming to them across an open field. We read, "His brethren therefore envied him.... And when they saw him afar off ... they thought to kill him.... And said one to another: 'Behold the dreamer cometh. Come, let us kill him, and cast him into some old pit: and we will say: Some evil beast hath devoured him: and then it shall appear what his dreams avail him.'"[152] Ruben and Judah persuaded their brothers not to kill Joseph, not to have family blood on their hands, but to abandon him in a dry cistern. They hoped to rescue him later. As it happened, a Midianite caravan of traders passed by at that moment on their way to Egypt. The brothers, instead of killing Joseph, sold him to the caravan as a slave for twenty pieces of silver. They then tortured their hapless father—victim of his sons' envy of Joseph, as well as

---

[149] Isa. 26:11.
[150] Matt. 27:17-18.
[151] Mark 15:9-10.
[152] Gen. 37:11, 18-20; see generally 37:3-20.

their violence and lying—by presenting him with Joseph's tunic, which they soaked in goat's blood to convince Jacob that the boy had been devoured by a wild animal. The distraught father rent his garments, girded himself in sackcloth, and mourned his son for many days. The wages of envy is often lying, violence, and death.

St. Paul was severely persecuted and driven from city to city, because of his mission to convert the Gentiles. The chief priests and Pharisees flagellated and sought to kill him out of envy, given his success with the Gentiles, as well as some Jews led into the Church. Scripture narrates, "And the Jews seeing the multitudes [listening to Paul and being converted] ... were filled with envy.... The Jews stirred up religious and honorable women, and the chief men of the city, and raised persecution against Paul and Barnabas: and cast them out of their coasts."[153]

On another occasion, when Paul was arrested in Jerusalem and held by the Romans awaiting trial, a group of Jewish men entered a conspiracy to assassinate Paul. The Acts of the Apostles relate, "Some of the Jews gathered together, and bound themselves under a curse, saying, that they would neither eat, nor drink, till they killed Paul. And they were more than forty men that had made this conspiracy. Who came to the chief priests and the ancients, and said: 'We have bound ourselves under a great curse that we will eat nothing till we have slain Paul. Now therefore do you with the council signify to the tribune, that he bring him forth to you, as if you meant to know something more certain touching him. And we, before he come near, are ready to kill him.'"[154]

Again, when Paul and Silas, by their preaching in Thessalonica, won over to the Faith some Jews and "of the Gentiles a great

---

[153] Acts 13:45, 50; see generally 13:45–50.
[154] Acts 23:12–15.

multitude, and of noble women not a few ... the Jews, moved with envy, and taking unto them some wicked men of the vulgar sort, and making a tumult, set the city in an uproar."[155] Then, too, Paul, in his Letter to the Romans, relates how God punishes idolaters by delivering them up to all forms of self-inflicted, violent, moral wickedness, envy included: "And as they liked not to have God in their knowledge, God delivered them up to a reprobate sense, to do those things which are not convenient; being filled with all iniquity, malice, fornication, avarice, wickedness, full of envy, murder, contention, deceit, malignity, whisperers, detractors, hateful to God, contumelious, proud, haughty, inventors of evil things, disobedient to parents, foolish, dissolute, without affection, without fidelity, without mercy."[156] Such are those spiritually sick with the disease of envy.

In writing to St. Timothy to beware of lying teachers, Paul indicates that heretics will be full of vices, envy included: "If any man teach otherwise, and consent not to the sound words of our Lord Jesus Christ, and to that doctrine which is according to godliness, he is proud, knowing nothing, but sick about questions and strifes of words; from which arise envies, contentions, blasphemies, evil suspicions, conflicts of men corrupted in mind, and who are destitute of the truth."[157] And St. James indicates that one source of wars and quarrels is the capital vice of envy: "From whence are wars and contentions among you? Are they not hence, from your concupiscences, which war in your members? You covet, and have not: you kill, and envy, and can not obtain."[158]

---

[155] Acts 17:4-5.
[156] Rom. 1:28-31.
[157] 1 Tim. 6:3-5.
[158] Jas. 4:1-2.

The Roots of Violence

The Modern Cult of Envy

The cult of envy saturates modern society, because it is found useful in eliminating the hierarchical spectrum of values. For envy, in perhaps its most destructive activity, attempts to level all persons to the same common denominator. If anyone is not equal in intelligence, good looks, talents, wealth, position, power, prestige, and in happy experiences, the envious conclude that a grave injustice has been imposed on the less fortunate. For envy acts like a spiritual law of gravity; it pulls down, puts down all into an egalitarian herd society. Talent, training, and hard work are condemned as excuses for this injustice. Envy seeks a society of mediocrity where everyone can do everything, have everything, and experience everything. Yet, in envy's breeding ground, a strange anomaly takes place. The lowly are persuaded they will arrive at the highest, while the highest are injected with a guilt complex over their hard-earned success. People content in their natural positions have their expectations for success and promotions cruelly and falsely promised, by the rise of the inner torment of envy. Out of envy, women claim they have a right to be priests; priests want to be married or, at least, be in politics, acting, music, dancing, or anything and everything. There is even a beer advertisement that says, if you drink this particular beer, "You can have it all." And when envy fails to fulfill its promises, it works to destroy all stages of excellence in an effort to satisfy its jealousy. Henry Fairlie, in his book *The Seven Deadly Sins Today* unmasks this tactic of envy:

> The legend of our times, it has been suggested, might be "The Revenge of Failure." That is what envy has done for us. If we cannot paint well, we will destroy the canons of painting and pass ourselves off as painters. If we will not take the trouble to write poetry, we will destroy the rules

of prosody and pass ourselves off as poets. If we are not inclined to the rigors of an academic discipline, we will destroy the standards of that discipline and pass ourselves off as graduates. If we cannot or will not read, we will say that "linear thought" is now irrelevant and so dispense with reading. If we cannot make music, we will simply make a noise and persuade others that it is music. If we can do nothing at all, Why! We will strum a guitar all day and call it self-expression. As long as no talent is required, no apprenticeship to a skill, everyone can do it, and we are all magically made equal, and failure has had its revenge.[159]

Envy among Celebrities

The habit of envy is fostered early by those who enter institutions that train them to attain success and become leaders. For example, a young man enters a seminary with the ardent ambition to become a scholar or bishop, or both. He left his father's grocery store, where life could scarcely be more plebeian than that of the commercial fisherman bringing to dock his daily catch. And he enters a palace of learning and culture, where his talents and whole personality are oriented toward vanquishing ignorance and attaining holiness through the fulfillment of spreading the good news of the gospel and administering the seven sacramental streams of divine life to the faithful. One would expect him to be filled with a blazing zeal, as he fulfills the commitments of his divine vocation. One would be almost certain that he would courageously challenge the softness, skepticism, and tepidity of his society. One would expect him to teach the truth enthusiastically, guide the faithful with the warmth of conviction, and open paths to the sweetness of harmony and

[159] Fairlie, *The Seven Deadly Sin Today*, 63.

peace so eagerly sought by his disillusioned and wicked generation. But, *no*! He trims his sails to the prevailing winds of the wicked generation. He tailors his thoughts to the dominant ideology of his professors and superiors, even though he knows that this ideology is against the holy Faith he must teach, defend, and spread. After all, that is what the majority of his confreres are doing. Why? Because, in joining the ruling ideologues, they all hope to attain academic honors now and prestigious, high-paying jobs in the future. He plays his cards close to the vest, guarding every glance, conversation, and relationship to see if they further or hinder his chances for fame and notoriety. He fawns upon the mighty, shuns the simple and forthright, and quickly abandons acquaintances once they become, or might become, liabilities. He has no friends. A loner, he is already insecure about the prospects of the race he has entered, even while the luxuriant head of hair attesting his youthfulness is still gleaming in its natural beauty.

But, as one listens to and observes him, one sees that already the green-eyed monster of envy has taken possession of him. He is obsessed with himself; he considers all others in his rising profession as rivals, almost as enemies, for they are in pursuit of the same goal he seeks. The competition is already a psychological war. To get ahead of the others, he twists the truth, sends out false rumors, and makes unhealthy alliances. He is preoccupied with marks, success, getting honors, and meeting the right people. He is almost paranoid about what others—especially those in positions of power, who can advance or hurt his career—are thinking and saying about him. He who promised to be a great apostle has become a self-serving sycophant.

What a tragedy for God, the Church, the faithful, and all mankind! Already living a life of lies motored by envy, our young priest has become a displaced person, closed in upon himself, with a siege mentality that has erected a barrier of hostility against all possible rivals. Such envy has reaped, and is still reaping, a great harvest of seared souls among clergy, professors, writers, actors, journalists, singers, artists, directors, scientists, and celebrities. Perhaps the instruments most often used in these professions—to further the attainment of their envious goals—is the lie in its infinite variety of forms. For fallen man has an infinite capacity for self-deception. And the envious, driven on by a mania and an illusion of grandeur, have this capacity to the second degree of infinity, if that is imaginable. For when they arrive at the pinnacle of position and fame, they continue to serve number one, themselves, so ingrained has become the habit of self-seeking and self-serving. And the poor people below can never enjoy their services or compassion, for the *nouveau* rulers cannot be bothered by a rabble for whom they have nothing but benign contempt. Yet all of these envious persons eventually experience bitterness of heart, for they become alienated, sullen, isolated, and feckless when someone in their field—whose success they count as their own failures—rises above them. Such envy is a real form of psychological violence, because it shatters interpersonal love and harmony, and creates a freezing social atmosphere in which Jean-Paul Sartre's aphorism becomes a frightening reality. Because, for such envious celebrities, "Hell is other people."[160]

Marxist Envy Masquerading as Justice

What is the vice that hides behind the facade of the Marxist claim, that it seeks only justice for the poor in its struggle against the superstructure of society? That vice is envy. Marx claims that the ultimate purpose of man's thinking is to change the world. In this statement,

---

[160] Jean-Paul Sartre, *No Exit.*

he shows his contempt for the primacy of truth, for to change things for the better requires that we first of all grasp the truth of things. Marx has the cart before the horse. He states that things must first be changed—by the violence of the proletariat—from private ownership to state ownership, to party ownership, and, finally, to no ownership at all in the classless society. But history demonstrates that, when the bureaucracy of the party is entrenched in power, the vast majority of people become destitute and remain destitute, being deprived not only of material necessities for life but also their spiritual rights and dignity. Only the rulers, and those high in the ranks of the party, enjoy a high standard of living. Yet, to attract the gullible toward a classless society, Marx had to play the role of economic savior and masquerade his vice of envy under the mask of justice.

For the ideology and practice of Marxism is characterized by aspects that clearly reveal its specific disease to be the capital sin of envy. There is hatred for the splendor of being, for the hierarchical order of being, an envy that flattens all into mere matter and imprisons this evolving matter in the straitjacket of time-space. Marxist envy denies the transcendent values in man and society, reducing them to the one disvalue of the classless society. There is thus contempt in Marxism for any other-worldly, eternal destiny for being, and for man in particular. That superstition is "the opium of the people." This envy explains Marxism's hatred of the Judeo-Christian God, because He is a God of goodness with a preferential love for man among all His creatures. In a war of spite, Marxism aims at replacing God with the proletarian masses under the direction of the party super-gods, even as Lucifer sought to seize God's throne with his legions of self-divinized demons. Marxism's envy is revealed in the enraged hatred of man for being the special object of God's love, the special object of God's redemption and glorification of him. This divine, ineffable love drives Lucifer and his Marxist minions into such envious madness that their whole activity is concentrated on seducing man to cooperate in a worldwide human uprising against God and His communion of the just upon the earth. Having imitated the Luciferian legions in their revolt against God, Marxists also imitate hell's angels in their efforts to destroy man as God's lover. They scheme to make mankind into a society of militant atheists, demoting men from their high position as children of God into an egalitarian "herd collectivity" and "termite colony." We witness here once again envy's reductionist tactics against any spectrum of excellence. For Marxist man, the meaning of world history is not the salvation of men through the life and deeds of the God-Man, Jesus Christ, but rather the re-creation, liberation, and salvation—indeed diviniza-tion—of man through his own efforts. To attain this goal, Marxism has insisted that the only instrument necessary and efficacious is ongoing class warfare.

And yet, despite this divinization of man, Marxist envy simply cannot be placated. It has even raised envy to the level of a salvific virtue, a virtue whose mission is to create ideal man in an ideal soci-ety. But, in order to achieve this ideal, Marxism has had to develop a huge bureaucracy that wields frightening centralized power and works zealously to wipe out all differentiations, whether of being or wealth. Marxism has welded together a far-flung political hege-mony: a terrifying, colossal, and technically advanced military ap-paratus; an omnipresent internal army of secret police; a worldwide system of spying; and a vast network of concentration camps—all instruments of institutionalized envy in a messianic campaign to conquer the earth, indeed the universe, for the establishment of a global atheistic classless society. Today, there is not an iota of moral idealism or humaneness in the Marxist system. Indeed, it is an act of the gravest, naive self-deception to believe that Marxism ever seriously sought to establish a just society. The testimony of Eugene Lyons, once a Communist enthusiast, dissolves the roseate myths of a Marxism dedicated to a humane secular humanism. He writes in his book *Workers' Paradise Lost*:

> By 1934 when I departed from Russia, nothing was left of the high mood of dedication, traces of which I still found among Communists six years earlier. The very vocabulary of idealism had been outlawed. "Equality" was lampooned as bourgeois romanticism. Excessive concern for the needs and sensibilities of ordinary people was punished as "rotten liberalism." Terror was no longer explained away as a sad necessity. It was used starkly and glorified as "human engineering." Means had blotted [out] ends and have held this priority ever since. The Marxist theory of permanent class struggle rules out compromise, reform, truce, common humanity, mutual respect, family loyalties.[161]

The book of Wisdom tells us, "By the envy of the devil, death came into the world."[162] By the envy of the Marxists, the devil's human agents, worldwide slaughter of millions of persons has been executed in the past and is still going on today. And there is no end in sight. St. Thomas Aquinas quotes Pope St. Gregory the Great on the other vices that have their sources in envy. Gregory holds that the capital vices are so closely allied to one another that one springs from the other. But they all find their ultimate source in pride. Now, the first offspring of pride is vainglory, which corrupts the mind and begets envy. How? Because the vainglorious person

---

[161] Eugene Lyons, *Workers' Paradise Lost*, 380.
[162] Wisd. 2:24.

craves in envy the power of an empty name; he torments himself for fear that another may acquire that good instead of himself. St. Thomas continues, "From envy arises hatred, tale-bearing, the effort to lower another's reputation secretly. Then there is detraction, the effort to lower a man's good name openly. There follows defamation that, if successful, leads to joy at another's misfortune. But when defamation fails, there is grief at another's prosperity in the maintenance of his good name. All these are rooted in hatred, because just as good that causes delight causes love, so does sorrow at another's good fortune cause hatred. These are envy's 'ugly daughters.'"[163]

They are rampant in Communist countries. The machinery for spying and repression is so vast that it strikes terror into the hearts of all of the more than a billion slaves. No regime in the whole of history has ever spawned such appalling systems of surveillance, denunciation, intimidation, and punishment. Communist countries have legalized an enormous number of "crimes against the state," for which the death penalty is extensively applied. Citizens' mail is opened and read by party authorities; phones are tapped; state spies, like vermin, infiltrate offices, factories, mines, farms, universities, libraries, hotels, railroad stations, churches, and homes. Even children are trained to report on their parents and relatives. Millions of youth are enrolled into party vigilante brigades to inform on their neighbors' ideas and practices. One segment of society is constantly informing on another, like rats preying on rats. Just about every family in the vast empire of Marxism has lost at least one member, many even more, to this insatiable beast. Moreover, the ugly practice of committing religious and political dissidents to mental institutions has increased, thus perverting professions and

---

[163] St. Thomas, *Summa Theologica*, q. 36, a. 4.

institutions established to cure the sick into prisons and procedures for breaking the minds and spirits of the brave and healthy. Then there is the violence and cruelty of the concentration camps. Elinor Lipper, a German prisoner, conveys this horror to us in her book *Eleven Years in a Soviet Prison:*

> A Soviet camp is an incubator for all the vilest human instincts. Its name "correction labor camp" is a mockery.... Not only does the camp provide no educational work, it gives the criminal the finest opportunity to practice his profession. The thief steals, the speculator speculates, the prostitute sells herself. The normal person is perverted, the honest man becomes a hypocrite, the brave man a coward, and all have their spirits and bodies broken.[164]

Marxism's greatest crime is that, after presenting itself as a messianic liberator, it then reveals itself to be a flaming dragon, no doubt an agent of the red dragon announced in the book of Revelation (see Rev. 12). It dethrones man's most civilized activities—the pursuit of truth and the practice of love. In their place, Marxism substitutes man's most primitive, monstrous deeds—the art of lying and the practice of hateful violence known as class warfare. It also fosters the eruption of social volcanoes of violence that such sins beget. Philip Spratt, a former British-Indian Communist leader, openly stated, "The Communist movement runs on hate—and hate is a powerful fuel."[165] Marx founded his ethics on the pseudo-science of historical materialism. Lenin added an emotional fanaticism to this morality by following the radical immoralism of Sergei Nechayev. Lenin encountered Nechayev's ideas

---

164 Elinor Lipper, *Eleven Years in a Soviet Prison.*
165 Quoted in Lyons, *Workers' Paradise Lost.*

before he ever engaged Marx's views. In 1868, Nechayev wrote his celebrated *Catechism of a Revolutionist*, in which he renounced all norms of civilized behavior and prescribed every imaginable depravity in the pursuit of the ideal. It is as fanatic and hate-packed a document as the human brain has ever produced. "The revolutionist," he wrote, "knows only one science, the science of destruction, which does not stop at lying, robbery, betrayal, and torture of friends, or murder of his own family."[166] His central dictum that "everything that contributes to the triumph of the revolution is morally good," has been accepted by Marx, Lenin, and their disciples to this day. Indeed, this document impacts every Marxist pronouncement on morality. Lenin advanced this standard of morality when he expounded on "The Tasks of the Youth League," in a speech delivered to the Communist youth congress October 20, 1920:

> In what sense do we repudiate ethics and morality? In the sense that they were preached by the bourgeoisie, who declared that ethics were God's commandments. We, of course, say that we do not believe in God.... We repudiate all morality that is taken outside of human class concepts.... We say that our morality is entirely subordinated to the interests of the class struggle of the proletariat.[167]

Max Eastman writes that "the confluence of these two streams of thought (Nechayev and Marx) is one of the greatest disasters that ever befell mankind."[168]

---

[166] Quoted in Lyons, *Workers' Paradise Lost*.
[167] Vladimir Lenin, "The Tasks of the Youth League," Third All-Russian Congress of the Russian Young Communist League, Oct. 20, 1920, in *Selected Works*, vol. 9, 474, 475, 477.
[168] Quoted in Lyons, *Workers' Paradise Lost*.

The Roots of Violence

Nor has Marxist, so-called justice attained for man an economic paradise. Rather, Marxism has a dreadful history of economic incompetence in the Soviet Union, China, the Iron Curtain satellites, Yugoslavia, Albania, Cuba, Cambodia, North Korea, Vietnam, and now Nicaragua. Far from achieving economic justice and human liberation, Marxism's envy has established universal economic destitution and slavery for the masses—their supposed beloved proletariat. Under these circumstances, a new class of undemocratic elite dominates and is ruthlessly engaged in violating human rights; and they are determined to bolster Marxism's continuance in power, with its ideological, inefficient, inhuman, and indeed impossible pursuit of the mirage of an unnatural industrial development founded on spiteful, enraged, and envious hatred.

In addressing justice in his *Summa Theologica,* St. Thomas Aquinas coherently demonstrates a truth proclaimed throughout Holy Scripture: *Opus justitiae pax* (The work of justice is peace). Peace between God and man; peace among men. On the other hand, the system of thought and conduct elaborated by Karl Marx and his fellow atheists—the system of Marxism which has dominated Russia now for seventy years and enslaves about a third of the world's population—demonstrates, with oceans of bloodcurdling violence, the terrifying truth proclaimed throughout history: *Opus invidiae bellum* (The work of envy is war). War between God and man; war among men.

Now Christ warned men to judge a tree by its fruit, not by its foliage. Marxism's pseudo-ideal of justice, equality, and classless fraternity presents a pleasant foliage to the unwary, who expect good fruit from its tree. But the tree of Marxism is fertilized with the metaphysical manure of the big lie, and it thrives on the sap of satanic envy. It can only produce the bitter fruits of hatred, violence, and war, and never the good fruit of justice, love, and peace.

7

THE VIOLENCE OF ANGER

Anger has no mercy, nor fury
when it breaks forth; and who can bear
the violence of one provoked?

—Proverbs 27:4

"Be not quickly angry: for anger resteth in the bosom of a fool," we are warned in Ecclesiastes.[169] And the poet Horace comments, "Wrath is a transient madness."[170] For sinful anger is an irrational outburst of emotion that is intent on wreaking savage vengeance on another. Anger flings words at its opponents with a violence that seeks to stone them to death psychologically or, in a modern fashion, to mow them down physically with a machine gun. Henry Fairlie writes on this subject:

> We think of anger in terms of fire: blazing, flaming, scorching, smoking, fuming, spitting, smoldering, heated,

---

[169] Eccles. 7:10.
[170] *Roget's International Thesaurus*, 616.

white-hot, simmering, boiling, and even when it is ice-cold, it will still burn.[171]

For the eruption of anger is likened metaphorically to a spiritual volcano, one which wildly spews molten violence out of the devil's furnace in the form of a demonic magma, creating a fiery river of moral corruption that boils with the kindred currents of envy, resentment, avarice, lust, scorn, obstinacy and sloth—a river that reduces to a burnt-out desert the garden of virtues which once flourished in the soul. Anger accuses; raises its voice; threatens; glares menacingly; jabs its fingers into alarmed, frightened faces; stamps its feet; froths at the mouth; strides back and forth furiously; and roars out a stream of denunciations and, often enough, a litany of curses. The book of Proverbs remarks, "A passionate man provoketh quarrels."[172] It continues its wise advice when it warns, "Be not a friend to an angry man, and do not walk with a furious man: lest perhaps thou learn his ways, and take scandal to thy soul."[173] Yet, not all demonstrations of anger are evil. In his Letter to the Ephesians, St. Paul advises, "Be angry, and sin not. Let not the sun go down upon your anger."[174] St. Thomas Aquinas makes a distinction between reasonable and irrational anger:

Properly speaking, anger is a passion of the sensitive appetite.... Evil may be found in anger when, to wit, one is angry more or less than reason demands. But if one is angry in accordance with right reason, one's anger is deserving of praise.... St. John Chrysostom says, "He that is angry

---

[171] Fairlie, *The Seven Deadly Sins Today*, 89.
[172] Prov. 29:22.
[173] Prov. 22:24–25.
[174] Eph. 4:26.

without cause, shall be in danger; but he that is angry with cause, shall not be in danger; for without anger teaching will be useless, judgments unstable, and crimes unchecked." Therefore, to be angry is not always evil.[175]

Many examples of justified anger are found in Holy Scripture. And the deeds performed under this anger are reported as being holy actions. Elijah, the prophet of God, was incensed against the 450 prophets of Baal, the god of fertility, in whose idolatrous service these prophets had seduced the Chosen People. In righteous anger against this religious abomination, he led these false prophets down to the torrent of Cison and killed them.[176] When Moses descended from Mount Sinai with the two tablets—on which were engraved the Ten Commandments—he found his people adoring and frolicking before a molten calf placed on an altar. Moses' wrath flared up immediately; he hurled the tablets down and smashed them at the base of the mountain. Then he seized the golden calf, fused it in fire, and reduced it to powder. He scattered the powder on the water, which he forced the Israelites to drink. Still enraged, he called forth the Levites who had resisted the seduction of idolatry. He ordered them to draw their swords and slay their own kinsmen, friends, and neighbors. There fell that day three thousand idolaters. For this action, the Levites were blessed by God, to whom they had remained dedicated in filial fidelity.[177]

Perhaps the most striking example of holy anger, however, is demonstrated Jesus Christ's cleansing of the temple. Jesus arrived in Jerusalem during the feast of the Passover. In the temple, He found merchants selling oxen, sheep, and doves. The money changers were

---

[175] St. Thomas Aquinas, *Summa Theologica*, II-II, q. 158, a. 1.
[176] 1 Kings 18:22–40.
[177] Exod. 32:15–29.

doing a great business at their tables. Infuriated at this abominable desacralization of his Father's temple, Jesus made a whip of cords, drove out all the merchants, sheep, and oxen, overturning the merchants' money tables and scattering their shekels. He sent the dove sellers out of the temple. And in an authoritative voice raised for all to hear, especially for the ears of the scribes and Pharisees who permitted these sacrileges, Jesus proclaimed this truth: "My house is the house of prayer. But you have made it a den of thieves."[178] It was then that His disciples remembered a prophecy about Him: "The zeal of thy house hath eaten me up."[179]

In all these examples, and in many more that could be cited, the zeal that is the intense love of God—and of one's neighbor for the love of God—is the driving power behind this holy anger. The strong action taken is the proper response of a person dedicated to God in the face of insults poured out against God and souls. Unfortunately, modern man has lost this intense love for divine and spiritual values. He has become habituated to insults, crimes, and sacrileges. He lives in a permissive age, in which all types of sins are tolerated and even considered normal. He is often a passive spectator to crimes inflicted on his neighbors, not moving a muscle to come to their aid, nor even summoning the police. Yet, at times, matters are far worse than this show of apathy. Indeed, instead of a show of justified anger, or even apathy in the face of a criminal act, modern man takes sadistic pleasure in witnessing such crimes. Our age is one in which modern man is convinced that he is not his brother's, nor his sister's, keeper. Fear, self-love, and personal convenience render him unavailable to his embattled neighbors. The poet Dante has written that evil prospers because good men

---

[178] Luke 19:46.
[179] John 2:17.

do nothing. But I question whether a do-nothing person can be called good. When one is impervious to evil, and to the divine-spiritual values that evil violates, can such a person be really a good person? Apathy, neutrality, indifference, and tepidity—in the face of wicked actions that call for righteous anger—show forth that the heartless, permissive society of our times has become, in reality, a post-Christian, corrupt pagan society. Even God is nauseated with such a spineless society. He testifies, "I know thy works, that thou art neither cold, nor hot. I would thou wert cold, or hot. But because thou art lukewarm, and neither cold, nor hot, I will begin to vomit thee out of my mouth."[180] Ours is an age that displays a strange spiritual paradox in man's conduct in the face of crimes. The majority of persons, especially our leaders, are infected with the spiritual disease known as cowardly irenicism, which renders them morally paralyzed: unwilling and unable to fight crime. On the other hand, the rebellious minority adheres to irrational anger as if it were an eighth sacrament, an essential means for the reform and salvation of a corrupt society.

Yet, even in the expression of justified anger, one must be careful not to sin by excess. In his famous work *Moralia*, Pope St. Gregory the Great says, "We must beware lest, when we use anger as an instrument of virtue, it overrule the mind, and go before it as its mistress, instead of following in reason's train, ever ready as its handmaid to obey."[181]

We are living in an Age of Anger. The conviction has gone forth that the modern world cannot be reformed or saved by intelligent and peaceful means. It must be angrily blown up, purged by fire, before man can build a world of justice on its ruins. Fire,

---

[180] Rev. 3:15–16.
[181] St. Gregory the Great, *Moralia*, bk. 5, ch. 45.

explosions, bombs, tanks, planes, missiles, nuclear submarines, aircraft carriers: any machine that produces smoldering, exploding, napalm purgations expresses the wrath of persons, groups, and international movements which seek revenge on a world founded on injustice. Violence and counterviolence, kidnapping and counter-kidnapping, spying and counter-spying, worldwide covert military activities, murder and reprisals all fill our daily newspapers and TV screens. Vendettas leap up from the fiery coven of anger, with a voracious intensity to consume men and nations. Everywhere the wrath of the terrorist, kidnapper, hijacker, looter, rapist, pedophile, homosexual, and satanic cultist — along with ideologically exalted masses with clenched fists — is tearing apart societies. And the authorities look on with benign indifference. It is as if the perpetrators of these crimes must be mollycoddled because they *are angry.* Wrath itself seems to have become a justification for their violence. As Yeats explains once again in his *Second Coming:*

> Mere anarchy is loosed upon the world
> The blood-dimmed tide is loosed, and everywhere
> The ceremony of innocence is drowned;
> The best lack all conviction, while the worst
> Are full of passionate intensity.[182]

In today's climate of pusillanimity, passionate intensity and blazing anger — because of their very outrageousness — are accepted as reasons for tolerating violent criminals. It seems as if the fiercer the wrath of the criminals, the greater the sympathy to grant them a license to torture their fellowmen. The causes and so-called rights of violent criminals are accepted by lily-livered politicians, milquetoast judges, and visionless, effete liberals, who are all intent on creating

---

[182] Yeats, "The Second Coming."

a humanistic utopia. But the victims of the violence are tabulated as depersonalized numbers, buried as statistics, and quickly forgotten. Henry Fairlie profoundly expresses this flight from responsibility to maintain order: "Society has allowed its fighting ability to be impaired, maliciously and permanently, on the ground that, just as wrath must be given our understanding, so violence to which it leads must be given our tolerance."[183]

Indeed, in shackling its law-enforcing agencies from restraining the violent anger of terrorists, society has become an accomplice in their violence. Because of its cowardice and flight from responsibility to maintain order and defend the citizenry from the brutal anarchy created by these nihilists, society only encourages the enraged groups to inflict even more frighteningly novel forms of violence. Undisciplined anger, because of its success, explodes into bolder, fiercer anger—thus begetting a chain reaction of more ferocious violence. St. Thomas Aquinas enumerates six vices as the ugly daughters of the capital sin of anger:

> Indignation or anger's arrogance in belittling its victim.
> The swelling of the mind with the accomplishment of its vengeance. Job asks the pertinent question on this vice: "Will a wise man ... fill his stomach with burning heat?" Blasphemy when an angry man uses injurious language against God. Contumely when an angry man uses injurious language against his neighbor. Quarreling which leads to all manner of injuries inflicted on one's neighbor. Clamor is when an angry man uses disorderly or confused speech against his neighbor, for example, when he calls his brother "Raca," that is, "You fool!" [Matt. 5:22].[184]

183 Fairlie, *The Seven Deadly Sins Today*, 91.
184 St. Thomas, *Summa Theologica*, II–II, q. 158, a. 6.

The Roots of Violence

Why is anger and violence saturating society the world over? It is because of the falsity, the hypocrisy, and the massive apostasy that have seduced nations—from the militant atheist countries of the East to the soft, hedonistic atheist countries of the West—to abandon the kingdom of Christ and to adhere to the kingdom of this world, i.e., the kingdom of Satan. Because of this worldwide apostasy, God has delivered up the world to a reprobate sense, that is, a sense of murderous treachery.

The Anger and Violence of Nazism

Perhaps the most powerful secular prophet and writer of the late nineteenth century was Friedrich Nietzsche. He announced that the decadent Christian world had finally "killed God." He proclaimed the end of the two thousand years during which Europe had been influenced and led by humane and Christian values. He stated that the time had come to enthrone the Will to Power, which transcends good and evil and will eventually create a new type of super-humanity. At that time, the masses had no inkling of the demonic forces that were undermining the depths of the Christian consciousness. At the same time, moreover, intense and angry national rivalries and colonial expansions were heating up the lust for international supremacy among the European competitors. The age had become one of fiercely competitive materialism: intellectually, economically, politically, and militarily. Moreover, crude theories of racial and national superiority fostered hatred and contempt among ethnic nationalities. Then, too, the new theories of biological evolution and natural selection as the survival of the fittest, were interpreted in a way that justified the hostile struggle for existence and success between states and classes. There already existed an economic psychology and political warfare as means to justify the survival of the fittest. National superiority became the new, liberal, and secularized religion that replaced Christianity in its pure Catholic or corrupted Protestant forms. International policies were inspired by imperialism, jingoistic nationalism, chauvinism, and militarism. Power politics were the order of the day. Such political games spawned communists, anarchists, nihilists, and fascists.

All this culminated in World War I. Germany—crushed in an overwhelming defeat, humiliated by a degrading treaty imposed mercilessly, and flattened by an exceptionally severe depression—turned to Hitler and National Socialism in a bitter rage with fanatical determination. Hitler's *New Order* now fulfilled Nietzsche's prophecy concerning European nihilism. Hitler became the very personification of Nietzsche's dream of the Will to Power. Christopher Nugent, in his book *Masks of Satan*, writes: "Barbara Tuchman, in her book *The Proud Tower*, a telling symbol of the Babel that Europe was becoming on the eve of World War I, wrote that 'Nietzsche bewitched his age.' Yes and this age has not yet ended."[185]

Hitler had become obsessed with the *libido dominandi*. He incorporated this lust for dominating into the Aryan race, whose idol was the "magnificent blond brute" produced by the purity of the German race. The time had come for the Aryan master to burst out of his prison, rise from the ashes of his humiliating defeat from his economic coma, and punish severely—in pitiless anger—its inferior conquerors. As Nietzsche wrote at the end of his *Birth of Tragedy*:

> Some day the German spirit will awaken from its deep sleep and then it will slay the dragons, destroy the malignant dwarfs, awaken Brunnhilde—and Wotan's spear itself will be unable to obstruct its course.[186]

[185] Nugent, *Masks of Satan*, 125, 126.
[186] Quoted in Nugent, *Masks of Satan*, 131.

The Roots of Violence

Thus, Germany in the 1920s was ready for the ascendancy of a charismatic dictator. She was submerged in the humiliation of a defeat, plagued by official guilt, and resentful of a punitive peace. She suffered the starvation of a blockade, the insurrection of the Bolshevik revolutions, disastrous inflation, a great depression, and the uprooting of its middle class. In all this, it was also experiencing the end of its empire. In fact, the break up of the supernatural tradition of the Hapsburg monarchy rendered the new Germany prone to its creation of a pan-German ideology, an ideology steeped in anti-Semitism and anti-Catholicism, and ferocious in its zeal to impose upon its citizens the cult of the pure Nordic race.

Spiritually, the nation reacted with resentment, rage, and despair. It abandoned, for the most part, Christianity and it embraced occult idolatries. It is written that, at that time, there were more astrologers in Germany per square mile than anywhere else in the world. The occult—with Karma, mystical visions, and demonic revelations—invaded all strata of society. Even many of the commanders of the German army participated in neo-pagan rituals, dressing in bear skins and hoping to make gold by way of alchemy. Women and the youth experienced full liberation from the shackles of Christian dogma and morality. There was a cult of nudity in an apocalyptic atmosphere. People abandoned themselves to promiscuous sexuality, while drugs and morphine were popular everywhere. The times were those of abandonment to eroticism in all its forms, deviant and otherwise. It was as if as much pleasure as possible had to be experienced in the short time remaining before the arrival of the apocalyptic end. Nugent, quoting a famous writer, reports on the conditions in Berlin in those days:

> I know Satanists when I see them.... In the whole of The
> Thousand and One Nights, in the most shameful rituals

of the Tantras ... you couldn't find anything more nauseating.... The city is doomed, more surely than ever Sodom was. These people don't even realize how low they have sunk. Evil doesn't know itself.[187]

Then, too, Stefan Zweig alluded to the ascendancy to demonocracy:

Berlin was transformed into the Babylon of the world.... What we had seen in Austria proved to be just a mild and shy prologue to this witches' Sabbath.... Even the Rome of Suetonius had never known such orgies as the pervert balls of Berlin, where hundreds of men, costumed as women, danced.... And in the collapse of all values, a kind of madness gained hold particularly in the bourgeois circles.... But the most revolting thing about this pathetic eroticism was its spuriousness.... The whole nation actually only longed for order.[188]

When Hitler came to power, he admitted that Nazism could not be understood as a mere political movement. He also admitted that he was inspired in all he did by the *Protocols of the Elders of Zion*, a fantastic forgery which predicted a Zionist plot for world domination. Moreover, he set out to destroy Christianity in Germany and to exterminate the Jews for, in his mind, they had plotted World War I against Germany. By this time, Hitler had become an addict of occult literature like *Ostara*, an anti-Semitic periodical published by Lans von Liebenfels, an ex-Cistercian monk. This periodical featured old German spells, number mysticism, and tales of Nordic women in the clutches of ape-like men, as well

---

[187] Quoted in Nugent, *Masks of Satan*, 144.
[188] Quoted in Nugent, *Masks of Satan*, 144.

as blood mysticism and Aryan religion. There is strong evidence that the inexperienced, down-and-out, socially-challenged Hitler of the year 1913—the man who became, within seven years, the dynamic, charismatic leader of National Socialism—experienced an amazing transformation because of a "psychic pact" or some kind of union with Satan. Hitler thus became a "diabolical mystic." Konrad Heiden's study of him at this stage recorded Hitler as being "the unhappiest of all men." Albert Speer described him as being "like a ghost pretending he was alive." This is not surprising for, along with the gifts of power that Satan grants his devotees, he also instills an all-pervading mysticism of deep depression. Hermann Rauschning, once a friend of Hitler, records Hitler's nightmarish struggles and screams:

> "He! He! He's been here!" he gasped. His lips were blue. Sweat streamed down his face. Suddenly he began to reel off figures, and odd words and broken phrases entirely devoid of sense. It sounded horrible. He used strangely composed and entirely un-German word formations (shades of Ostara). Then he stood quite still, only his lips moving. He was massaged and offered something to drink. Then he suddenly broke out: "There! There! In the corner! Who's that?"[189]

The Furious Violence of Hitler

Hitler was driven by a mad lust for power. His gods were *Nature* and *Self*. Like Nature, he knew no pity. He put it thus: "Nature is cruel, therefore we, too, can be cruel."[190] He became the god of

---

[189] Quoted in Nugent, *Masks of Satan*, 148–150.
[190] Quoted in Nugent, *Masks of Satan*, 170.

the Aryan race, which he identified with his mission to create "a violently active, domineering, intrepid brutal youth. That is what I'm after.... Strong and handsome must my young men be ... for Man is becoming God. That is the simple fact. Man is God in the making."[191] Hitler was the very incarnation of the *furor teutonicus*, that is, the Teutonic Rage against all races, with a paranoid hatred against the Jews. One day in the Bavarian town of Tolz, before a beer-drinking crowd of workers, Hitler launched his battle cry:

> Aryans and anti-Semites of all nations, unite in the struggle against the Jewish race of exploiters and oppressors of all nations.[192]

He was obsessed with blood during his whole career—from his fatal, abortive beer hall putsch, his ghastly purge of his private army, the storm troopers who brought him to power, to his boast in his last political testament that the extirpation of the Jews in the death camps was his greatest achievement. A shocked Gernal Halder, who was with Hitler during the Polish blitzkrieg, recalls Hitler's ecstatic call for drowning people in blood:

> Then his eyes popped out of his head, and he became quite a different person. He was suddenly seized by a lust for blood.[193]

And Hugh Trevor-Roper concludes,:

> In his last days ... Hitler seems like some cannibal god, rejoicing in the ruins of his own temples. Almost his last orders were for execution: prisoners to be slaughtered, his

[191] Quoted in Nugent, *Masks of Satan*, 155, 157.
[192] Quoted in Konrad Heiden, *Der Fuehrer*, 124.
[193] Quoted in Heiden, *Der Fuehrer*, 156.

old surgeon was to be executed, his own brother-in-law was executed.[194]

In addition, through an *earlier* blood purge—the "Night of the Long Knives" in June 1934—Hitler wiped out possible rivals in his private army, which finally enabled him to gain absolute mastery over his party and Germany. He was now completely unfettered to strike out against his internal enemies, the Jews, and all Christians that opposed Nazism. Moreover, he could now prepare his war machine to conquer all of Europe. Thus, in reality, those firing squads in the Stadelheim Prison in June 1934 fired the first shots of the Second World War. Eventually, the blitzkrieg on Poland in 1939 exploded a volcano of violence that engulfed the whole world with its floods of fire and magma from sky, earth, and sea. In the end, World War II took a tremendous human toll: fifty-four million dead, and untold millions more wounded, including many maimed for life. The desire for revenge on Europe and the world was perhaps the most fiery impetus Hitler had for wreaking his anger in an all-out war. Moreover, the very war fed Hitler's hatred and anger against the Jews. In his madness, he performed many senseless acts. After all, the Jews were not very numerous in Germany, a minuscule group and no clear menace to the Nazi regime. Yet, against all reason and intelligent wartime necessities, Hitler had trains, which were needed to carry men and supplies to the front lines of the war, diverted for the more diabolical work of delivering millions of his enemies—Jews and Christians—to death camps. Only the madness of violent hatred could have made such irrational action an end in itself.

And here we would like to correct a false rumor that has been bruited about by misinformed agents. It has been maintained that

[194] Hugh Trevor-Roper, *The Last Days of Hitler*, 156.

Hitler's Holocaust was inspired by Christianity, that it was the Christians' revenge against Jews for the sin of deicide. But here one must remember that, historically, Christians had their differences with the Jews on religious grounds. Hitler's hatred and anger against them was grounded on racial reasons. Christians have never had the desire to liquidate the Jews. In fact, they always embrace them in Baptism. Adolf Leschnitzer, in *The Magic Background of Modern Anti-Semitism*, emphasizes this truth:

> An anti-Semitism intent on the extermination of the Jews was irreconcilable with medieval Church dogma, if for no other reason than that divine Providence required preservation of the Jews until the end of time.[195]

The Church still teaches that doctrine. At any rate, a perversion of Christianity did lay the groundwork for a form of passive anti-Judaism. But Hitler hated and persecuted Christians not for racial reasons, but for religious and political ones. Thousands of the clergy and faithful were victims in the Holocaust. In a letter sent to me by the Very Rev. Bernard Goebel, pastor of Immaculate Conception Church in Panna Maria, Texas, and dated in 1987, we read, "I am fifty-six years in the priesthood, 5.5 in German concentration camps, 4.5 in Dachau in the company of twenty-five hundred Catholic priests. There were no turncoats among them."[196] In principle, therefore, Christianity is completely incompatible with anti-Semitism. As a matter of deeper understanding of this question, it becomes clear that, in order to be anti-Semitic, one must first be anti-Christian. Thus, the Holocaust was not the action

---

[195] Adolf Leschnitzer, *The Magic Background of Modern Anti-Semitism*, 178.
[196] Fr. Bernard Goebel, letter to the author.

of Christianity, but of Hitler mystically in league with the devil as his forerunner of the Antichrist. For it was Hitler, using the demonic forces of Nature, who planned to change man, made in the image and likeness of God, into man made in the image and likeness of the Beast, his animal god, his superman, his brutal, youthful satanist. Christopher Nugent, in his *Masks of Satan*, sums up clearly the diabolical purposes of Hitler's National Socialism:

> With nationalism (Nazism), the purpose was to establish the divine origin of particular peoples at the expense of the common divine origin of mankind as handed down in Judeo-Christian faith. The logic of nationalism rendered the Jews alien.... Despite pretensions, Hitler was not Christ, and Voltaire, Nietzsche, de Gobineau, Renan, Schoenerer, Wagner, Chamberlain, von Liebenfels, Eckart, Hess, Himmler, and Rosenberg were not the twelve apostles. They were all anti-Christian, as well as anti-Semitic (or anti-Hebraic).[197]

Whenever Hitler spoke of power, higher culture, or the "New Order," he really was alluding to the torturing, murdering, and—finally—extermination of all the races groveling as slaves beneath the German Master Race. Yet, he even once indicated in an offhanded, yet cold-blooded manner that the weak, defective, backward German progeny should also be purged:

> If Germany should get a million children each year and eliminate seven to eight hundred thousand of the weakest, in the end the result would be an increase of power. These murders would be done "in accordance with racial law." ... The clearest racial state of history, Sparta, carried out these racial

---

[197] Nugent, *Masks of Satan*, 169, 167.

laws systematically. By our modern humanitarian drivel, we strive to preserve the weak at the expense of the healthy.... We slowly cultivate the weak and kill the strong.... It does not cost more blood to win the land that we need for bread than is now removed from life and suppressed by artificial reduction of life.[198]

Hitler's Medical Violence

In the New Order created by Hitler, there were many bizarre medical experiments made on humans. These were exercises in sheer sadism. They increased the already functioning lust for mass murder. Concentration camp inmates and prisoners of war were used as human guinea pigs. Some two hundred murderous, medical quacks—some even considered eminent in the medical world—were supposed to be advancing medical science through what they learned in torturing their victims. Science was to leap ahead through cruel, bizarre experiments on innocent humans.

Jews were by no means the only victims of these medical tortures. Russian, Polish, and Slavic prisoners, including men, women, and even children were victims. The experiments were of great variety. Prisoners were thrown into pressure chambers and subjected to high altitude tests until they ceased breathing. Some were injected with lethal doses of typhus and jaundice, and some to freezing experiments in icy water—or exposed naked in the snow outdoors until they froze to death. Poison bullets were tried out on them as well as mustard gas. In a camp for hundreds of Polish women—the "rabbit girls," as they were called—gangrene-gas wounds were inflicted on some, while others were subjected to the operation of bone grafting.

[198] Quoted in Heiden, *Der Fuehrer*, 323.

The Roots of Violence

At Dachau and Buchenwald, gypsies were chosen to see how long—and in what manner—they could survive on salt water. Sterilization experiments were carried out on a large scale—at many camps and by a variety of means—on thousands of men and women, especially young Jewish girls. To rationalize these experiments, the S.S. physician, Dr. Adolf Pokorny, wrote Himmler that "the enemy must not only be conquered but exterminated."[199] Men and women were collected at Auschwitz whose heads and skeletons, studied while they were yet alive, were to furnish the Nazi doctors with "scientific measurements." They were later murdered. Not only skulls and skeletons of victims were collected, but also the skins of victims were used for decorative value. Tattooed skins were much sought after. At the Nuremberg Trials, it was revealed that some four hundred "freezing experiments" were performed on three hundred persons: 80 or 90 percent died directly, and the rest were executed, some having been driven insane first. This lust for blood in the New Order was justified by the Nazi supermen's attempt to become God, masters of life and death, creators of quality life through their exaltation of the idols of Race, Blood, and Science, an unholy trinity if ever there was one. In the end, the mark of Cain—that is, the mark of the Beast and the Antichrist—was branded forever on their criminal foreheads.

Hitler's Mania for Mass Murder

On May 29, 1942, midway in the existence of the Nazi New Order, two Czechs—Jan Kubis and Josef Gabeik, members of the free Czech army in England who had parachuted from an R.A.F. plane, tossed a bomb of British make into the Mercedes sports car of Reinhard Heydrich, known as "Hangman Heydrich," as he was

---

[199] William L. Shirer, *The Rise and Fall of the Third Reich*, 979.

driving from his country villa to the castle in Prague. Heydrich was chief of security police and chief deputy of the Gestapo, and known for his cruelty and ruthlessness in the slaughtering of thousands of the conquered peoples. The two Czech freedom fighters were performing an act of justified retribution against this gangster-style aggressor of the New Order. Heydrich died of his wounds on June 4, 1942. There followed a pitiless, savage German revenge, a frightening mass human sacrifice of the whole population of the Bohemian village of Lidice (current Czech Republic), a sacrifice to the Teutonic idols of Blood and Race.

On the morning of June 9, 1942, ten truckloads of German security police arrived at Lidice and surrounded the village. No one was allowed to leave. But anyone who lived there and happened to be away could return. A boy of twelve, sensing the danger, tried to sneak away. He was mowed down by machine-gun fire. A peasant woman, seeking escape, ran towards the outlying fields. She was shot dead in the back. Then the entire male population was locked up in the farm stables and cellars of a farmer named Horak, who was also the mayor of the village.

The next day, from dawn to 4:00 p.m., the men were taken into the garden behind the barn in batches of ten and shot by firing squads of the security police. A total of 172 men—and boys over the ages of sixteen—were executed. An additional nineteen male residents, who were working in the Kladno mines during the massacre, were arrested and dispatched to Prague. Seven women, who were rounded up at Lidice, were taken to Prague and shot. All the rest of the women, 195 in number, were transported like cattle to the Ravensbrueck concentration camp, where they were executed or otherwise killed: most gassed, three "disappeared," and forty-two died of ill-treatment. Four of the women of Lidice were about to give birth. They were taken to a maternity hospital in Prague, where their newborn infants were murdered; and they themselves were then shipped back to Ravensbrueck.

Then the children had to be disposed of, for their fathers were dead and their mothers imprisoned. Miraculously, the Germans did not shoot them, not even the male children. But they were carted off to a concentration camp in Gneisenau. Seven of these who were less than a year old were selected by the Nazis—after a thorough examination by Himmler's "racial experts"—to be sent to Germany and brought up as Germans with German names. The Czechoslovak government, which filed an official report on Lidice for the Nuremberg Tribunal, stated that "every trace of them had been lost"[200] Lidice itself was wiped from the face of the earth, for the security police burned the village, dynamited the ruins, and leveled every construction in a scorched-earth madness. Though Lidice is the most widely known example of Nazi savagery, it was not the only village that underwent such a barbaric destiny. There was another in Czechoslovakia—Lezhaky—and several more in Poland, Russia, Greece, and Yugoslavia. Moreover, in the French village of Oradour-sur-Glane, a detachment of the S.S. division *Das Reich* massacred 642 inhabitants: 245 women, , 207 children, , and 190 men. Oradour, like Lidice, was never rebuilt. It remains a monument to Hitler's idolatrous New Order, which massacred whole populations in the service of its man-made gods, idols created by man's arrogant, raging Will to Power: the satanic gods of Sex, Blood, Race, and Science.[201]

Hitler's Violence against Religion

"Gods" without an altar, liturgy, priests, preachers, dogma, and morals—indeed a church—could have very little influence on the

---

[200] Shirer, *The Rise and Fall of the Third Reich*, 992.
[201] Ibid.

German population, on the New Order which was to educate, dominate, and guide them to their racist utopia. So Hitler's New Order created The National Reich Church of Germany. Thus, Hitler's government drew up a thirty-point code of religious laws for this National Church. The laws were drawn up during the war by Alfred Rosenberg, an outspoken, dedicated pagan who—among his many other official duties—held that of "the Fuehrer's Delegate for the Entire Intellectual and Philosophical Education and Instruction for the National Socialist Party." A few of the thirty religious articles convey the violent essentials of this secularistic, pagan, and naturalistic religion:

1. The National Reich Church of Germany categorically claims the exclusive right and power to control all churches within the borders of the Reich; it declares these to be national churches of the Reich.

5. The National Church is determined to exterminate irrecoverably ... the strange, foreign Christian churches imported into Germany in the ill-omened year of A.D. 800.

7. The National Church has no scribes, pastors, chaplains, or priests, but National Reich orators are to speak in them.

13. The National Church demands immediate cessation of the publishing and dissemination of the Bible in Germany.

14. The National Church declares that to it, and therefore to the German nation, it has been decided that the Feuhrer's Mein Kampf is the greatest of all documents. It ... not only contains the greatest—but it also embodies—the purest and truest ethics for the present and future life of our nation.

18. The National Church will clear away from its altars all crucifixes, Bibles, and pictures of saints.

19. On the altars, there must be nothing but Mein Kampf—the most sacred book to the German nation and therefore to God—and, to the left of the altar, a sword.

30. On the day of the National Church's foundation, the Christian cross must be removed from all churches, cathedrals, and chapels ... and it must be superseded by the only unconquerable symbol, the swastika.[202]

As Martin Bormann, one of the men closest to Hitler, said publicly in 1941, "National Socialism (Nazism) and Christianity are irreconcilable."[203] That is because the *New Paganism* of the Nazi butchers could only exist and function with violence, genocide, and terrorism—all of which worked to torture and murder not only the bodies of its victims, but also, even more tragically, their souls.

[202] Shirer, *The Rise and Fall of the Third Reich*, 993.
[203] Shirer, *The Rise and Fall of the Third Reich*, 240.

8

THE VIOLENCE OF AVARICE

Her princes in the midst of her [the house of Israel],
are like wolves ravening the prey to shed blood, and to
destroy souls, and to run after gains through covetousness.

—Ezekiel 22:27

Covetousness, also known as avarice, is the inordinate desire for temporal goods, whether it be a lust for gold, land, the neighbor's wife, success, economic prestige, political rank and power, or any other professional possession. Avarice becomes the capital sin of covetousness when, because of its insatiable cupidity, a greedy person violates the laws of justice, charity, or any other law guaranteeing the rights of one's fellowmen.

Silas Marner, the fictional character in George Eliot's eponymous novel, ceaselessly counting his shekels in the solitude of the night, is doing violence to his own humanity. His avarice is not so much a maniacal love of gold, as it is his lust for merely possessing it. He has made an idol of his gold, and his pathological counting and fondling of it is his liturgy that honors this graven image. His idolatry is a form of self-abasement before a thing, a creature, which is totally unworthy of such adoration. That is why the covetous person is called a miser. In his book *The Seven Deadly Sins Today* Henry Fairlie expertly observes that there is a profound metaphysical relationship, and not merely an etymological one, between the reality of being a "miser" and being "miserable."

> It is not an accident that "miser" comes from the same root as "misery"—or that the first meaning of "miserable" given in the dictionary is "stingy, miserly," and that the first meaning of "miser" is "a wretched person."... Scrooge stays in our minds as the portrait of a miserable man.[204]

It is written in the book of Ecclesiastes that "a covetous man shall not be satisfied with money: and he that loveth riches shall reap no fruit from them."[205] St. Thomas Aquinas enumerates seven ugly daughters that are begotten by the capital vice of covetousness:

> Now since covetousness is excessive love of possessing riches, it exceeds in two things.... It exceeds in retaining, and, in this respect, covetousness gives rise to insensibility to mercy, because a man's heart is not softened by mercy to assist the needy with his riches. In the second place, it belongs to covetousness to exceed in receiving, and in this respect covetousness may be considered in two ways. First, as in thought (*affectu*). In this way it gives rise to restlessness, hindering man with excessive anxiety and care.... Secondly, it may be considered in execution (*effectu*). In this way, covetousness in acquiring other peoples' goods sometimes employs force that pertains to violence, sometimes deceit, and then, if it has recourse to words, it is falsehood, if it be mere words; it is perjury if he confirms his statement by

---

[204] Fairlie, *The Seven Deadly Sins Today*, 133.
[205] Eccles. 5:9.

oath. If he has recourse to good deeds and the deceit affects these things, we have fraud; if the deceit affects persons, then we have treachery, as in the case of Judas who betrayed Christ through covetousness.[206]

The Lord Himself, in His parable of Dives and Lazarus, demonstrates the insensibility to mercy that hardened the heart of Dives, the affluent miser. This devotee of the Goddess Success, who was clothed in purple and fine linen and feasted daily in splendid fashion, heartlessly denied Lazarus—the sick, starved, sore-infested pauper—even the crumbs that fell from his table (Luke 16:19–31). Concerning the vice of restlessness to which avarice gives rise, we need only consider modern man's mania for possessing and acquiring more and more. Our shopping malls are getting larger and larger; some have become small cities. Larger and larger crowds are invading them, buying more and more superfluous objects that only cause increasing anxiety over their care and preservation. The affluent society buys what it does not need, not merely for the pleasure of possessing and counting its wealth but, above all, to flaunt its many holdings in the face of its competitive neighbors. This is a form of runaway avarice in the service of one's self-aggrandizement. It is often, too, avarice in the service of snobbery. The poet William Wordsworth has captured this avaricious rat race for possessions in words of memorable wisdom: "Late and soon, getting and spending we lay waste our powers."[207]

---

[206] Thomas Aquinas, *Summa Theologica*, II–II, q. 118, a. 8, emphases added.

[207] William Wordsworth, "The World Is Too Much with Us," as given at https://www.poetryfoundation.org/poems/45564/the-world-is-too-much-with-us; Wordsworth was the Poet Laureate of England from 1843–1850.

The Roots of Violence

What powers? Our spiritual, immortal powers, of course. When a person idolizes things as the most precious possessions of life, he depersonalizes himself; he dehumanizes himself for the sake of material possessions, security, and status. Instead of growing up in spiritual maturity in an *ascent to being* by subordinating things to a transcendent, spiritual, and intimate relationship of love and service to God and his fellowmen—as the Divine Persons and human persons to whom he would be willing to surrender himself and possessions—the avaricious person chooses to immerse himself in the fall, into the infantile *descent of having*, losing his personhood in a sea of transitory possessions which he must eventually leave behind. The Psalmist comments on the inanity of such a way of life: "The senseless and the fool shall perish together: And they shall leave their riches to strangers: And their sepulchers shall be their houses for ever. Their dwelling places to all generations: they have called their lands by their names. And man when he was in honor did not understand" (Ps. 48[49]:11–13). For the miser treats himself and others as objects, not as persons. He completely misses the wonderment and exhilarating mystery of human beings made in the image and likeness of God. The avarice of the miser leads to self-annihilation, to a narcissistic love that empties him of all spirituality, making him become a displaced person, bored with the monotony of collecting things, and sick with the ennui of manipulating others or with avoiding being manipulated by others. The danger is that such an avaricious style of existence—we cannot dignify it with the title of life—will finally bring man down to despair, to social suicide and—who knows?—even to physical suicide. Could the disillusionment of covetousness partly explain why so many youngsters are committing suicide today? Perhaps they've had and experienced it all at a very young age. There is nothing left to acquire or experience to satisfy their excessive greed. They are bored with the inanity and absurdity of a life that gets its only meaning from things and the pursuit of things. So they dismiss themselves from this madly consumeristic, coarsened, and heartless world. It is reported that Sweden, which satisfies its citizens' needs and desires completely from the womb to the tomb, nevertheless, registers the highest percentage of all nations in suicides among its youth. "Not in bread alone doth man live, but in every word that proceedeth from the mouth of God" (Matt. 4:4). Mammon is a cruel god who devours its devotees.

When we consider violence as an evil effect of avarice, we discover two forms of this evil fruit: psychological and physical violence. Philosophers and psychologists have recorded that the mystic bond of friendship has been all but lost in the West, especially in the United States. Americans do not usually cultivate friends and, as a result, they themselves do not easily become friends. A mere disagreement on some issue and acquaintances stop talking to each other. There is the lust to dominate minds as well as actions in others. We see this especially in the colleges and universities and, perhaps, in its worst form, in those so-called conservative colleges who boast that they are orthodox Catholic and better than all others, even while they act as tyrants over their students. Thus, Americans make useful contacts or allies, even spending money to acquire them. These promising contacts are manipulated opportunistically to help Americans scale the backs of their competitors in economic, political, academic, clerical, or even sports rivalries, so as to gain the top of the pyramid of conquered opponents. Thus, often enough today's contacts and allies become tomorrow's implacable adversaries. For a real friend gives *himself* to his friend, not merely his possessions, prestige, or social clout. But in the highly organized consumeristic society, people are not available to enter into friendship with others. Too much sacrifice is entailed in becoming not numero uno, but even *numero secundo* in everyday life. Rather, Americans are eager to use (consume?) others as means for the goal of increasing their assets. This age is called the "Me Generation," and with good reason. Americans, and unfortunately their silly imitators in other countries, are detached spectators, investigators of other peoples' lives and talents, calculating how they can exploit them to their own advantage. Such self-centered peoples are seldom true participators. They never dream of developing a bond of sympathetic brotherhood that could create a union of spirits and a marriage of hearts among nations. For avaricious nations have their heads and appetites in other peoples' lives, but not their hearts nor affections. Why are such opportunistic contacts called violence? Because the avarice they display toward mankind degrades their fellowmen by violating their own spiritual dignity, and that of the whole human race.

We come now to analyze avarice or covetousness as the source of some other vices, and here especially of physical violence. An historical and biblical example will graphically reveal its sinful developments. One of the commandments that God engraved on the tablets He gave to Moses for the moral guidance of His Chosen People—and, indeed, all men—proclaimed, "Thou shalt not covet thy neighbor's ... wife."[208]

King David, while walking upon the roof of his house one afternoon, caught sight of a woman bathing. The woman was stunningly beautiful. David was strongly attracted toward her; he inquired about her and learned she was Bathsheba, the wife of Uriah. Now the woman's beauty so fascinated David that the temptation to possess her conquered his will. He coveted her for pleasurable intercourse. The king sent for her and he slept with

[208] Exod. 20:17.

her. Then he sent her back home. Beauty seduced David through the concupiscence of the eyes, and then covetousness aroused lust in his heart, leading, in turn, to the unwise and unjust summoning of Bathsheba to his royal chambers by royal authority. All this led finally to the sin of adultery. Beauty had seduced David and lust perverted his heart. But the trail of corruption did not stop there, for one serious sin embraced usually leads to others.

Bathsheba reported to David that she had conceived as a result of their union. Then began David's frantic efforts to cover up his covetousness and sins. He had Uriah called back from the front, where he was fighting the enemies of Judah. He urged Uriah to go home to his wife and, to make his return certain and pleasurable, he sent a mess of meat from the royal table as a gift. But Uriah, moved by a deep spirit of loyalty to the king and patriotism to his nation, refused the blessings of a furlough back home into the loving arms of Bathsheba. Instead, he slept before the gate of the king's house. It was then that David tried another tactic to cover up his adulterous, impregnating adventure. He made Uriah drunk at a royal banquet, hoping to get him to go home to his wife in a drunken stupor, so that he could sleep with her. Here again, we have the sin of deceit compounded by the king's seducing Uriah into the state of drunkenness. Despite these tactics, Uriah refused to go home to the joys of matrimonial life. He protested he could not enjoy family life while "the ark of God and Israel and Judah dwell in tents, and my lord Joab and the servants of my lord abide upon the face of the earth."[209] While drunk, Uriah slept upon a couch in the company of the other servants of the king.

It was then that David, in desperation, had recourse to physical violence. He sent Uriah back to the war front, bearing a letter to

[209] 2 Sam. 11:11.

Joab his military lord. Unbeknown to Uriah, he was delivering his own death warrant. The letter to Joab read, "Set ye Uriah in the front of the battle, where the fight is strongest: and leave ye him, that he may be wounded and die."[210] Sure enough, in the ensuing battle, the abandoned Uriah was killed. Thus, David completed his sins of covetousness, seduction, adultery, and fraud with the violent sin of murder. Bathsheba was now totally in his possession. Fortunately, David repented of his serious sins, did hard penance, begged God's forgiveness with a broken, contrite heart, and was reinstated to God's good graces. But he had to suffer experiencing the death of his child as a punishment. In Judas's selling of Christ for thirty pieces of silver, we witness the capital sin of avarice culminating in treachery—and accomplishing the violence of deicide and the ghastly self-destruction of the traitor.

Collective Avarice and Collective Violence

But avarice and its accompanying violence are not restricted to being only personal evils. There are many underworld crime associations—or "families" as they are sometimes called—that avariciously rake in billions of dollars through drug trafficking, pornography peddling, prostitution rings, loan-sharking, price-fixing, union controlling, bribe arrangements for the outcome of sports events, and many other sleazy rackets too numerous to mention. And woe betide the "canary" who sings to the law-enforcement authorities. He or she will be mercilessly killed. Moreover, there are deadly wars between mobs who compete to monopolize certain areas of criminal moneymaking activities. These wars take their toll of violent deaths on both sides. And they create an atmosphere of violence and insecurity in the major cities of all nations. Heads

[210] 2 Sam. 11:15.

and lieutenants of criminal families seldom die in bed. True, they are usually given gala farewells in sumptuous funerals, attended often by their murderers, that follow their unsolved violent deaths. But the surviving greedy ones, caught inescapably in the meshes of these rackets, return to the avaricious hunt for riches and power. They undergo degradation, perpetual fear, and slavery. For them, human life is cheap and expendable for the baubles of the god Mammon. Yet, long before they themselves are "liquidated," they must suffer the daily psychological violence that reduces them to being, not human persons, but targets for the weapons of their enemies and of the law. And they work for the transitory end of enriching their bosses and themselves. Such domination of their souls by material things extinguishes the spirituality of their intelligence, eradicates their freedom to pursue virtue, and robs them of any transcendent dignity.

The Avarice and Violence of Colonialism

Massacres of whole peoples were brought about by the *avarice* that drove Western nations to collect colonies. The centuries of colonization and imperialism provide plenty of examples of the "administrative massacres" that flowed from the avaricious lust to dominate indigenous peoples overseas, and to exploit the untapped resources found in their lands. Western mercantilism ruthlessly grasped the precious metals found there as a basis for strengthening their own economy, including through establishing trading stations, plantations, and power centers. Then, too, political power loomed large in the drive to acquire more and more colonies. For colonies were also a source of prestige and increased military power, adding important manpower reserves to offset the competition of other colonial powers. Often the natives were treated as if they were subhuman. Blacks were sold in the West as slave laborers. Indians were oppressed to the point of extinction in some areas, and to the point of destitution everywhere. For a long time, no one contested the right of advanced Western colonial nations to dispossess, dominate, and rule over these native inhabitants. They were regarded not as human persons, but as property. Eventually, theologians such as Bartolomé de Las Casas insisted that the Indians of the New World were true human beings with corresponding human rights.

Almost two hundred years ago, Britain was the world's leading slave-trade nation. Other nations, for instance Spain and Portugal, were also in this avaricious business. What emphasized the brutal inhumanity of this business was the famous Zong case of 1783 in England. We read in Garth Lean's book *Brave Men Choose* some of the details of that case:

> Both sides (in Britain's government) in the Zong case of 1783 ignored the loss of 132 lives—thrown overboard by the owner to profit by the insurance. "It was," said the Attorney General, "a case of goods and chattels, a throwing of goods overboard to save the residue," and the law, said Chief Justice Mansfield was "exactly as if horses were thrown overboard." The Solicitor-General deprecated the "pretended appeals" to "humanity" and agreed that the master had the unquestioned right to drown as many as he wished without "any shew or suggestions of cruelty" or a "surmise of impropriety." All the Court allowed to be investigated was the "precise distribution of costs and losses." The Earl of Abingdon was stating a settled conviction of the age when he replied hotly to Wilberforce: "Humanity is a private feeling, and not a principle to act upon."[211]

[211] Garth Lean, *Brave Men Choose*, 10.

British slave ships sailed from Liverpool, Bristol, and London to the West African coast and there—by direct seizure, purchase from Arab traders, or barter with local chiefs—gathered their black cargo. The male slaves were jammed between decks in pairs on shelves with barely 2.5 feet of headroom. Women and children, when not chained, were packed equally tight with no room to lie down and exposed to the savage lusts of the crew. Three hundred to six hundred would be the normal cargo for a ship of 100 or 150 tons. By the time they reached their destination in the Americas or West Indies, 10 percent had died, while many others were desperately ill. There, brutal merchants would fetch as many as forty pounds a head, while the sick and the wounded would be sold off in cheap lots with women and children. The profit on these trips was well over one hundred percent of the original costs. Millions of human beings were sold in this violent fashion. This trade was not just successful business for the Western nations, it was a national policy. Eventually, by the Treaty of Utrecht, Britain wrested from France and Spain a virtual monopoly of this trade with America, on condition that she supply at least 144,000 slaves to the Spanish colonies within thirty years. "The Institution,"[212] as slavery itself was called, was regarded as "the great pillar and support of the British plantation trade in North America."[213] It is estimated that, before the year 1776, Britain supplied three million black slaves to the French, Spanish, and British colonies.

It took the great British statesman William Wilberforce—a man fearless, tactful, and unseeking, who had taken his seat in Parliament at the age of twenty-one in 1780—twenty years of

[212] Lean, *Brave Men Choose*, 1.
[213] Lean, *Brave Men Choose*, 2.

herculean struggle against fierce opposition in Parliament, and the all-pervasive apathy of the masses, to achieve success on March 23, 1807, with a vote of 283 to sixteen that finally abolished slavery in England. Then, at the Congress of Vienna, Britain persuaded Spain and Portugal to ban the slave trade. This ban was completed in 1817.[214]

The Violence of Mass Deportations

Then there is the heartless crime that seeks to annihilate native populations. This crime permits the invader to expand his possessions, power of domination, and moral-political ideologies. Communist Russia seized Latvia, Lithuania, and Estonia during World War II and perpetrated the horrible crime of spiritual genocide. There were mass deportations of millions upon millions of these people. They were swallowed up in Siberian slave labor camps or lost in the interior of the Soviet Union. The efforts to eliminate these peoples as nations are still continuing today. Families are ruthlessly torn apart as the intense Russification, denationalization, and displacement of whole nations scar the modern age with this new crime against humanity. The Communists not only aimed at extinguishing the social-political identity of these nations, but, above all, they worked to destroy their Christian religion—destroying their churches, seminaries, and schools.

In a similar ferocious fashion, Hitler established his policy of "the Final Solution" for the Jews in all of Europe. Here the genocide was physical and ethnic. The Jews were to be annihilated, not for any utilitarian purpose, nor to gain more territory or riches from them, but simply because they were a hated ethnic group, that is, Jews. Hitler's actions in the "killing camps" were aimed at

[214] Lean, *Brave Men Choose*, 10–11.

getting rid of the whole Jewish population in all of Europe. To do this, even prisoners of war were mistreated and executed. For its part, Communist Russia engaged in mass murders for political, military, and religious reasons, not for racial motives. Reliable investigations prove that the Communist Russian army murdered fifteen thousand Polish officers, whose bodies were found at Katyn Forest in the neighborhood of Smolensk in Russia. The Allies themselves participated in the obliteration of civilian populations, the saturation bombing of open cities and, above all, the dropping of atomic bombs on Hiroshima and Nagasaki in Japan. These actions clearly constituted massive crimes against humanity, for they annihilated entire cities with innocent and defenseless men, women, and, children being wiped out. Thus, the violent West was open to the *tu quoque* accusation leveled by the Axis powers: "You, too, committed crimes against humanity."

Hitler's extermination of Jews via gas factories grew out of his euthanasia program, which was in full swing in the first weeks of World War II. This program was undertaken to eliminate the mentally sick, physically handicapped, gypsies, the asocial, and, of course, "potential enemies." The Nazi and Communist mass murderers justified their massacres by claiming that these crimes were, in fact, great deeds for history: grandiose, unique tasks for bettering the human race. Men and nations have an infinite capacity for self-deception. These criminals claimed that they were "superhumanly inhuman" in order to produce, for the Nazis, a perfect human race and, for the Communists, a prosperous, classless society. They were purifying physically and socially the human race of miscreants, who were given the honor of experiencing "mercy deaths." Unfortunately, by the end of World War II, everybody knew that technical developments in the instruments of violence had made the adoption of "criminal warfare inevitable." There was no longer any distinction between soldier and civilian, army and home population, military targets and open cities.[215]

Violence and the New Nationalism

Scripture warns man, "Thou shalt not covet thy neighbor's house."[216] Now this commandment holds true for nations as well as individuals. We have indicated how the European nations exploited the peoples and lands of foreign cultures, though, to complete the picture, they also did these lands much good—especially in the realm of the Christian religion. However, unfortunately, it is part of human experience that, once a certain type of activity has been enacted before the eyes of the shocked world—no matter how cruel, unjust, or unnatural the activity may be—the deed remains in man's memory to be potentially repeated in the future. Because no punishment for a specific crime that has appeared for the first time is adequate to erase that crime forever. Its reappearance is more likely than its initial appearance could ever have been. For mankind gets acclimated, habituated, and tolerant of the most abhorrent, ghoulish crimes. Thus, many of the crimes initiated by the Nazis and the Communists are back with us today. To take just one example, the Nazi medical murder of hundreds of thousands—under the euphemistic rubric of "mercy deaths"—is being legally repeated in many of the democratic nations of the West.

The same truth holds for the recurrence of exaggerated political ideologies with all the crimes they have committed in the past. Thus, the exaggerated nationalisms of the early twenties—and later in Italy—led to many horrible wars. For these nationalisms drove these nations to expand avariciously their power and influence

---

[215] Hannah Arendt, *Eichmann in Jerusalem*, 256–257.
[216] Exod. 20:17.

over new territories of indigenous peoples. And these expansions clashed among the colonial powers, who often went to war to establish their superiority.

Conclusion

The avarice of stealing the house and home of one's neighbor must inevitably lead to violence and war. All colonialism is really a secular form of exaggerated nationalism that attempts to justify—through a specious patriotism—the economic, political, even military rape and exploitation of indigenous peoples.

9

The Violence of Vengeance

Revenge not yourselves, my dearly beloved; but give place unto wrath, for it is written: Revenge is mine, I will repay, saith the Lord.... Be not overcome by evil, but overcome evil by good.

—Romans 12:19, 21

Vengeance consists of an action in which an avenger inflicts a punishment upon his adversary who had previously inflicted, or was planning to inflict, an injury upon him. Of its very nature, vengeance is not necessarily an evil or unlawful act. Man must look to God for nothing but what is good and lawful. But Scripture tells us that we are to look to God for vengeance. "Will not God revenge his elect who cry to him day and night: and will he have patience in their regard? I say to you, that he will quickly revenge them."[217]

St. Thomas Aquinas looks to the Old Testament to provide examples for acts of vengeance that were justified:

Sometimes a wrong done to a person reflects on God and the Church. Then it is the duty of that person to avenge the

[217] Luke 18:7–8.

175

wrong. For example, Elijah made fire descend upon those who sought to seize him. Likewise, Elisha cursed the boys who mocked him. And Pope Sylverius excommunicated those who sent him into exile.[218]

The principle of action directing such vengeful conduct is expressed by St. John Chrysostom: "Let us learn after Christ's example to bear our own wrongs with magnanimity, yet not to suffer God's wrongs, not even by listening to them. For it is praiseworthy to be patient under our own wrongs, but to overlook God's wrongs is most wicked."[219] In the natural order of human events, St. Thomas also defends the right of sovereign rulers (legitimate governments) to take vengeance on the wicked, in keeping with the order and rank that does not usurp what belongs to God. For in his Letter to the Romans, St. Paul writes of the earthly prince, that "he is God's minister: an avenger to execute wrath upon him that doth evil."[220] But if the ruler inflicts vengeance outside the order of divine ordinance, he usurps what is God's and therefore sins.

Now what makes the act of vengeance morally good or evil is the mind of the avenger. If his intention is directed primarily to inflict evil on the persons on whom he takes vengeance, and remains there in hatred and cruelty, his vengeance is criminally sinful. For to take pleasure in another's evil is the sin of hatred, contrary to charity whereby we are bound to love all persons — even our enemies upon whom we may be avenging our wrongs. But if the avenger's intention is directed to some good to be obtained by means of the punishment inflicted — for example, the rehabilitation

---

[218] St. Thomas Aquinas, *Summa Theologica*, II–II, q. 108, a.1.

[219] St. John Chrysostom, in Thomas Aquinas, *Summa Theologica*, II–II, q. 108, a.1.

[220] Rom. 13:4.

of criminals or that justice may be restored or God honored—then the act of vengeance will be morally good, provided other due circumstances be observed; i.e., that the common good be obtained, the multitude be shielded from grave scandal, and more harm than good not be the outcome of the punishment. St. Thomas also reminds us that, when a whole nation or multitude sins continually or habitually, then vengeance must be taken on them. Thus the Egyptians were drowned in the Red Sea for stubbornly opposing God and His Chosen People. The children of Sodom and Gomorrah, though they were invincibly ignorant, perished with their corrupt parents. Even parts of multitudes can be avenged for their sins, as is demonstrated by the mass execution of those Israelites who worshipped the Golden Calf.

But, as a rule, individual persons may not perform acts of violence on their own determination. This is the sin of taking the law into one's own hands. Persons may not do evil, because evil has been done to them. St. Paul gives instruction for morally just conduct for Christians in the event they have to suffer wickedness from evil persons:

> To no man rendering evil for evil. Providing good things, not only in the sight of God, but also in the sight of all men. If it be possible, as much as is in you, have peace with all men. Revenge not yourselves, my dearly beloved; but give place unto wrath, for it is written: "Revenge is mine, I will repay, saith the Lord." ... Be not overcome by evil, but overcome evil by good.[221]

St. Thomas answers the objection that vengeance should not be inflicted with punishments that are customary to men thus:

[221] Rom. 12:17–19, 21.

Vengeance is lawful and virtuous so far as it tends to the prevention of evil. Now some who are influenced by the motive of virtue are prevented from committing sin, through fear of losing those things which they love more than those they obtain by sinning, else fear would be no restraint to them. Consequently vengeance for sin should be taken by depriving a man of what he loves most. Now the things which man loves most are life, bodily safety, his own freedom and external goods, such as riches, his country and his good name. Wherefore according to Augustine's reckoning,[222] Tully writes that the laws recognize eight kinds of punishments namely: death, whereby man is deprived of life; stripes, retaliation, or the loss of an eye for an eye whereby man forfeits his bodily safety; slavery, and imprisonment, whereby he is deprived of freedom; exile, whereby he is banished from his country; fines, whereby he is mulcted in his riches; ignominy, whereby he loses his good name.[223]

Now there are two vices that render what would normally be a justified taking of vengeance into the crime of the violence of vengeance. The first is the sin of hatred, cruelty—even brutality—which exceeds the rational use of vengeance. The second is the vice of the excessive toleration of evil, for Scripture warns that "he that spareth the rod hateth his son."[224] God punished the holy high priest Eli because he tolerated abuses by his two sons against the holy liturgy of the temple. The two sons were killed in battle and Eli, on hearing of their deaths, fell back, broke his neck, and

---

[222] St. Augustine, *De Civitate Dei* (The City of God), bk. 21, ch. 11.
[223] Thomas Aquinas, *Summa Theologica*, II–II, q. 108, a. 3.
[224] Prov. 13:24.

died. The day before these events took place, the prophet Samuel predicted these punishments to Eli for his negligence in disciplining his sons.

In this chapter, we can only analyze some of the more fanatically brutal and vengeful events of recent history. By no means do we justify these acts of violence, whoever may perpetrate them. For vengeance is never cured by counter-vengeance, nor one evil crime cured by another evil crime.

The Vengeance of the Black September Organization

The Black September Organization (BSO) took its name from the Berim and Ikrit Christian villages in northern Israel that had surrendered without resistance in the 1948 war. The authorities persuaded the villagers to leave their homes on "security grounds." They promised the villagers they would be able to return to their homes within fifteen days. Instead, the Israeli authorities betrayed the villagers. The Christian Arabs not only were not allowed to return to their villages and their homes in Berim and Ikrit, but their homes were demolished in their absence and settlers had seized their land and were cultivating it. It was a clear case of the treacherous violence of avarice. The BSO planned an operation of vengeance.

Eight members of the BSO were trained and chosen to launch a television spectacular by capturing Jewish athletes in Munich, West Germany, where the 1972 Summer Olympics had opened on August 26. The publicity profits for calling the world's attention to their cause were enormous. Nearly five thousand journalists and television crews were present to photograph and record the games. Thus, on Tuesday September 5, 1972, eight figures disguised in sportsmen's track suits, while carrying traveling bags, climbed over the metal mesh fence that surrounded the Olympic Village. The group was seen by a cleaning woman and a postman, but no one paid any particular attention to them for, as one Olympic official later related, "Anyone dressed in a track suit could get in with no questions asked." The eight commandos, after stripping off their track suits, opened their traveling bags and drew forth AK-47 automatic rifles and grenades. They crept silently along, seeking the residence of the Israeli Olympic team. They carefully opened doors that were unlocked and knocked gently on those that were locked, whispering in perfect Hebrew, "Is this the Israeli team?" They soon found the team's residence, but the door to the apartment was locked. However, one Israeli was awake, expecting his companion to return very late. He had agreed to let him in. On hearing the knock, he thought it was his friend. So he unlocked and partly opened the door. He realized his mistake too late. The terrorists muscled their way in. There followed a scuffle and they shot and killed the Israeli at the door, and another who tried to run past them. Awakened by the shots, the remainder of the Israeli team in another room escaped over their own back balcony. But those in whose room the commandos had entered, nine in number, were taken as hostages with their hands tied behind their backs.

By later that same Tuesday morning, the news had spread throughout the Olympic Village and around the whole world. The Germans established a crisis staff to deal with the situation. The leader of the terrorists, shrouded in a black hood, appeared on the balcony for all the world to see and learn of his demands. He demanded the release of two hundred Arabs held in Israeli jails, in exchange for the safety of the hostages. He also demanded an aircraft to fly the commandos and the hostages to an Arab capital other than Amman or Beirut. The crisis staff tried to bribe the commandos with large sums of money, and they even offered "to provide them with beautiful German blondes." This obscene, materialistic offer of the German crisis staff clearly demonstrated their total incomprehension of the spiritually vindicative nature of this project. The response of the terrorists should have enlightened them: "Money does not matter, neither do our lives." The crisis staff then brought up marksmen and then decided to take a hard line against the commandos. The crisis staff informed the commandos that it agreed to supply a single aircraft to take them out of Germany with the hostages. But the terrorists were suspicious and demanded three helicopters, so as to break up the hostages and foil any full-scale attack upon themselves. Then they demanded an airport bus to take them and the hostages from the ground floor level of their building to the helicopters some hundred yards away. The crisis staff agreed to supply the bus. Then the terrorists and their blindfolded hostages entered the bus. The hostages were tied together and, for the first time, the Germans realized that there were eight rather than five commandos. The three helicopters were waiting at the selected site; four commandos and four hostages entered one; four commandos and five hostages entered the second. Israeli General Zvi Zamir and his assistants got into the third, hoping to surprise the commandos and destroy them on arrival at what the staff said would be the Munich airport. Thinking they were being flown to the Munich airport, the Arabs promised not to hijack the helicopters while in flight. But the helicopters were flown not to Munich but to the Furstenfeldbruck military airport, where the helicopters came to rest some fifty yards in front of the control tower. They were guided by two policemen disguised as airport ground staff. Five policemen were hidden about 150 yards away in a shadowy place near the floodlit *Lufthansa* Boeing 727, which was to take the commandos and their hostages out of Germany. These policemen were poised to fire, with one being on the roof of the control tower. He would be the first to fire, signaling the others to shoot as well. Two Arabs jumped from the helicopters and went to examine the *Lufthansa*. Satisfied there were no booby traps, they walked back to the helicopters where their companions were holding the hostages at gunpoint. When they were halfway back the Germans made a terrible mistake. The control tower policeman fired killing the Arab accompanying his commander. The commander dove into the shadow of the helicopter and fired back, killing the policeman on the roof of the control tower. Then all hell broke loose. The terrorists jumped from the helicopters and fired into them at the hostages. One threw a grenade which set the helicopters on fire. The gun battle flared up in full fury between the policemen and the commandos. When it was all over, seventeen people were dead: the two Israeli athletes killed in the Olympic Village, the nine Israeli athletes taken hostage, five Arab terrorists, and one policemen. The next day, the Israeli dead were flown back to Israel. The three terrorist survivors were taken to West Germany for trial. Colonel Muammar Gaddafi accepted the bodies of the dead Arabs and gave them a "hero martyrs" funeral. The Munich massacre was roundly condemned by all Western nations. On Friday September 8, since violence begets violence and revenge creates a tornado of counter-revenge, the Israeli Air Force made its expected reprisal raids that lasted twenty minutes, hitting seven camps in Syria and three in Lebanon, causing heavy casualties: "sixty killed, two hundred wounded, not counting the innocent civilians killed." In both projects of violence, victims innocent of previous violent crimes were killed out of a vengeful madness and brutal fanaticism. So true is it that avaricious and vengeful violence prove to be their own executioners.[225]

[225] Edgar O'Ballance, *Language of Violence*, 115–125. All of the exploits and many more are narrated in full detail in these pages.

The Japanese Red Army's Exploit in Arab Vengeance

In October 1971, the Popular Front for the Liberation of Palestine (PFLP) sent Ruyshi Ghanem and Bassam Abu Sharif to Japan to the Japanese Red Army (JRA) leadership to plan violent episodes for the Arabs against the Israelis. The PFLP agreed to train the Japanese terrorist agents. Three Japanese terrorists were involved as the action men. The leader was Takeshi Okudaira; the second man was Yasuyuki Yasuda; and the third was Kozo Okamoto. Near Baalbeck in the Lebanese mountains, they practiced firing live ammunition, throwing grenades, setting aircraft on fire with phosphorous bullets, and other murderous techniques. When they completed their training, the three Japanese men arrived in Rome from Germany, where they had gone to pick up forged passports. They passed through inspection without arousing any suspicion. Their suitcases were checked in and put on the conveyor belt without being opened or examined. Holding valid tickets to Tokyo via Lod airport in Tel Aviv, they passed through a newly installed metal screen and came out "clean," indicating they had no weapons concealed. But the JRA terrorists' weapons were in their checked luggage and went undetected. They boarded an Air France Boeing 707, leaving Rome at 6:50 p.m. and arriving at Lod Airport in Tel Aviv at 10:00 p.m. local time. At Lod, their false passports were accepted as genuine and stamped by the official on duty. This gave them the right to stay as tourists in Israel for up to three months.

When their suitcases appeared the Japanese stepped forward, took them from the conveyor belt, and walked away, spreading out from each other as they did. Then they stopped, put down their suitcases, stooped down, unfastened them, took out from each a Czech 726-mm automatic rifle (the VZ-58), several magazines—each filled with thirty rounds of ammunition—and two or three grenades. Straightening up, they commenced firing into the crowded customs hall. Death, injury, and painful bloodshed filled the room. Instant pandemonium broke loose. The rattle of automatic fire and crackling thuds created an atmosphere in that concentrated area seldom experienced even on a battlefield. Within seventeen seconds, twenty people were killed and eighty wounded. After this massive carnage, the three moved toward open doors leading to the tarmac, determined to destroy two aircraft, one a passenger jet operated by El Al, the chief Israeli airline company, and the other a Swedish-based Scanair plane. Both had passengers aboard. As they approached the planes, Okudaira, the leader, came within fire of his comrades and was killed. Yasuda tripped as he opened his grenade; it exploded and blew him to pieces. The third terrorist, Okamoto, after throwing two grenades and firing his rifle at the stationed aircraft, was seized by an airport official and secured as a prisoner with the help of other security guards. Instantly nurses, doctors, and ambulances began to arrive and attend the injured. PFLP claimed full responsibility for the massacre at Lod Airport, saying it was a reprisal for the death of two Black September commandos killed by Israeli security forces on May 5, 1971, when they forced a hijacked plane into Lod Airport. Here is proof to demonstrate how the vengeance networks are cooperating on an international scale, with allies dedicated to their plans for brutal, fanatical terrorism.[226]

1973: A Litany of Hijacks and Horrors

The year 1973 produced an explosion of violent vengeance. There was a sequence of fifteen Arab terrorist acts; the October Yom Kippur War between Egypt, in a united front with Syria and Jordan,

---

[226] O'Ballance, *Language of Violence*, 147–162.

against Israel; and also attacks on embassies and airport facilities. In almost all of these incidents, innocent hostages were taken, with many of them murdered or injured. It all started on December 28, 1972. On that day, four BSO commandos occupied the Israeli embassy in Bangkok, Thailand, holding it for eighteen hours. They seized six hostages, including the Israeli ambassador to Cambodia who was on a visit there. After much negotiation and a guarantee of a safe flight for the BSO team to Damascus, the hostages were freed. Fortunately, no one was killed or injured in this episode.

Then on February 21, 1973, a terrible tragedy took place. A Libyan Boeing 727, on a regular commercial flight from Tripoli to Cairo with a French crew, strayed too far eastward due to a navigation error. The weather was very bad and the pilot attempted to get back on course, But the Israelis shot the plane down, killing all 106 passengers. In this eye-for-an eye, tooth-for-a-tooth madness, not even innocent civilians from many peaceful countries are safe.

On March 21, 1973, Israeli aircraft raided Fatah camps in Lebanon, killing 108 persons. The next BSO exploit ended in tragedy. On March 1, 1973, eight BSO commandos seized a Saudi Arabian embassy in Khartoum, Sudan and held five diplomats as hostages, among them George Moore, the retiring American ambassador to Sudan. To ensure the safety of the hostages, the BSO agents demanded the release of Abu Daoud, a BSO leader, and fifty other Palestinian Fedayeen held in Jordanian prisons, Sirhan Sirhan who had assassinated Robert F. Kennedy in June 1968, held in an American jail, all the Baader-Meinhof members in West German jails, and the release of all female guerrillas held in Israeli prisons. When negotiations failed, the Arabs reduced their demands to the release of Abu Daoud. The terrorists were calm until they received a radio message from their leaders. It read, "Why are you waiting? The blood of the people of Nahr al-Bared cries out for vengeance." Then the commandos suddenly became hard and cruel, indeed brutal. They gave the two Americans and Belgians time to write last letters to their families. Then they shot them to death. Later evidence showed that George Moore had been beaten and kicked in the face before being killed. The terrorists, on orders from their leaders in Beirut, finally surrendered and had to stand trial in the Sudan. King Hussein conferred the death sentence on Abu Daoud and his colleagues in Amman, although Daoud would live until 2010.

On April 9, 1973, three Arab agents placed explosives on the ground-floor of a two-story apartment where the Israeli ambassador to Cyprus lived. Cypriot police opened fire. In the exchange of shots, one policeman was killed. The explosion damaged the first floor but left unharmed those who had been on the second floor, as the wife and children of the ambassador had left only minutes before. The terrorists were captured. In a second plot, Arab terrorists attempted to hijack an Israeli Arkia Viscount aircraft. They drove through the barrier at Nicosia Airport. One vehicle circled the airport firing at the plane. An Israeli security guard and the Cypriot police were able to kill one terrorist and capture seven. One of the terrorists' vehicles contained fifty pounds of explosives. Luckily, they were captured before the terrorists could ignite them.

On April 14, 1973, four masked men overpowered guards at the Zahrani terminal of the TAP Oil Pipe Line in Sidon, Lebanon. They held hostage with other employees, taking them to a nearby beach where they were joined by fourteen other men. Explosives were then affixed to eighteen oil storage tanks and detonated. Only two tanks were destroyed. The other devices either failed to detonate or were defused by Lebanese army experts. The terrorists scattered nails on the main road that ran through the oil installation complex, which delayed pursuing vehicles and thus enabled them to get away.

Another Greek episode took place on July 19, 1973. An Arab agent, armed with automatic rifle and grenades, attempted to enter an El Al Airlines office at Athens. He was seized by bystanders, but he escaped and ran to the nearby Amelia Hotel and took twenty people hostage. After four hours of negotiations, the Arab released the hostages upon being guaranteed safe conduct to Kuwait. Again in Greece, the BSO struck on August 3, 1973, in a crowded transit lounge at Athens International Airport. Two Arabs suddenly took grenades from their suitcases and threw them across the floor. They then produced automatic weapons and fired them indiscriminately into the crowd. Three persons were killed and fifty-six injured. One of the injured died later from his wounds. Three of the dead were Americans, one an Austrian. The two raiders then herded fifty hostages into a corner and attempted to bargain with the police. After two hours, they surrendered. They revealed they were on this mission to attack passengers embarking on an Israeli-bound TWA flight, but had mistakenly attacked those waiting to take a flight to Geneva and New York. They were sentenced to death by a Greek court on January 24, 1974.

On September 5, 1973, the first anniversary of the Munich Massacre, five BSO members broke into a Saudi Arabian embassy in Paris, seized control of the building, and held fifteen hostages, including four women. They demanded the release of Abu Daoud and his colleagues, as well as safe conduct from France via aircraft to an Arab capital. Otherwise they would blow up the building. After much negotiating, the terrorists freed all the hostages at the Paris-Le Bourget Airport, except for five Saudi Arabians. After receiving a Syrian Caravelle aircraft, they flew to Kuwait. However, at the Kuwaiti airport, the BSO raiders demanded that the Syrian Caravelle be replaced by a Kuwaiti Boeing. This being done, the hostages and the terrorists flew toward Riyadh, the Saudi Arabian capital. During the flight over the desert, the terrorists threatened to throw their Saudi hostages out of the plane one by one unless Abu Daoud was released. When they got no response from Riyadh or Amman, they ordered the aircraft back to Kuwait. When they landed it was surrounded by troops and police. After more negotiations, more deadlines, and more threats, the Arabs released the Saudi hostages and surrendered to the Kuwaiti authorities. Luckily, no one was killed or injured.

On the same day, September 5, 1973, Italian police surrounded and arrested five Arabs who were planning to shoot down—with ground-to-air missiles—an El Al airliner bound for Rome. Later, another four Arabs who were connected with this plot were arrested at a Rome hotel. These Fedayeen terrorists were brought to trial and sentenced to imprisonment by a Rome court. The police who raided an apartment in Ostia, near the airport, uncovered in their possession two SAM-7s, complete with launchers and missiles. Two of the terrorists were released and deported to Libya. The remaining three were expelled from Italy on March 1, 1974, after a sum of money was paid the court by an unrevealed source.

On September 23, 1973, two Syrian commandos boarded a train called the Chopin Express, which ran from Moscow, through Kiev (then in the Soviet Union) and Bratislava (then in Communist Czechoslovakia), to Vienna, Austria. There were seventy passengers on the train, thirty-seven of them Jews emigrating from Russia. At this time, the Soviet Union had eased its emigration restrictions against the Jews and about seventy thousand Russian Jews had traveled on this train to the West. The terrorists seized the two Austrian customs officers when the train crossed the frontier into Austria. As the train got under way again, the Arab commandos went into the sleeping coaches and seized four Jews as hostages. The commandos had forged passports, and they also had automatic weapons and grenades. They carried out this operation because the immigration of Soviet Jews to the West and Israel was increasing Israel-based opposition to the fight for their Palestinian homeland. Thus, the terrorists demanded that the Schonau Castle transit camp near Vienna be closed down, and that all facilities the Austrian government provided to help Jews emigrate be withdrawn. Bruno Kreisky, himself a Jew and Austrian chancellor, agreed to comply with the terrorists' demands. His government also promised safe conduct via aircraft out of Austria. Libya allowed the Cessna airplane to land in its country "for humanitarian reasons." On September 29, the two commandos were presented at a press conference during which one stated, "Moshe Dayan has stated publicly that he would attack the Palestinian Fedayeen wherever they may be. Therefore, we are determined to attack Zionists everywhere in the world."

Then, on October 6, 1973, the Yom Kippur War between Egypt, in a united front with Syria and Jordan, surprised Israel and tumbled back the Israelis, for the Egyptians and Syrians simultaneously attacked on two fronts. The Arab advance shocked Israel, as the myth of the invincibility of the Israeli Army was shattered. The early success in the war was a terrific morale builder for the Arabs. Eventually, the war developed into a stalemate with attrition lasting thirty-four days on the Syrian front, and 129 on the Egyptian front, before a truce on both sides took hold. It was a war in which there was no victor and no vanquished, though the loss of lives for the Israelis was much higher proportionally, since they have a much smaller nation in comparison with the Arabs.

On November 25, 1973, three Arabs hijacked a Dutch KLM jumbo jet with 288 persons aboard as it left Beirut. They demanded that the Dutch government close the transit camps on its soil for Russian Jews, stop Soviet emigration through Holland, stop Dutch volunteers fighting for the Israelis, and stop Dutch arms deliveries by air to Israel. The Dutch rejected all the demands, except it did announce that Dutch volunteers fighting with Israeli armed forces would lose their Dutch citizenship. The jumbo jet landed in Malta, where the hijackers released 247 hostages and three hostesses in exchange for being refueled. In the end, the jumbo jet landed at Dubai, in the United Arab Emirates, where the Arabs surrendered to the authorities. The nine-man crew, a relief pilot, and a KLM representative were released unharmed.

To mark the end of this year with its long chain of hijacks and horrors, one of the worst vengeful exploits was committed on December 17, 1973. Five Arabs at the Rome airport took out automatic weapons and grenades and opened fire indiscriminately. Then they rushed out onto the tarmac toward an Air France aircraft about to leave for Beirut, which had aboard Ahmad Osman, the prime minister of Morocco. The crew managed to slam the door shut before the Arabs could enter. The terrorists then made for a Pan American airliner that had 90 passengers aboard, including Moroccan ministers, and which was waiting for the signal to depart. They threw incendiary bombs at the plane, hoping to kill U.S. Secretary of State Henry Kissinger, whom they mistakenly thought was aboard. Within seconds, the plane was a blazing inferno. Thirty-four persons died and another forty were injured; the dead included two Moroccan ministers. Then the terrorists seized several Italian airport guards as hostages, took over a Lufthansa plane standing by, and killed an airport worker in the process. The Lufthansa took off with the five terrorists, six Italian hostages, and a crew of seven. The terrorists demanded the release of two Arabs who had killed four people and injured fifty-five in August 1973. The plane was told to fly to Athens, where the Greeks refused to release these two prisoners, so the hijackers selected at random one of the six Italian hostages, shot him, and flung his body out onto the tarmac. During the flight, the hijackers threatened to kill their hostages one by one if their demands were not met. From

Athens, the Lufthansa took off again, and, after refueling at Damascus, forced a landing at Kuwait, damaging the plane thereby. No one onboard was seriously hurt. After three hours of negotiations, the hijackers surrendered, freeing the remaining hostages unharmed. The five terrorists were handed over to the Palestinian Liberation Organization (PLO) and were never prosecuted or even questioned. Thus ended the year 1973 in the Middle East and Europe, the year of the chain-reaction of hijackings and horrors.[227]

Massacre of 241 Marines, 58 French Soldiers

Perhaps the most vengeful crime that Arab terrorists perpetrated occurred on October 23, 1983. American Marines and UN multinational forces were stationed in Lebanon in a peace-keeping effort. The Israeli invasion, undertaken against the will of the West and especially by the United States, left war-tortured Lebanon in a shambles. Thousands of innocent Lebanese were killed; hundreds of family residences were destroyed; many hundreds of thousands more were left homeless, starving, and facing death from sickness. Moreover, when the PLO forces evacuated Lebanon in 1982, they were persuaded to do so by an agreement made with the West, particularly with the United States, that the Palestinian refugees left behind, many of them families of the PLO, would be protected and that the besieging Israeli forces would not be allowed to enter Beirut or the camps of the refugees. That the agreement was not honored is testified to by the gruesome massacres perpetrated by Israeli-directed forces in the camps of Sabra and Shatila, which were detailed in the previous chapter. The Arabs, betrayed and seething for revenge against the West, and especially against the

---

[227] O'Ballance, *Language of Violence*, 187–203. Here, too, the details are most revealing.

United States—whom they considered the stubborn and treacherous ally of their deadly enemy, the Zionists—struck back in a bloodcurdling event. On that fatal October morning, while the Marines were still asleep, an Arab driver of a truck entered the U.S. barracks uncontested, detonating a powerful bomb which killed 241 Marines. The terrorist behind the wheel, apparently affiliated with a fundamentalist Islamic sect, was most willing to sacrifice his life for a cause which he saw as a retaliation against injustice and treachery to the Arabs. Two minutes later, a second bomb at the French paratroop barracks two miles away exploded, killing fifty-eight French soldiers. Here was another Arab zealot willing to blow himself up in order to avenge crimes against his people.[228]

Achille Lauro and Carlos "The Jackal"

Then, in early October 1984, four Palestinians pirated the Italian cruise ship *Achille Lauro*. All aboard were held as hostages, but the Palestinians, before getting their demands accepted and releasing the ship and the hostages, wantonly murdered and threw overboard a vacationing American invalid simply because he was Jewish. The episode was reported to have been masterminded by Mahmoud Abbas in cooperation with Abu Nidal, leader of the breakaway Fatah Revolutionary Council, which belonged to that block of Arab revolutionaries which sought a hard line taken against Israel and its international supporters.[229] The other organization of revolutionaries, under the command of Yasser Arafat, wanted to restrict their vengeful violence to what they called the private Arab-Israeli war, and not to make enemies of other nations by perpetrating violence in their territories. Also involved

---

[228] *The World Almanac & Book Facts 1983*, 891.
[229] *The World Almanac & Book Facts 1983*, 889.

in the *Achille Lauro* piracy was the mysterious Carlos "The Jackal," a very successful terrorist for Arab causes. Carlos's real name was Ilich Ramirez Sanchez, a Venezuelan whose father was paradoxically both a rich lawyer and convinced Marxist. During the '70s, Carlos ravaged France as he led Palestinian raids in Paris with great success. But the event that made Carlos world famous was his television spectacular. With five terrorists, one woman and four men, he burst into the headquarters of the Organization of the Petroleum Exporting Countries (OPEC) in Vienna where the ministers were holding an important meeting. His group killed an Austrian doorman and two other people, while two others were wounded. They held the eleven oil ministers and their staffs hostages. The nations represented were Algeria, Ecuador, Gabon, Indonesia, Iran, Iraq, Kuwait, Libya, Nigeria, Saudi Arabia, and Venezuela. They demanded revolutionary sanctions against the Zionist presence on Palestinian territory. Their eight demands were: 1. no treaty, no recognition, no negotiation with Israel; 2. a denunciation of all compromise with Israel; 3. a condemnation of attempts to persuade the Palestinians to go to the negotiating table in Geneva; 4. a condemnation of the disengagement agreements and the reopening of the Suez Canal; 5. the formation of a Northeast Front comprising Syria, Iraq, and the PLO; 6. Arab states to work for unification; 7. a declaration of full sovereignty over oil; and 8. a declaration of support in Lebanon against Zionists.

The text of these demands was read over the Austrian radio in French. The Austrian cabinet, in emergency session under Chancellor Bruno Kreisky, agreed to their demands. It also supplied a plane for the terrorists and thirty-three hostages to fly to Algiers. There Carlos released the so-called neutrals, that is, the ministers of Ecuador, Gabon, Indonesia, Nigeria, and Venezuela, but he refused to allow the other hostages to leave the plane. Then the aircraft took off for Tripoli, Libya. In an interview at the Tripoli airport, Carlos said, "The aim of this exploit was twofold: to extract a pro-Palestinian statement from each of the oil ministers, and to execute the Iranian and Saudi Arabian oil ministers, because they were selling oil and trading with the enemy, Israel and its allies." Because the PFLP was appalled by what it saw as the surrender of some Arab oil states to Western (thus indirectly to Israeli) interests. In the negotiations, the governments of Saudi Arabia and Iran agreed to pay a ransom amounting to $25 million each for the safe return of their ministers. With this arrangement, the terrorists released the Algerian and Libyan oil ministers, but retained nine hostages, including both the Iranian and Saudi Arabian oil ministers. With them still onboard, they ordered the plane to return to Algiers, where they accepted the ransom money from the Iranians and Saudi Arabians and released the remaining hostages. When Carlos was questioned thus, "But you are not an Arab. Why do you perform such violent acts?" He replied, "We are revolutionaries, not criminals. We are The Arm of the Arab Revolution. And my name is Carlos. They all know me. I am the famous Carlos." He stated that he carried out operations that involved killing and injuring innocent people, "because violence is the one language the Western democracies can understand."[230]

The Violence of Arab Vengeance

US News and World Report, April 25, 1988—"Again, Iran Revs Up the Hijack Murder Machine":

When Kuwait Airways Flight 422 lumbered down the runway at Bangkok on April 5, carrying 112 people, it flew

---

[230] O'Ballance, *Language of Violence*, 205–220.

straight into a plot hatched four months earlier in Tehran by Shiite radicals from Bahrain, Lebanon, and Iran. Mideast intelligence sources say that one of the chief plotters is Shiite terrorist boss Imad Mughniyeh—mastermind of the bloody bombings of the US embassy and US Marine headquarters in Beirut, and the man behind a number of kidnappings of Americans in Lebanon. The hijackers demanded the release of seventeen Shiite terrorists imprisoned in Kuwait.... The demand for the freedom of these seventeen was already made in a 1984 hijacking of another Kuwaiti jet that resulted in the murder of two US government employees, and this demand was made once more in a 1985 TWA hijacking, with its equally brutal killing of a US Navy diver. When Kuwait refused to release the seventeen prisoners, the terrorists murdered two innocent Kuwaiti citizens who were passengers on the plane, and dumped their bodies onto the tarmac. Eventually, in a deal made in Algeria, the terrorists allowed the passengers to go free and they themselves flew to safety.

These actions are cases of pure vengeful terrorism. They cannot be justified under any circumstances. In his book *Terrorism*, Benjamin Netanyahu reflects wisely on the irrational madness of terrorism:

> Terrorism gradually *conditions* [emphasis original] us to lawlessness and outrage. We are by now almost resigned to attacks on airline offices, seizure of embassies, hijacking of airplanes, bombing of government buildings, assassination of political leaders, machine-gunning of children.... Terrorism not only cuts across political boundaries with impunity, it violates our most precious moral and ethical boundaries. For the deliberate targeting of innocent civilians—shoppers, tourists, passengers, students—has gradually eroded the

crucial distinction between combatant and non-combatant. It is not only that the terrorist breaks down this distinction. It is that we begin to accept his standards. With each fresh terrorist attack, the public is conditioned—first by the terrorists, then by his own compliant interpreters in the press—to equate innocent hostages with jailed terrorists and to accept the notion that the murder of children is a regrettable but understandable expression of the terrorists' purported grievance ... (Terrorism, 202–203). Unlike natural catastrophes, terrorism is neither purposeless nor fortuitous. It is deliberately planned, organized, initiated, and launched by people who wish to dramatize the powerlessness of governments (Terrorism 200).

The answer to terrorism must never be counterterrorism. For such reactions are utterly futile and irrational conduct. Counterterrorism only intensifies the maddening spiral of violence, begetting a senseless exchange of savage massacres which lead to mutual psychological and eventual physical suicide.

Bombs and Booby-Trapped Cars Take Their Toll in the Eastern Areas[231]

Forty-seven explosions, 323 dead, and 1,631 wounded. These are the results compiled over a thirteen-year period, from January 1976 through June 1988.

These are the results of booby-trapped cars, bombs, and explosive devices that have exploded in East Beirut and its suburbs. To most, these are but figures and statistics, but to the residents of these areas, these are loved ones who were killed, or maimed for life.

[231] *Lebanon News*, June 30, 1988, 5.

Date	Place	Device	Dead	Wounded
Jan. 16, 1976	Akkawi	Bomb	0	12
June 4, 1977	Nahr al-Kalb	Bomb	1	14
Aug. 25, 1977	Martyr's Square	Bomb	8	7
Feb. 26, 1978	Ashrafieh	Car	7	6
May 13, 1979	Mtyab Road	Bomb	0	1
Feb. 23, 1980	Akkawi	Car	6	3
March 12, 1980	Daoura	Car	1	4
April 22, 1980	Jdeideh	Car	0	5
July 30, 1980	Ashrafieh	Car	3	16
Aug. 17, 1980	Ashrafieh	Car	1	4
Nov. 10, 1980	Ashrafieh	Car	10	70
Sept. 14, 1982	Ashrafieh	Bomb	24	75

The Roots of Violence

Date	Place	Device	Dead	Wounded
Sept. 20, 1984	Awkar	Car	12	96
Jan. 9, 1985	Sin al-Fil	Car	0	0
March 21, 1985	Daoura	Car	0	4
May 22, 1985	Sin al-Fil	Car	42	177
Aug. 14, 1985	Sid Bouchrieh	Car	13	118
Aug. 17, 1985	Jal al-Dib	Car	31	85
Nov. 12, 1985	Awkar	Car	3	25
Jan. 21, 1986	Furn al-Chebak	Car	30	123
Feb. 3, 1986	New Jdeidheh	Bomb	9	20
Feb. 3, 1986	Jeitawi	Bomb	0	0
Feb. 12, 1986	Ain al-Remaneh	Bomb	2	17
Feb. 24, 1986	Sloumi	Car	5	15

Date	Place	Device	Dead	Wounded
March 8, 1986	Rmeil	Car	3	0
March 26, 1986	Ashrafieh	Car	10	0
April 8, 1986	Jounieh	Car	11	89
May 23, 1986	Sin al-Fil	Car	7	118
May 24, 1986	Sabtieh	Bomb	0	0
May 23, 1986	Sin al-Fil	Car	7	118
July 28, 1986	Ain al-Remaneh	Bomb	25	140
Aug. 3, 1986	Jal al-Dib	Bomb	0	5
Aug. 14, 1986	Bourj Hammoud	Bomb	2	30
Aug. 14, 1986	Daoura	Car	20	100
Aug. 20, 1986	Daoura	Bomb	0	3
Dec. 30, 1986	Zalka	Attaché case	2	25

The Roots of Violence

Date	Place	Device	Dead	Wounded
Jan. 7, 1987	Nahr Highway	Car	2	50
Jan. 30, 1987	Zalka	Car	6	48
Feb. 2, 1987	Chevrolet Area	Bomb	0	8
Feb. 19, 1987	Hirjtabet	Bomb	0	9
April 12, 1987	Daoura	Car	0	25
April 15, 1987	Jal al-Dib	Car	1	1
May 21, 1987	Daoura	Car	1	1
July 3, 1987	Moamiltaine	Car	0	1
Nov. 27, 1987	Hayek Circle	Bomb	0	3
May 30, 1988	Rmeil	Car	20	80

Chinese Communist Vengeance

Although we have for the most part demonstrated the malignant evil of hateful, violent vengeance from examples in Europe and the Middle East, this scourge exists in the whole world in our age of modern violence. Perhaps the headquarters of world violence and planned vengeance is to be found in the Communist capital of Moscow. In her excellent book *The Time of the Assassins,* Claire Sterling does a magnificent unmasking of the Communist plot—worked through Bulgarian lackeys—to assassinate Pope John Paul II, because of his enormous moral influence in working for the economic and religious freedom of his Polish countrymen. Vladimir Lenin tells the world that the entire Communist system of totalitarianism is founded on the use of terror and violence: "We can achieve nothing unless we use terror. The energy and mass nature of the terror must be encouraged." Well, the Chinese Communists have obeyed Lenin's orders in a frightful manner. For in Communist China we have recorded unspeakable vengeful actions of the Reds against student and adult followers of Chiang Kai-shek. In his book *The Enemy Within,* Fr. Raymond J. De Jaegher, who spent nineteen years as a missionary in China living among the Communists, witnessed the horrible cruelty the Communists inflicted upon their own people, including as they established the practice of burying their victims alive. They would tie victims' hands behind their backs, bury them up to their navel, and then leave them there under the evil eye of a sentinel, who made sure no one brought them food or drink. Victims lasted two or three weeks, depending on their strength and the fierceness of the sun's rays. In speaking to Communist General Ho Lung about the barbaric aspect of this torture, Fr. De Jaegher received this response: "That is the death we must mete out to the capitalists, comrade, because it is slow and they suffer much."[232] On another occasion, Fr. De Jaegher recalled, the whole town—young, old, men, women, and children—were signaled by a big town bell to come to an open

---

[232] Fr. Raymond De Jaegher, *The Enemy Within,* 192.

place. The Communists summoned them to witness the ghastly beheading of thirteen young students of the Seu-tsuen School, the anti-Communist school in Chang Tsun. Here is Fr. De Jaegher's eyewitness description of this vengeful barbarity:

> The Communists forced the children in the front row to sing patriotic songs. Then the Communist leader gave the signal for the execution to the swordsman, a tough, compact-bodied young soldier of great strength. The soldier came up behind the first kneeling victim, lifted his great, sharp, two-handed sword and brought the blade down cleanly. The first head rolled over and over, and the crowd watched the bright blood spurt up like a fountain. The children's voices, on the thin edge of hysteria, rose in a squeaky cacophony and garbled words. The teachers tried to beat time and bring order into the tumult of sound. Over it all, I heard the big bell tolling again. Moving quick as light from right to left as we watched him, the swordsman went down the line, beheading each kneeling student with one swift stroke, moving from one to the next without ever looking to see the clean efficiency of his blow. Thirteen times he lifted that heavy sword in his two hands. Thirteen times the sun glinted off the blade, dazzling at first, then dully as the red blood flowed down over the shining steel and stained and dimmed its glow. Thirteen times the executioner felt steel pierce cartilage and flesh slide between small neck bones. Not once did he miss. Not once did he look back at what he had done. And when he came to the thirteenth, the last man, and chopped his head off, he threw the sword down on the ground and walked away without looking back.[233]

[233] Fr. De Jaegher, *The Enemy Within*, 128–131.

Conclusion

The practice of vengeful violence is an exercise in a maddening, hate-driven futility. It arises from the basest, blackest dregs of the human heart steeped in barbarity. When the terrorists have succeeded in a project of revenge, they experience a visceral, exhilarating, and wicked joy. But this malignant satisfaction lasts a very short time. For there are so many wrongs to be repaid that the terrorists feed on their own vengeance. They are consumed with such blazing passions that they are deliriously galloping across the stage of history on mad horses. Mr. Winston Churchill, who in a blaze of vengeance ordered saturation bombing of German cities—in which every citizen, man, woman, child, non-combatant was a target for fire from the skies—had a change of heart about the usefulness or efficiency of vengeance. Speaking in the British Commons on October 28, 1948, when Europe was threatened by Communist Russia with its policy of "the Cold War," he said, "Revenge is, of all satisfactions, the most costly and long drawn out; retributive persecution is, of all policies, the most pernicious. Our policy should henceforth be to draw the sponge across the crimes and horrors of the past and look, for the sake of all salvation, towards the future." Unfortunately the future is a non-person—an abstraction—and mankind will never be saved by abstractions, but only by Jesus Christ, but more of this in the final chapter.

The terrorist acts reported in this chapter—and these are only a few of thousands more which could have been cited—are crimes of hate that have driven their enraged perpetrators to the extreme of irrational murderous violence. A crime suffered at the hands of a criminal does not give the victim the right to repay crime with crime. And there is absolutely no justification for engaging in hijacking and violence against innocent citizens. Such actions, besides being counterproductive and criminal, antagonize nations that tended to be understanding of the terrorists' cause. They abandon that cause when they see it defended by immoral means and mount a thorough hunt against the terrorists. Nor does it advance the inimical parties one step toward the table of negotiation, where there might be achieved a mutual forgiveness of crimes and a just, charitable reconciliation. For the evil method of constantly returning violence for violence, evil for evil, blow for counterblow, aggression for counter-aggression, creates a hardening insensitivity to the horrors of the most gruesome crimes. Moreover, there is developed in the souls of the terrorists and their enemies an indifferent, habitual callousness to the sacredness of human life. And from their hardened hearts, both sides will attack anyone—innocent or not, sacred or not—who is indifferent to their cause or an ally of their enemy. What results is that a hit-and-run guerrilla war is mounted against cities, civilians, and societies. Moreover, even normally more humane societies slowly become habituated to the violent destruction of innocent life. They lose that necessary, reasonable reaction of horror at the murder of innocent life. And they easily approve, in their despiritualized mentality, the legal killing of innocent, defenseless babies in the womb. Indeed, they move on to work for legislation that allows for the killing of innocent, defenseless aged persons. So true is it that vengeance begets vengeance, violence begets violence, and crime begets crime, and "all that take the sword shall perish with the sword" (Matt. 26:52). Hateful vengeance is a self-destructive activity. It will never attain justice and lasting peace. However, within the vengeful violence which is scourging the modern world, there is more than meets the secularized eye of the worldly intellect. After all, fallen humans are much too insignificant and limited to produce—all by themselves—the hurricane of barbaric violence that tortures mankind today. There exists in society today a general apostasy from God and His Holy Church and a rush to enroll again in the kingdom of Satan. Thus, the powers and principalities of his demonic kingdom, who are behind the scenes fanning the fires of hateful vengeance, are clearly in force among men (Eph. 6:12). These have taken over the "world," whose prince, Satan, man has also chosen for his own prince. When mankind abandons fidelity to Christ, the Prince of Peace, it must inevitably become the slave of the Prince of Violence and Terror. There is no neutral ground, no no-man's land between Christ and Satan. The essence of Satan's campaign is to infect mankind with his own hatred and violence of vengeance against the God-Man, who died to bring all men together into the peace and happiness of the communion of saints. With the fire of vengeance, Satan aims to establish among men a perpetual war of fratricidal hatred, a mankind in history that would ape his own kingdom of dissention, darkness, and despair.

10

From Barbarism to Terrorism

Terrorism is the prolongation of barbarism from the massacre of
civilians in a war to the massacre of any nation's civilians anytime.

—The Author

In primitive times, warrior kings engaged in savage warfare. They burned down cities, massacred their inhabitants, tortured prisoners, and deported—as well as enslaved—whole populations. If deemed not sufficiently famous to merit trial and execution, prisoners of war were reduced to slavery, working for their conquerors for an indefinite period. Cruel, brutal, and ferocious wars were considered by the primitives to be natural for mankind. Peace was considered to be an abnormal, even unnatural, phenomenon. In the minds of the primitives, war and barbarism existed in an ambiguous position; they were never clearly defined. They were considered the ineluctable, fatalistic destiny for man, outside of all restraints and laws and subject only to their political usefulness. So they were accepted as human activity and strategy, however brutal and cruel, for destroying one's enemies. We can recall here some of the bloodcurdling acts perpetrated by ruthless, merciless leaders.

In the book of First Samuel, the prophet relates this message from God to Saul, king of Israel:

> Thus saith the Lord of hosts: I have reckoned up all that Amalec hath done to Israel: how he opposed them in the way when they came up out of Egypt. Now therefore go, and smite Amalec, and utterly destroy all that he hath: spare him not, nor covet any thing that is his: but slay both man and woman, child and suckling, ox and sheep, camel and ass.... And Saul smote Amalec.... And he took Agag the king of Amalec alive: but all the common people he slew with the edge of the sword.
>
> And Saul and the people spared Agag and the best of the flocks of sheep and of the herds, and the garments and the rams, and all that was beautiful.[234]

But God abandoned Saul because he did not execute King Agag, and because he took booty for himself and his people against the will of God. Then Samuel the prophet had Agag, the king of Amalec, brought before him and, in the presence of Saul and all the people, "Samuel hewed him in pieces before the Lord in Gilgal."[235] When King Saul was unsuccessful in pursuing the fleeing David to kill him, he heard that David spent time in the city of Nobe. There David was received and treated royally by the priest Achimilech and his family. Enraged, King Saul summoned Achimilech and his family before his throne, accused them of conspiracy, and ordered Doeg, his chief servant, to kill them in his presence:

> And the king [Saul] said to Doeg: Turn thou, and fall upon the priests. And Doeg the Edomite turned, and fell upon

---

[234] 1 Sam. 15:2–3, 7, 8–9
[235] 1 Sam. 15:33.

the priests and slew in that day eighty-five men that wore the linen ephod [sign of the priesthood].[236]

Now the empire of Assyria was totally dedicated to total warfare. It was unequaled as the incarnation of implacable, untiring, and efficient military barbarism. The record of its warrior kings fills readers with uncomprehending horror, as they learn of the awesome details of atrocities so proudly described. Their kings, beginning with Asshurnazirpal, and his successors, are seen as the forerunners of our modern sadistic monsters. They impaled, blinded, flayed alive, burned, and otherwise tortured to death prisoners and enslaved whole populations. The Assyrians felt a perverse pride in collecting military trophies and carefully recorded the erection of any huge pyramid made of skulls. They derived keen satisfaction from the gruesome rites of their victory days. To them, a good, totally barbaric war was its own satisfaction. They never sacked a city, nor executed an enemy, without piously associating their gods with the deed. But they never allowed their warlike activities to become subservient to religion like the Aztecs of Mexico, whose wars were fought mainly for the purpose of making prisoners for use as human sacrifices in honor of their god, Huitzilopochtli, and as cannibalism for their people.[237]

When King Nebuchadnezzar of Babylon besieged the city of Jerusalem in 586 BC, he captured its king, Zedekiah, and his family. He slew the sons of Zedekiah before their father's eyes, and he killed all of his nobles as well. Nebuchadnezzar also put out Zedekiah's eyes, bound him with fetters, and took him prisoner to Babylon. Moreover, he carried off the sacred vessels from God's

---

[236] 1 Sam. 22:18–19.
[237] F. J. P. Veale, *Advance to Barbarism*, 35–36.

temple in Jerusalem, and he used them in paying homage to his idolatrous gods in Babylon. He also took captive to Babylon much of the Jewish population, where they were to remain for seventy years as slaves.[238]

In the AD 200s, 300s, and 400s, the Goths, Visigoths, and Vandals—barbaric hordes of Germanic tribes—invaded and overran the corrupt Roman Empire with ferocious violence. The Vandals sacked Rome in 455, and also ravaged Gaul, Spain, and Northern Africa. The Visigoths set up a kingdom in France and Spain, which lasted until about 700. In the ninth century, the Franks, another member of the Germanic tribes, overran with fire and sword what is today France, Germany, and Italy, and they established a Frankish empire. All of these barbaric tribes recognized no restraints in carrying out their atrocities. Also, in the fifth century, Attila the Hun—known as "The Scourge of God"—ravaged Christian Europe and arrived at the gates of Rome, which he intended to destroy. But he was met by Pope St. Leo the Great, who pacified him, persuaded him to leave Rome unharmed, and thus saved the city and Western civilization. We have here, perhaps for the first time, the initial influence of Christianity through a saintly pope on the madness of barbaric war. For "civilized warfare" is entirely a product of Europe and Christianity, and for many centuries restrained the wars among Europeans.[239]

But among the Byzantine emperors in the East, who were Christian, war continued to be conducted strictly in accordance with the ancient barbaric tradition. Basil, the Bulgar-Slayer, put out the eyes of fifteen thousand prisoners. Moreover, in the West during the Albigensian Crusade of 1209, the number killed is put at fifty thousand.

[238] Jer. 39:1–9.
[239] Veale, *Advance to Barbarism*, 43.

At Beziers, almost the entire population—twenty thousand men, women, and children—were slaughtered "by reason of God's wrath wondrously kindled against it." Pope Innocent III, one of the greatest popes, was determined to root out heresy in southern France. After the capture of Minerve, in place of the usual massacre, 140 leading heretics were burnt together in one huge bonfire.[240] The Thirty Years War (1618–1648), one of the most protracted struggles of ferocious barbarity, caused one-third of the population of Central Europe to perish. The population of Bohemia was reduced from three million to eight hundred thousand. The important city of Augsburg had a population of seven hundred thousand at the beginning of the war; at the end, it had only 18,000. Such appalling massacres, as that perpetrated at Magdeburg in 1631, bear comparison with ancient barbarities. "Some twenty-five thousand people were butchered in this massacre, not one in fifty of whom was armed."[241]

Since the downfall of the Roman Empire, Christian Europe had been menaced three times by primitive warfare on a grand scale. The Saracens (Muslims) made the first attack at the close of the Dark Ages. They were notorious for their orgies of slaughter and rapine. But they were repulsed at Poitiers by Charles Martel and Christendom was spared. The second occasion was in the early thirteenth century at the very peak of Christian medieval civilization. This time Genghis Khan, the great Mongol conqueror, threatened Europe with a formidable military machine. With his wild horsemen of the steppes, he conquered, in turn, the great empires of China and Persia. Then he crushed the Russian principalities at the great battle of Kiev. There fell before his might Germany, Poland, and Silesia, with the Teutonic Knights

---

[240] Veale, *Advance to Barbarism*, 42.
[241] Francis Watson, *Wallenstein*, 326.

annihilated at Liegnitz. Then Breslau was taken and sacked. Then another wing of the Mongol hordes defeated the great crusading army under the king of Hungary near Tokay on the Sayo river. Not even the assistance of the veteran Knights Templar could prevent this defeat, for they perished to a man on the field. Then Buda (modern-day Budapest) was stormed and sacked. City after city was captured and their inhabitants methodically massacred. The Mongol hordes had reached the Adriatic, a day's march from Venice, when an act of God saved Europe. The "Great Khan" died in far-off Karakoram on the edge of the Gobi Desert. And this caused the recall of the Mongolian armies. Thus Europe was saved again and with it Christian civilization. For Europe was no match for the Mongolian hordes and trembled at their advance.

The Mongols dealt with conquered populations with an unwavering brutality. When a city was taken, the inhabitants were brought forth, tied together with ropes, and divided into three groups—men, women, and children. Skilled craftsmen and attractive women were carefully selected for dispatch to Central Asia; from there, if they survived the frightful journey, they went to labor as slaves or serve as concubines. Lastly, those remaining were forced to kneel with outstretched necks in rows down which Mongol soldiers proceeded, expeditiously cutting off with their long sabers the bent heads, which were then gathered in great pyramids to facilitate the work of the scribes, whose duty it was to supply the Great Khan with accurate statistics of the carnage. The Christians at that time were filled with speechless horror at this barbaric procedure. But we have already recorded how the Chinese Communists of today continue to employ this type of atrocity against their enemies.

Several centuries later—in the sixteenth and seventeenth centuries—Europe was again menaced by primitive warfare. This time, the Ottoman Turks were the enemy. After conquering the Byzantine Empire in 1453 and having firmly established themselves at Constantinople, the Turks conquered the whole of the Balkans, Greece, Hungary, and twice besieged Vienna. A divided Europe was helpless before their armies, which were also helped by Christian renegades. But the strategic ability and courage of John Sobieski, king of Poland, defeated the Turkish army at the gates of Vienna in 1683. Once again, Europe and Christian culture was spared. So much for the barbarism of primitive violence and warfare.[242]

Civilized Warfare

As Europe developed its national states, it gradually established a humane code for waging war. Its nations agreed to subject themselves to this code so as to eliminate all the primitive atrocities of barbarism. Popes and Church councils did their best to encourage this advancement in civilized war conduct. Civilized war could thus be defined as warfare conducted in accordance with certain rules and restrictions, which the nations of Europe became accustomed to wage their wars with each other. When they conquered in war, they also insisted that these rules and restrictions should be observed by non-European states in wars with Europeans.[243] Regulations were thus laid down from time to time to conduct the wars in Christendom according to reason and a Christian spirit. This code won general acceptance in Europe about the beginning of the eighteenth century. In his book *Advance to Barbarism*, Mr. F. J. P. Veale gives us the main purpose of these rules of war: "The fundamental principle of this code was that hostilities between civilized peoples must be limited to the armed forces actually

---

[242] Veale, *Advance to Barbarism*, 47–50.
[243] Veale, *Advance to Barbarism*, 43.

engaged."[244] This meant that the code drew a distinction between combatants and noncombatants, emphasizing that the sole business of combatants is to fight each other and, consequently, they were to exclude noncombatants from the scope of military action. Thus, much needless violence and many atrocious massacres would be prevented. Much earlier, both St. Augustine and St. Thomas Aquinas taught that war, as a human activity, was subject to the laws of reason and the moral law concerning the natural rights of men and societies. Thus the fatalistic, inevitable, amoral approach to war as the natural destiny of man the warrior, exempt from all rules and laws, was now rejected.

In this era, the ideals of chivalry had considerable influence in formulating a reasonable approach to mitigate the violence of war. For chivalry became a collective term embracing a code of conduct, manners, and etiquette, a noble system of ethics, and a distinctive Christian philosophy of life. When this code of chivalry was adopted as the standard for the military caste in all European states, it provided a common bond among them. The European knight lived the code of the Christian warrior. His reputation depended on his fidelity to it. Such a knight would never think of using the capture of a prisoner as an opportunity to indulge his resentment, revenge, or wrath against a helpless enemy in the manner of a Mongol barbarian. Sadism could no longer masquerade as moral indignation. Prisoners, no matter their nationality, were treated with honor and courtesy, as were the inhabitants of conquered cities. For chivalry had been described as the product of Christian idealism. Professor R. B. Mowat said, "Chivalry had two outstanding marks, two things that were as its essence: It was Christian and it was military."[245] Thus

---

[244] Veale, *Advance to Barbarism*, 58.
[245] Veale, *Advance to Barbarism*, 59.

"civilized warfare" was waged in Europe for some two hundred years, from the beginning of the eighteenth century down to our present generation. This, of course, does not include the "holy wars" between Christians—and between Christians and infidels—which we will examine shortly. Moreover, the eighteenth century was called the Age of Reason, Poise, and Moderation. Balance and urbanity were the qualities it most admired. Warfare conducted with clarity, for reasonable and limited ends, and with limited military means, came to be known as "civilized warfare." Military violence, atrocities, and horrors were now abhorred and outlawed.

Holy Warfare

The notion of a "holy war" was conceived and developed by the Jews from the time they were liberated by Moses from Egyptian slavery. In their destiny to occupy the "land that floweth with milk and honey" (Exod. 3:8; Num. 14:8), which God promised them through their leaders, prophets, and judges, they also received from the Lord the vocation to wipe out by wholesale homicide the idolatrous tribes that inhabited that land. We read in 1 Samuel that Saul, guided by the advice of Samuel, God's prophet, "slew the Ammonites ... so that two of them were not left together."[246] He conquered Agag, king of Amalec, but was punished by God for not executing the king and annihilating his people and possessions. King David achieved a glorious chain of victories in his holy wars against the idolatrous nations. He wiped out the Moabites, Philistines, the kingdom of Zobah (Soba), the Syrians, and many other Gentile idolatrous peoples.[247] The Jews then possessed the lands and properties of the defeated peoples as

---

[246] 1 Sam. 11:11.
[247] 2 Sam. 8:1–15.

their own, for God had promised to give these to His Chosen People. Thus, in "holy wars," the old primitive barbarism with its wholesale slaughter and scorched-earth policy was considered justifiable — in fact, meritorious — because religious issues were involved, and God willed it so.

The Church employed the reality of "holy war" to justify the Crusades in the Middle Ages against Muslim imperialists. In addition, "holy wars" known as the Albigensian Crusade and the Thirty Years War pitted frenzied Catholics, Protestants, and other heretics against each other in barbaric, fratricidal, no-holds-barred ferocities. The return of primitive barbarity in "holy wars" was piously justified, because God willed such deeds to be performed with traditional religious zeal for his honor and glory. Thus, in "holy wars," the cruelties and crudities of primitive warfare were considered holy deeds. For pious enthusiasm was considered to justify any war deed, including a variety of gratuitous carnage. Even today, there are religious millenarian sects who are convinced that the creation of a utopian paradise can only be achieved through the hell of holy wars. This doctrine was the driving force of Israel's wars against the Canaanites. It is the driving force of the PLO for the repossession of their homeland. Then, too, Islam also has its own special conception of the "holy war" called *jihad*. And Iran is presently fighting just such a war to recall all Arab nations back to their fundamental religious ideals. In his Peoples Temple, established in lush Guyana in South America, Jim Jones organized a religious mass suicide to keep his millenarian cult faithful from the "corrupting" contacts of the outside world. In their book *The God Makers*, Ed Decker and Dave Hunt unmask the "holy war" that Joseph Smith, founder of the Mormons, also known as the Latter Day Saints, planned to wage against the United States and the whole world:

In spite of the fact that every time he opened his mouth to "prophesy" he only further confirmed that he was a false "prophet," Joseph Smith's giant ego wouldn't allow him to quit. Revenge upon the "Gentiles" became his obsessive madness. That revenge was to work itself out in two ways: the destruction of all his enemies throughout the entire United States, and the establishment of his Independence, Missouri, "Zion," which was the key to reigning over the entire world.[248]

As one former teacher at Brigham Young University has said:

The Mormons do intend to take over the world.... There is no secret about that. It's in the writings of Joseph Smith right on down. The Constitution of the United States will "hang by a thread" and the [Mormon] Church will save it by establishing a theocracy.[249]

Cranmer's Violence against England's Catholics

In his brilliant little book *Cranmer's Godly Order*, Michael Davies documents the wars of violence that the religious revolutionaries, mistakenly called "Reformers," waged against Catholicism in England to establish the Anglican heresy as that nation's religion. The reformers devised and imposed the new liturgy on June 9, 1549, casting out the Sacrifice of the Mass as a "blasphemous fable and dangerous deceit," and reducing ministerial priests to men who merely read prayers, preached, and presided "over a table at which to feast, not an altar on which to offer sacrifice." As a result, Davies writes, there broke out a number of armed uprisings among

[248] Ed Decker and Dave Hunt, *The God Makers*, 224.
[249] Decker and Hunter, *The God Makers*, 230.

enraged Catholics, who were determined to defend the Mass and the Faith of their fathers:

> Even Protestant historians conceded that the Western rebellion (of the Catholics) was genuinely religious. The Catholic rebels were attacked by a propaganda campaign as well as with military forces. The government propagandists warned the Western countrymen that they were deceived by their priests, "whelps of the Romish litter." It had, in fact, been the laity who had forced or shamed their priests into making a stand for the Faith. Nicholas Udall, a Protestant scholar who had gained the favor of [King] Edward VI through the patronage of [Queen] Catherine Parr, derided the rebels for their pronouncements against heresy which, he claimed, they did not understand. The changes were, he insisted, based on the "most godly council ... with long study and travail of the best learned bishops and doctors of the realm." Had the rebels had the learning or debating skill of St. Thomas More, they could have pointed out that the traditional religion had the support of a numberless host of the best learned bishops and doctors, stretching back in time to the apostles themselves.
>
> The religious nature of the rebellion is made clear by the demands of the rebels. "First we will have the general council and the holy decrees of our forefathers observed, kept, and performed, and, whoever shall gainsay them, we hold them as heretics.... We will have the Mass in Latin, as before.... We will have the sacrament hang over the high altar, and there to be worshipped as it was wont to be, and those who will not consent thereto, we will have them die like heretics against the Holy Catholic Faith.... We will

have palms and ashes at the times accustomed, images to be
set up again in every church and all other old ceremonies
used heretofore.... We will not receive the new service because it is like a Christmas game, but we will have our old
service of matins, Mass, evensong (vespers) and procession
in Latin, not English, as it was before.

Davies relates what happened when the enraged Catholics
proclaimed their ultimatum:

The Western rebels had demanded that those who refused
their demands should "die like heretics against the holy
Catholic Faith." In the event, of course, it was the rebels
who died when the rebellion was eventually crushed by
Lord Russell and Lord Grey de Wilton, who had joined
him after putting down another religious uprising in Ox-
fordshire. The only reliable troops were the mercenaries,
Italians, Spaniards, and Germans. When they eventually
discovered the religious nature of the campaign in which
they had fought, many of them sought absolution. "There
was a fierce battle at Clyst St. Mary and another at Clyst
Heath where the rebels died by hundreds. And then, in the
night of August 4 and 5, the rebels withdrew from Exeter.
Lord Grey had never fought against Englishmen before and
marveled at "such stoutness.... Never in all the wars did
he know the like."

The rebellion was far from over, however, and the final
battle took place at Sampford Courtenay where the rebellion had begun. Groups of rebels still kept up the fight,
retreating into Somerset, and at least four thousand west
countrymen died at the hands of the royal army. Thomas
Cranmer's Prayer Book [Book of Common Prayer] had

had its baptism of blood. "By the end of August it was all over," writes Professor [S. T.] Bindoff. "Some thousands of peasant households mourned their menfolk slaughtered on the battlefield, some hundreds those who expiated their treasons on the gallows of a dozen counties.". . .

Terror was everywhere struck into the minds of the people by the sight of the executions, fixed for the market days, of priests dangling from the steeples of their parish churches, of the heads of laymen set up in the high places of the towns. The parish priest of the Church of St. Thomas (Exeter) was hanged on a gallows erected on his high church tower in his Mass vestments, with "a holy water bucket, a sprinkler, a sacring bell, a pair of beads and such other like popish trash hanged about him.". . . The last act in the Western tragedy was the execution of the leaders at Tyburn on January 7, 1550. The very objective Venetian envoy reported that "had the country people had only a leader, although they had been grievously chastised, they would rise again."

It happened, therefore, with violence and executions, that the ungodly, heretical liturgy of Anglicanism was imposed upon a Catholic people striving to persevere in the traditions of the Holy Mass in Latin, and in fidelity to the Faith they received from the holy apostles. Their rebellion represented the most dramatic and heroic rejection of the Anglican *Book of Common Prayer*, which had reduced the Holy Sacrifice of the Mass to being a mere *symbolic* feast of sacred communion at a common table, and with Christ being present only spiritually in the members attending. Moreover, further penalties were promulgated for anyone attending the Catholic "administration of sacraments, making of ministers or (priests) in the churches, or any rite at all otherwise done than is set forth in the (Anglican)

Prayer Book." Upon conviction, first offenders went to prison for six months; on the second offense, they went for a year, and for a third offense they were put in prison for life. Fr. Philip Hughes writes on this matter in his three-volume masterpiece *The Reformation in England*: "Such are the first penalties to be enacted in England for the new crime of hearing Mass, or of receiving the sacraments *as they had been received ever since St. Augustine came to convert the English, nearly a thousand years before*" (emphasis added). And Professor S. T. Bindoff, in his book *Tudor England*, explains the evil fruits of this heretical, religious lie that was imposed upon the English:

> The facts themselves are indisputable. Wherever we look, from the Royal Court and the circles of government down to the villages and parish, and whatever type of evidence we choose, from [Anglican chaplain Hugh] Latimer's sweeping denunciations to the detailed facts and figures yielded by the records of royal and diocesan visitations, we are confronted by the same black picture of irreligion, irreverence, and immorality on a terrifying scale.

It appears then that the true religion will always have to resort to spiritual, and sometimes physical, force to maintain its revealed dogmas, morals, and most reverent and beautiful liturgy this side of Heaven. Whereas heretical religions will always find a pretext for violently imposing their false dogmas, evil morals, and wicked rites against the rights of the loyal faithful. The result of this confrontation is very often the so-called "holy wars" that are steeped in barbaric orgies.

Just Warfare

The conditions for a "just war" have been worked out over the centuries, helped greatly by theologians, moralists, popes, and philosophers. A basic truth presupposed about a "just war" is that war, as a human activity, is not in itself an intrinsic evil: that is, not an act forbidden under any circumstances. War is a morally indifferent reality when considered notionally. But a war receives its morality from three characteristics: the nature of the act of war, the intention for which the war is waged, and the conditions—or circumstances—of how the war is conducted. If any one of these conditions is evil, the war is evil. For example, *the act*: Russia's invasion of Afghanistan in the 1980s is an aggression aimed at subjecting another nation to the intrinsically evil ideology of Communism; its war is an internationally criminal act. It is criminal on two accounts: aggression and intention to enslave. *Intention*: Hitler's invasion of Poland had the goal of wresting a seaport from Poland by an unjust war. *The circumstances*: after entering World War II to assist Poland in a just defense against the aggression of Hitler, England decided in 1940 to use "saturation bombing" indiscriminately against wholly defenseless noncombatants, thereby leveling German cities like Dresden, which had no military targets as legitimate objects for attack. These circumstances vitiated England's war effort and made this military activity a crime against humanity, and also set a horrible precedent for future conflicts.

Thus, a necessary requirement for a "just war" is that one party is seen to be morally culpable, while the offended party intends to rectify the crime. It would seem then that only self-defense justifies waging a "just war." This doctrine has been incorporated into the UN Charter. However, if another nation comes to the aid of an ally defending itself against aggression, it is clear that this nation's entrance as a combatant is morally justified, granted that its intentions and method of conducting the war remain morally good. But because the immediate aim of a "just war" seeks to restore international justice by punishing the aggressor, it follows that a "just war" must be regulated by reasonable rules and limitations. In addition, the ultimate aim of a "just war" is to reconcile the warring parties, so that a lasting peace based on justice and goodwill may be achieved. This means that whichever party is defeated, including even the offending one, that party still has the right to live with a recognition of its national dignity, honor, and economic welfare. It is evident from this analysis of a "just war" that absolute pacifism is an irrational position in response to a military aggressor who, by brute force, would deprive an innocent nation of liberty and rule. Such pacifists hold that war can never be justified for any reason or under any circumstances. Hidden beneath this fallacy is an abdication of all moral and social responsibility for the common good and a craven submission to some manner of historical determinism.[250] Pacifism is not peace.[251]

Nowhere does the New Testament exhort mankind to endure the loss of personal and civil liberties—to submit to tyranny—as a means of avoiding destruction and the horrors of war. The Sermon on the Mount was not an invitation to disregard the ugly necessities for preserving civilization. God, our Creator, wills that men live in civility, under public laws dedicated to the requirements of justice. Thus, the Christian, in establishing the conditions for a "just war," founds his conviction on the reasonable principle that a war should be waged only as an assertion of a moral right, a right rooted in the inherent moral claim of every individual and collective society for self-defense.[252] Popes, famous theologians like Sts. Thomas and Augustine, and many outstanding philosophers have upheld this truth. On September 10, 1954, Pope Pius XII said:

---

[250] Fr. John Courtney Murray, S.J., *Morality and Modern Warfare*, 84.

[251] Fr. Joseph F. Costanzo, S.J., *Political and Legal Studies*, vol. 2, 391.

[252] Fr. Costanzo, *Political and Legal Studies*, vol. 2, 392.

One cannot even in principle ask whether atomic, chemical, and bacteriological warfare is lawful other than when it is deemed absolutely necessary as a means of self-defense under the conditions previously stipulated.[253]

For a war of self-defense to be deemed morally legitimate, all seven conditions for a waging of a "just war" must be fulfilled. The war must be: (1) undertaken in a just cause; (2) waged by lawful authority; (3) directed with a just intention; (4) resorted to as the only means remaining to check unjust aggression; (5) engaged in with morally permissible means; (6) assured of a reasonable hope of success; (7) directed toward attaining a good that outweighs the evil it brings about.[254]

Pius XII never allowed his horror of nuclear war to blur his vision or weaken his will. In an address to military doctors, he upheld "the absolute necessity of self-defense against a very grave injustice that touches the community, that cannot be impeded by other means, that nevertheless must be impeded on pain of giving free field in international relations to brutal violence and lack of conscience." In the tragic aftermath of the Hungarian Revolution, when the brutal deeds of Communist violence shocked a complacent world, Pius XII recalled his warning of 1953:

When the threat is made to use atomic arms to obtain concrete demands ... it becomes clear that ... there may

---

[253] Pope Pius XII, "Address to the Eighth Congress of the World Medical Association," September 30, 1954; as given at https://www.vatican.va/content/pius-xii/en/speeches/1954/documents/hf_p-xii_spe_19540930_viii-assemblea-medica.html.

[254] Mark S. Latkovic, "Just-War Theory: Catholic Morality, and the Response to International Terrorism," *The Catholic Faith*, May–June 2002, 33–44; as given at https://www.catholicculture.org/culture/library/view.cfm?id=4644.

come into existence in a nation a situation in which all hope of averting war becomes vain. In this situation, a war of efficacious self-defense against unjust attacks ... cannot be considered illicit.[255]

I accept the conclusion of Fr. John Courtney Murray, S.J., as the only valid Catholic response to the threat of nuclear war: "One cannot ... uphold the simple statement that atomic war as such, without further qualifications, is morally unjustifiable, or that all use of atomic weapons in war is, somehow, in principle evil."[256]

Regression to Barbarism

With the outbreak of the French Revolution in the later 1700s, wars in Europe—especially the Napoleonic wars—became "Peoples' Wars." For the first time, there was the appearance of large "mass armies" raised by conscription, thus making modern wars much more savage and lethal. Second, there was an advance in the scientific propaganda of "social engineering," a tactic developed to whip citizens and nations into a frenzy for helping the conscripted army fight with enthusiasm, and for arousing the hearty support of the population at home. Previously, wars were fought by small armies of professional soldiers who obeyed strict orders. Now "Peoples' Wars" were fought by huge armies of conscripted civilians who, in order to fight with zeal, had to be hoodwinked into imagining they knew what they were fighting for. To meet this need, the modern science of "emotional engineering," as Aldous Huxley has labeled it, was gradually developed.[257] Wars fought by professional soldiers had low death statistics. In 1704, the English had only five

---

[255] *Acta Apostolicae Sedis* (1953), 748–749.
[256] Fr. Murray, *Morality and Modern Warfare*, 79.
[257] Veale, *Advance to Barbarism*, 82.

thousand killed for the whole year. Whereas Napoleon's wars had become mass murders. In the Battle of Borodino alone, he lost forty thousand men, for Napoleon was the most prodigal of men in battle. His Russian campaign started with roughly four to five hundred thousand men; it ended in total defeat with a retreat to Paris, with less than forty thousand of that grand army. At first, the rules of civilized warfare were observed in Peoples' Wars. But this new type of warfare, with its massive armies, inevitably contributed greatly to increased savagery, ferocity, and mortality. Moreover, the propaganda of "emotional engineering" worked on the principle that—to win wars—it was necessary to generate hatred. Thus, a technique of propaganda was devised to arouse frenzied fear in the people, a fear that begot hatred and a condition of public hysteria. The population must "see red" when the enemy was so much as mentioned. It was thought the mass armies would fight better if aroused to a state of blind hatred. Thus, though World War I was fought according to the rules of civilized warfare with limited objectives and limited military means, nevertheless the propaganda of "emotional engineering" succeeded in spreading the big lies that "the enemy is committing atrocities; the enemy has become uncivilized; we must fight to save civilization." The ferocity of the war increased and a bitter, harsh, dictated peace was eventually imposed by the Allies on Germany. This aroused a determination in defeated Germany to reverse that ignoble, unjust treaty, and Adolf Hitler became the vengeful incarnation of that determination. Yet, during World War I, there were no burning of cities, no massacre of noncombatants, and no lack of discipline among the soldiers. There was some looting of civilian property, but this was still a major military crime. One of the worst conditions imposed on Germany was to pay the cost of the war. In previous small wars, the conquered could rather handily do this.

In 1919, Peoples' Warfare had become so fabulously costly that it was simply beyond the capacity of the vanquished to meet this impossible condition. Insistence by the Allies on the performance of this impossible condition only aggravated and perpetuated wartime bitterness. In the end, Germany repudiated this condition, and then the rest of the entire treaty.

By 1933 and 1938, by threats of force, Adolf Hitler rejected one by one the main provisions of the Treaty of Versailles. During this same general time frame, the Soviet Union developed into a great military power. It had far-reaching territorial ambitions, driven by its Communists' lust to conquer the whole world. But between Western Europe and the Soviet Union lay the newly created state of Poland. Poland was a valuable buffer against Russia, and self-preservation linked Poland to Germany. The Polish ruling class depended on their ability to keep Communism in check. But one of the many blunders of the Treaty of Versailles had been to create the so-called Polish Corridor. To rectify this absurdity, Hitler was ready to sacrifice Poland as a buffer state. For their part, the Polish leaders were ready to defend the Corridor by force, although the price of victory would inevitably mean the ultimate absorption of Poland by the Soviet Union, along with the Soviets' own brand of ghastly liquidation. In order to guarantee the integrity of Poland, Great Britain and France fulfilled a treaty they had made to come to Poland's assistance in case it was invaded, and they declared war on Germany when Hitler's Luftwaffe made a blitzkrieg on Poland.

Even before World War II began, and as a result of what it called a "brain wave," the British Air Ministry decided that, in the event of a future war, nonmilitary objectives should be bombed. Thus, during World War II, which started in September 1939, the British Air Ministry made what it called "the Splendid Decision" on May 11, 1940, and therefore early in the war. That decision was to initiate "saturation bombing" against German cities and citizens. Consequently, on May 11, 1940, eighteen Whitley bombers attacked a part of Germany that was significantly outside the area of military operations. Up to that date, only places within the area of military objectives had been attacked by both sides. In his famous book *Advance to Barbarism*, Mr. Veale documents the West's terrible retrogression of civilized humanity towards the worst cruelties as they had been known and practiced by Sennacherib, Genghis Khan, and Tamerlane:

> This raid on the night of May 11, 1940, although in itself trivial, was an epoch-making event since it was the first deliberate breach of the fundamental rule of civilized warfare that hostilities must only be waged against the enemy combatant forces.[258]

It was not until April 1944 that the strict taboo of total silence about the British "Splendid Decision" was made public to the world. Mr. J. M. Spaight, former principal secretary of the British Air Ministry, was permitted to make known the barbaric decision in his book *Bombing Vindicated*. People were shocked by what they read:

> Because we were doubtful about the psychological effect of propagandistic distortion of the truth that it was we who started the strategic bombing offense, we have shrunk from giving our great decision of May 11, 1940, the publicity which it deserved. That, surely, was a mistake. It was a splendid decision. It was as heroic, as self-sacrificing, as Russia's decision to adopt her policy of "scorched earth." It

[258] Veale, *Advance to Barbarism*, 122.

gave Coventry and Birmingham, Sheffield and Southampton, the right to look Kiev and Kharkov, Stalingrad and Sebastopol in the face. Our Soviet Allies would have been less critical of our inactivity in 1942 if they understood what we had done.[259]

It is one of the greatest triumphs of modern social engineering that, in spite of the plain truth of the case, which could never be disguised or even materially distorted, the British public and that of the whole Western world—throughout the blitz period of London (1940–1941)—remained convinced that the entire responsibility for the sufferings which the Londoners were undergoing rested on the German leaders. For the blitz was unanimously accepted as proof positive of the innate wickedness of the Nazi regime. Yet, even Mr. Spaight agrees that Hitler only undertook the bombing of the British civilian population reluctantly, three months after the Royal Air Force had commenced bombing the German civilian population. He states, "Hitler assuredly did not want the mutual bombing to go on."[260] General recognition that it could have been brought to an end at any moment by Britain's ceasing its "saturation bombing" atrocity was never even suspected by the Londoners. Moreover, for the record, it must be stated that the French general staff, as well as the German air staff, rejected the policy of "saturation bombing" as a barbaric activity. It was still their moral conviction that the use of a bombing force should be exercised only to extend the range of artillery-supporting armies in the field. But the new British decision allowed its bombers "to roam" and destroy everyone and everything. As the British Air Force grew in numbers with

---

[259] J. M. Spaight, *Bombing Vindicated*, 74.
[260] Spaight, *Bombing Vindicated*, 74.

the aid of the United States, ever-increasing quantities of bombs continued to descend and decimate civilian populations. Upon Germany alone, 5,000 tons were dropped in 1940, 23,000 tons in 1941, 37,000 tons in 1942, and 180,000 tons in 1943. But the collapse of German morale and fighting spirit, which "saturation bombing" was to effect speedily, never occurred. The Germans fought more fiercely and, after the war, the British admitted that this barbaric policy was a failure because they lost from the air more than fifty thousand men.

The war then became unspeakably horrible. The "Splendid Decision" led to an unparalleled slaughter of human life. As far back as 1932, Winston Churchill recommended to the British government of that date that the Disarmament Conference, then sitting at Geneva, should draw up a code of formal rules to protect noncombatants by restricting bombing to the fighting areas. "Yet," Captain B. H. Liddell Hart soberly commented, "When Mr. Churchill came into power, one of the first decisions of his government was to extend bombing to the noncombatant area."[261] Churchill was not, therefore, announcing any change in policy, but was merely reviewing the past when he told a complacent House of Commons on September 21, 1943, "To achieve this [the extirpation of the Nazi tyranny], there are no lengths of violence to which we will not go."[262] Evidently at this time, in the mind of Mr. Churchill, hatred of the Nazis had obliterated any reasonable consideration for conducting the war in a civilized manner. Mr. Veale makes this pregnant observation about Churchill's decision for barbaric war: "In the light of this remark, and the deeds of violence on the part of the British Air Force which Mr. Churchill approved, it is easy to predict how he would

---

[261] B.H. Liddell Hart, *The Revolution in Warfare*, 79.
[262] Veale, *Advance to Barbarism*, 150.

have fared had the Nazis triumphed and Mr. Churchill been tried by a Nuremberg Tribunal conducted by the Nazis according to the principles and procedure followed in 1945-1946."[263]

Then there was the most unspeakable atrocity—the mass bombing of the city of Dresden by some two thousand heavy bombers on the night of February 13, 1945. At the time of this crime against humanity, the normal population of this large and splendid city was swollen by a terrified flood of women and children who were fleeing from the eastern provinces of Germany, given the advancing Russian barbarians, and who thus hoped to escape death or slavery. The raid on the artistic city of Dresden was useless, because by February 1945, the war had been won. No military purpose remained to be served by such horrific bombing. From the East, the Russian hordes were advancing steadily, irresistibly destroying all before them. In the center, they had reached the Oder River on a wide front on each side of Frankfurt an der Oder, only fifty miles from Berlin. On the right wing, the greater part of East Prussia had been subdued. On the left wing, lower Silesia had been overrun. In the west, the US armies of General Dwight D. Eisenhower were advancing on a wide front to the Rhine. The campaign had now become a mere race with the Russian hordes, a race in which anything the Germans could do to retard the progress of the Russians would be of enormous political value to the Western powers. Despite this fact, the British and Americans, in one of the most cruelly immoral actions of the war, launched a mass air attack on Dresden, a nonmilitary city. The *Times* of London reported:

> Dresden, which had been pounded on Tuesday night by eight hundred of the fourteen hundred heavies sent out

[263] Veale, *Advance to Barbarism*, 130.

by the RAF [Royal Air Force], and was the main object of 1,350 Fortresses and Liberators on the following day, yesterday received its third heavy attack in thirty-six hours. It was the principal target of more than 1,100 US Eighth Army Air Force bombers.[264]

Here are some of the horrendous statistics about those bombings, which the *Times* did not report. On the morning of the fateful February 13, 1945, fast Allied planes were seen flying over the city. The inhabitants of Dresden had no experience of modern air warfare. They watched the planes with curiosity rather than apprehension. Having been so long outside the theater of the war, the city had no antiaircraft defenses. Thus, the Allied planes observed all in complete safety. They must have seen that Dresden and all roads leading to it were filled with dense crowds moving westward away from the frantic orgy, murder, rape, and arson of the Soviet hordes. Some hours after nightfall, the first wave of bombers attacked Dresden. Terrific fires flared up and were still blazing when the second wave arrived shortly after midnight. The resulting slaughter was appalling, since the normal population of the city of some 600,000 had been swollen by the multitude of refugees, mostly women and children, their menfolk having remained behind to defend their homes. Every house in Dresden was filled with these innocents; every public building was crowded with them; many, too, were camping in the streets. Then, the third wave of bombers roared over with their bombs. A unique touch was added to the general horror. The wild animals in the zoological gardens, maddened by the noise and flames, broke loose. These animals, along with terrified groups of refugees, were machine gunned by

---

[264] The *Times* of London, February 16, 1945.

low-flying planes as they tried to escape across the Grosser Garten (Great Garden park), and many bodies riddled by bullets were found later in the park. The number of casualties will probably always remain a subject of speculation, the exact number being known only by God. Most of the victims were refugee women and children. So enormous was the number of the dead that nothing could be done, except to pile them on timber collected from the ruins and there to burn them in batches of 500 each. This lasted over a period of several weeks. Some put the figure of the casualties as high as 250,000. For, at the time of the attacks, over a million people crowded into the city that had no air-raid shelters.

The British press tried to represent these bombings as a great and glorious achievement about which there was no reason for modesty or reticence. Howard Cowan, Associated Press correspondent at the supreme headquarters in Paris, reported thus in *The People*:

Allied war chiefs have made the long-awaited decision to adopt deliberate terror bombing of German populated centers as a ruthless expedient to hasten Hitler's doom. More raids such as those carried out recently by heavy bombers of the Anglo-American Air Force on residential sections of Berlin, Dresden, etc., are in store for the Germans with the avowed purpose of keeping more confusion on Nazi road and rail traffic and to sap German morale.

The all-out air war on Germany became obvious with the unprecedented assault on the refugee-crowded capital two weeks ago, and the subsequent attacks on other cities, jammed with civilians fleeing the Russian tide in the East. The decision may revive protests in some Allied quarters against "uncivilized warfare," but it is likely to be balanced by the satisfaction in certain parts of the continent and Britain.[265]

The indiscriminate bombing of civilians, enemy cities, and civilian property brought about a terrifying and unprecedentedly destructive retrogression to primary and total warfare. But it remained for the war crimes trials, after 1945, to further degrade the process of administering justice. One phase of primary and total warfare had been the liquidation of enemy leaders. Such practices had become unthinkable during the 250 years of civilized European warfare. The abandonment of the civilized military code inevitably facilitated a return to this barbaric, primary warfare. The policy of "saturation bombing" means that, in future wars, no type of destructive technique and terrorization will be withheld. And the war-crimes trials, by demonstrating that the leaders of defeated nations will be exterminated, means that in later world wars there will be a recurrence of this atrocious precedent. If defeat means the liquidation of the leaders of the defeated nations, then these leaders will withhold no means, however deadly and appalling, by which defeat can be avoided. Concerning another bombing, the atom bomb dropped on Hiroshima, Japan, by U.S. forces, Fr. Ronald Knox—a British Catholic priest—confessed himself somewhat disturbed by the thought that tens of thousands were sent to their death without an opportunity to utter a prayer. The same fate fell upon tens of thousands of German civilians. In America, only one voice rose in protest against the immorality of "saturation bombing." That was the voice of Jesuit moral theologian, Fr. John Ford, who wrote an article in *Theological Studies* condemning the practice. Not one Catholic bishop, as far as I can ascertain, spoke

[265] *The People*, February 18, 1945.

up against this criminal act. It was thought to be unpatriotic to do so. But this was false irenicism and wimpish thinking.

Concerning the Nuremberg war trials, the Anglican Rev. William Ralph Inge wrote appropriately:

> I dislike the Nuremberg trials for three reasons. First, trials of the vanquished by the victors are never satisfactory and are generally unfair. Secondly, the execution of political and military leaders of a beaten side by the victors sets a most dangerous precedent.... Thirdly, one of the judges—Russia—ought certainly to have been in the dock and not on the bench.[266]

Britain—which launched the bombing of civilian centers—should also have been in the dock. Then, too, Russia liquidated fifteen thousand Polish officers and leaders in the Katyn Forest. How could such ferocious criminals be expected to administer justice to a vanquished foe? Also, the origin of the war-crimes trials can be traced to the proposal of Stalin, the murderer of untold millions, at the Tehran Conference in late 1943, in which the Soviet premier met with Churchill and President Franklin Roosevelt. It was Stalin, also, who suggested at the same conference that fifty thousand German officers and technicians be liquidated at the end of the war. Well, the chickens that hatched from the eggs of the barbarisms of World War II have already come home to roost. The horrors of the Korean War and the Vietnam Wars have already surpassed those of the Second World War in proportion to the forces engaged. In the December 30, 1952, issue of *Look* Magazine,. U.S. Supreme Court Justice William O. Douglas wrote a sobering account after visiting Korea the previous summer:

[266] Veale, *Advance to Barbarism*, vii.

I had seen the war-battered cities of Europe; but I had not seen devastation until I saw Korea. Cities like Seoul are badly mangled; but a host of towns and villages, like Chorwon on the base of the Iron Triangle, are completely obliterated. Bridges, railroads, dams are blasted.... Misery, disease, pain and suffering, starvation—these are all compounded beyond comprehension.[267]

To many, something more frightful than this appalling picture was the report that the Chinese Reds threatened to impose "the universal principles of justice established at Nuremberg" on the prisoners they captured in Korea from UN forces.[268]

Violence and Terrorism

Just as chapter four describes how violence and force are similar and comparable in certain respects, yet quite different in many others, so now we wish to point out the differences between violence and terrorism, though they are also similar and comparable in certain respects. The major difference between violence and force is that violence is always morally evil, while force is not. For violence degrades man by coercing his freedom, stealing his property, imposing upon him its own thought process, attacking his person, treating him as an enemy, and even taking his life. On the other hand, force is employed to protect rights, punish criminals, assure the security of citizens, repulse aggression, and work for the common good. Yet, in achieving these noble goals, force—in how it functions—often has an accidental similarity to the activity of violence. But when we consider the analogues of

---

[267] As quoted in Veale, *Advance to Barbarism*, xiii.
[268] Veale, *Advance to Barbarism*, xiv.

violence and terrorism, we can clearly see that both are always essentially morally evil. Just as rape and theft are diverse species of sin, and hence always essentially evil, just so violence and terrorism are diverse species of injustice, yet both always essentially crimes, despite their accidental differences. Here we can consider some of these accidental differences.

Terror is a special species of violence, which is its generic parent. The act of terror, in its most brutal and violent manifestation, is directed against innocent victims. Hence, terror is an arbitrary act of violence in which victims are used as instrumental means to the furtherance of some proximate end, for example, the release of confrere terrorists from prison, or the generation of fear and intense anxiety on the part of others. Terrorists employ a variety of means for indiscriminate destruction, such as poison gas, saturation bombing, shelling of population centers of no appreciable military significance, and biochemical and mass-destruction devices. Some of these forms of terrorism have been used by Great Britain and her Western ally—the United States—in World War II, as previously demonstrated, because using deadly violence against noncombatants in wartime is an act of terror. The poor, innocent victims have had no voluntary say or decision that would reduce the probability of their death or injury. Terrorism is also characterized by its surprise, sporadic, and indiscriminate use of deadly violent action against innocent persons. For terrorists, the wanton execution of some innocents will do very well in revengeful reprisal for the capture or execution of some of their own fellow terrorists.

Carlos Marighella, in his *Minimanual of the Urban Guerrilla*, wrote of "terrorism, an arm the revolutionary can never relinquish." He specified some of the terrorists' actions. He urged the "kidnapping of personalities outstanding as artists, sports celebrities, or famous in other fields, but who showed no interest in political affairs, so as to make their agony a useful form of propaganda. He precisely mentioned the kidnapping, and, if necessary, execution of North American residents," helplessly innocent and unarmed. The reason for doing this is to make some point, to achieve some success in the "war of nerves" against the "establishment."[269] Thus, outside of war itself, terrorists commit themselves to the surprise, indiscriminate bombing of banks, embassies, airport facilities, the random downing of commercial aircraft in transit, the hijacking of planes, seajacking of cruise ships, and the taking of hostages to serve as examples. Terrorists make no distinction between criminal violence and their own special type of violence. Whatever they do, however brutal, is justified by the nobility and righteousness of their causes. Terrorism neither barters with its victims nor offers them any escape from deadly coercion or loss. The victims can do nothing to better their chances of liberation, despite their innocence; they depend entirely for their liberation on the terrorists having their demands met. For terrorists are not concerned with changing the conduct of their victims, but they aim to influence others; they seek the world's public awareness of the justice of their cause. Victims are used to demonstrate the urgency of meeting the demands of the terrorists.[270]

In his perceptive article, "Fascism's Philosophy of Violence and the Concept of Terror," A. James Gregor provides these insights on terrorism:

[269] Carlos Marighella, *Minimanual of the Urban Guerrilla*, in A. James Gregor, "Fascism's Philosophy of Violence and the Concept of Terror," in David C. Rapoport and Yonah Alexander, eds., *The Morality of Terrorism*, 152–168.

[270] Gregor, "Fascism's Philosophy of Violence and the Concept of Terror," in Rapoport and Alexander, eds., *The Morality of Terrorism*, 159.

Any individual, or individuals, irrespective of anything they may or may not choose to do, can become the objects of terror. Nor is there any compliance behavior that would reduce the probability of their falling victim to terror. The object of terroristic violence is not a select and proper object. Terroristic violence has as its purpose not coercive sanction directed against culpable parties, but some proximate end. Instrumental terror is employed to impair the functioning of some system or institution. Demonstrative terror is used to bend entire populations to the purpose of others. Prophylactic terror is employed in anticipation of resistance or rebellion. Incidental terror involves those criminal acts—assaults, armed robbery, kidnapping, and so on—that impact upon innocent victims in the service of the perpetrators' pathology, profit or advantage.

One of the most salient traits of terrorism is its *indiscriminate* and *arbitrary* character, in the sense that there is no piece of voluntary behavior that would increase or decrease the probability of finding oneself the object of terror. Terrorist acts are like natural catastrophes—they strike anyone, the guilty and the innocent alike. There are few precautions that one might take to avoid becoming the object of terror. Its onset is incalculable, and its termination unpredictable for those who are its victims.[271]

In contrast, violence is distinguished from terror as being a universal phenomenon, not a sporadic one. We will always have

---

[271] Gregor, "Fascism's Philosophy of Violence and the Concept of Terror," in Rapoport and Alexander, eds., *The Morality of Terrorism*, 159, emphasis original.

violence with us; terror arises against certain specialized political situations. For the most part, violence assaults enemies; terror assaults innocents perhaps even more than enemies. Violence will negotiate terms with its victims, allowing them an opportunity to obtain freedom from captivity and injury; terror does not negotiate with its victims, using them merely to wrest demands from its enemies. Violence is ordered in its attacks; terror is sudden, arbitrary, and indiscriminate. Violence seeks secrecy; terror seeks the limelight and worldwide publicity. Violence has particularized, localized enemies; terror will choose the whole world as its victim. Violence still regards its victims as persons; terror reduces its victims, innocent or otherwise, to being pawns, instruments, objects, symbols, animals, or agents of corruption. Violence works to obtain practical needs; terror aims to instill insecurity, dread, fear, and shock in the whole world. Violence is usually fueled by greed—material and power goals; terror is fueled by a burning ideology that seeks utopia or paradise through the gates of hell. Violence is usually practical and political; terror is often messianically religious. Violence aims to justify, to get even, and punish; terror aims to obliterate, torture, and degrade its enemies. Violence seeks personal satisfaction; terror aims to provoke and enrage the whole world. Violence observes some accepted rules; terror rejects all bourgeois laws in seeking reprisals. Violence makes limited use of technological means to attain its evil goals; terror puts no restrictions on the use of technological means to attain its wicked goals. Violence is often restrained by natural and state laws; terror is unrestrained by such laws, but is guided by the will of its people. These are just some of the phenomenological differences between violence and terrorism as forms of criminal activity. A tabular scheme may help to focus the contrast among their characteristic marks.

Characteristics of Violence	Characteristics of Terror
Violence Is:	*Terror Is:*
Universal, everywhere	Sporadic, for specialized situations
Assault on enemies	Assault on innocents and enemies
Negotiates with victims	Refuses negotiation with victims
Ordered in attack	Sudden, arbitrary, indiscriminate
Seeks secrecy	Seeks limelight, world publicity
Has particular, local enemies	Whole world as enemy
Its victims are still persons	Victims as pawns, symbols, animals
Seeks practical needs	Seeks fear, dread, shock for all
Fueled by greed, power	Fueled by ideological revenge
Practical, political	Religiously messianic
Aims to justify, punish	Aims to torture, degrade, obliterate
Seeks personal satisfaction	Seeks to provoke, enrage world
Observes some rules	Rejects all rules

The Roots of Violence

Characteristics of Violence	Characteristics of Terror
Moderate use of modern weapons	Unlimited use of modern weapons
Restrained by certain laws	Unrestrained, follows will of people
Produces justifiable anger	Produces panic, paralyzing fear

11

THE CHRISTIAN ANSWER TO VIOLENCE

Why is there such a flood of violence and terrorism throughout the world today? Why has a counterculture of hatred and terror replaced the culture of Christian civility and love? The basic reason is that nations have rebelled against God and His Christ. In Christ, we were all invited by God to participate by faith and observance of His laws in the sanctity of the Holy Trinity. "Be ye holy, because I the Lord your God am holy" (Lev. 19:2). But the nations have chosen the darkness of atheism—militant in the East, hedonistic in the West. They have abandoned the kingdom of light for the kingdom of darkness and given their allegiance to the "the prince of this world" (John 12:31), Satan, the violent terrorist *par excellence*. Christ came to establish among men a civilization of holiness, love, and divine justice. But the nations have preferred to return the cultural disease known as the lust for primitive hatred, violence, and terror against human life. Witness the multimillions of innocents slaughtered in wars, butchered in abortion mills, snuffed out in euthanasia programs, and abused in child centers and broken homes. Witness the untold millions dying from diseases willfully brought on by sexual deviancy. Even Christian theologians of liberation have been fascinated by the use of violence and terror to attain a temporal economic utopia, forgetting all about the salvation of souls for eternity. For them, there seems to be a virtuous activity known as "holy violence," even "holy terror," no doubt leading eventually to "holy wars." Just what is the solution to this fascination of modern man for the kingdom of darkness, hatred, violence, and terror?

Christ and His way of life are the solution. For Christ, the Prince of Peace, in His Sermon on the Mount, was not giving men an invitation to disregard the basic necessities of civilization. As the author of human life, He willed that men live civilly under public laws designed to maintain a just social order. Nor was Christ in that sermon merely giving a Christian ethics more heroic than that advanced in the Old Testament. Naturally, there is an ethos in that existence. But we have in the Sermon on the Mount a transvaluation from "above," from the heart of God so great and so revolutionary that this can be expressed only by a complete reversal of man's natural understanding of moral values. Jesus did not come to destroy the law and the prophets, but to fulfill them (Matt. 5:17–18). Hence, His code of holiness does not destroy natural moral values, but rather develops them Godward to their highest fulfillment. With His grace, God builds on human nature to divinize it. Jesus goes straight to the heart of man's problems; He does not any longer simply draw a line between right and wrong, true and false, but He draws a line much deeper in man's conscience—between divine truth and human truth. We have already seen that the taproot of violence is hatred of truth, God's truth. But Christ calls man to a most profound love of God's revelatory truth. He assures man that "the truth shall make you free." Free from what? From slavery to sin and Satan, the Father of Lies, prince of violence, and "murderer from the beginning" (John 8:44). The old moral standards called for "an eye for an eye, a tooth for a tooth" (Matt. 5:38; see Exod. 21:24). But Christ calls for conquering the enemy with deeds of love (Matt. 5:39–48). Forgive, even if it has to be "seventy times seven times" (Matt. 18:22). Of course, this merciful love and forgiveness is never meant to cancel out a person's right to justice in his social, political, cultural, religious, and economic life. Refugees have a right to their homeland, citizens to religious freedom, innocent noncombatants to immunity from attack, and workers to economic freedom, just wages, and safety on the job.

The old commandment said, "Thou shalt not kill" (Exod. 20:13). But Jesus seizes the wickedness expressed by violence and terror and traces it back to its origin in the terrorist's heart. For what breaks out in violence is already present in the hostile resentment, harsh word, and wicked intention. First the heart has to be purged of murderous intentions before violence or terrorism can be eradicated among men. Notice that Jesus did not even mention downright hatred. A brother's irritation, or that he "hath any thing against thee" (Matt. 5:23), is enough to sow the dragon seeds of violence and terrorism. For from irritation against injustice grow suspicion, resentment, hatred, the works of emotional engineering known as lying propaganda, and, finally, the deeds of violence and terrorism. Hence for Christ, even if anyone calls his brother "Thou Fool" (Matt. 5:22), he exposes himself to the fires of Gehenna, whose lord is Satan, the super-violent terrorist.

Old Covenant law used justice as its norm of behavior. As others treat you, so shall you treat them; violence must be returned for violence, evil for evil. But sinners do this. How does such conduct make men imitators of God's love? It does not. So Christ told men, "That is not enough." For as long as a person clings to mere justice alone, he will never be guiltless of injustice. As long as man is entangled in wrong and counter-wrong, blow and counterblow, vengeance and counter-vengeance, aggression and counter-aggression, terrorism and counter-terrorism, he will be permanently trapped in the spiral of escalating barbarism. For passions always extinguish and surpass reasonable moderation. In any case, the claim to vengeance by non-authorized persons or groups is, in itself, the height of *hubris*, for it usurps a right which belongs to God alone. The avenger, the terrorist, the agent of violence tramples justice, never restores it. How can man extricate himself from this vicious circle of mounting violence and terrorism? A new force, superior to man's abilities, must be introduced into human affairs. Man must give up his absolute self-assertion; he must seek utter selflessness. For the peace he seeks is impossible to achieve by himself. It must come from God, from Christ the Prince of Peace, with whom all good is possible. Christ continues:

> You have heard that it hath been said, "Thou shalt love thy neighbor, and hate thy enemy." But I say to you: Love your enemies: do good to them that hate you: and pray for them that persecute and calumniate you: that you may be the children of your Father who is in heaven, who maketh his sun to rise upon the good, and bad, and raineth upon the just and the unjust.... Be you therefore perfect, as also your heavenly Father is perfect. (Matt. 5:43–45, 48)

Again, the Old Law taught man to render love for love, hate for hate. But this rendered love a captive, unfree, for it was leashed to the response of the other. Hence it was trammeled, unsure of itself, uncreative. It was not genuine love, for true love is so all-inclusive that there is no room for any other selfish sentiment. True, full justice is based on untrammeled love, not on emotions; it is independent of the attitude of the other, capable of loving like God when it has apparently solid grounds for hating. Such is the love of Christ for men. For "when we were enemies, we were reconciled to God by the death of his Son" (Rom. 5:10). Such divinely inspired love has the power to unseat and overcome hatred and violence. Here is established a justice that enables a man to look into the heart of his adversary, forgive him wholeheartedly, to accept him as a brother in Christ. Again, the Old Law said to the ancients, "Thou shalt not commit adultery" (Exod. 20:14). But Christ again goes to the heart of the problem: "But I say to you, that whosoever shall look on a woman to lust after her, hath already committed adultery with her in his heart" (Matt. 5:28). Thus, the root of all evil action is seen to be in the attitude of the heart, which is expressed in a glance, a word, an intention. With ethical treaties founded on mere natural justice, adversaries will never be able to extinguish violence, hatred, and terrorism. Only in divine love is the fulfillment of justice and peace historically possible. Christ tells us that man must *risk* love as a response to hatred, charitable deeds as a response to injustices, if he is to attain the goodness and peace promised by Christ. Such love is found only in Christ, as demonstrated in His life, death, and Resurrection as narrated in the New Testament, the testament of perfect love and peace.

Admittedly, the eradication of violence and terrorism is beyond human power. As Fr. Romano Guardini indicates in his masterful work *The Lord*, this must be the work of God inspiring men to cooperate with His grace-filled love:

> To purify the heart so completely that from the very start respect for the dignity of the other controls natural passions; to disarm hatred, surrounding it and overcoming its would-be violence in the perfect freedom of love; to return good for evil, benefit for enmity, all this surpasses human strength.... We are invited to participate in the sanctity of

him whose omnipotence and holiness are contained in the pure freedom of love; hence, of one who stands above good and evil, just and unjust. Truly, this is no longer a question of mere ethics—ethics which made such demands would be immoral—but faith, of self-surrender (by all parties) to a command that is simultaneously a promise, promise of grace, without which all hope of fulfillment would be futile.[272]

In the measure that man returns to God, and cooperates with Him to adhere to and attain His truth and holiness, will he be successful in diminishing—perhaps eradicating—the scourges of violence, terrorism, and, who knows? perhaps even war; certainly uncivilized war.

In his book *The Violence Within*, Paul Tournier gives a very succinct and profound solution to the scourge of violence, barbarism, and terrorism, which points to Christ as the sole Savior:

Christ broke into the vicious circle of violence by taking upon himself the violence of men, and then refusing—though he knew how to be violent!—to pay back violence for violence. He is literally a Savior, as we still call Him without really understanding the significance of the word: a sacred Savior from human violence, breaking its fatal determinism.... The martyrs in the Roman arena, in common with Christian martyrs throughout the ages, were conscious of being identified with Him, of uniting their fate with His in death, transfiguring death into victory over violence.[273]

---

[272] Fr. Romano Guardini, *The Lord*, 79–85.
[273] Paul Tournier, *The Violence Within*, 76.

Appendix

Pope St. John Paul II on Violence

"Human affairs must be dealt with humanely, not with violence. Tensions, rivalries, and conflicts must be settled by reasonable negotiations and not by force. Opposing ideologies must confront each other in a climate of dialogue and free discussion. The legitimate interests of particular groups must also take into account the legitimate interests of the other groups involved, and of the demands of the higher common good. Recourse to arms cannot be considered the right means for settling conflicts. The inalienable human rights must be safeguarded in every circumstance. It is not permissible to kill in order to impose a solution."

—Message for World Day of Peace, January 1,
1979: "To Reach Peace, Teach Peace"

"Admittedly the din of battle dominates history. But it is the respites from violence that have made possible the production of those lasting cultural works that give honor to mankind. Furthermore, any factors of life and progress that may have been found even in wars and revolutions were derived from aspirations of an order other than violence; aspirations of a spiritual nature, such as the will to see recognition given to a dignity shared by all mankind,

The Roots of Violence

and the desire to save a people's soul and its freedom. Where such aspirations were present, they acted as a regulator amid the conflicts; they prevented irreparable breaks; they maintained hope and they prepared a new chance for peace. Where such aspirations were lacking or were impaired in the threat of violence, they gave free play to the logic of destruction, which led to lasting economic and cultural retrogression and the death of whole civilizations."

—Message for World Day of Peace, January 1,
1979: "To Reach Peace, Teach Peace"

"Why is there so much violence today? Perhaps it is necessary to go back farther, to the concepts, to the groups who have proclaimed and inculcated, and who continue to proclaim and inculcate—above all into the minds of the young—a struggle against others; hate for those who think or act differently as ideals of life, and violence as the only means of social and political progress. But violence breeds violence. Hate breeds hate. Both one and the other humiliate and degrade the human person."

—Address to the Regional Government
of Latium (Italy), January 20, 1979

"The Gospels clearly show that, for Jesus, anything that would alter his mission as the Servant of Yahweh was a temptation. He does not accept the position of those who mixed the things of God with merely political attitudes. He unequivocally rejects recourse to violence. He opens his message of conversion to everybody, without excluding the very publicans. The perspective of his mission is much deeper. It consists in complete salvation through a transforming, peacemaking, pardoning, and reconciling love."

—Address to Latin American Episcopate (Puebla), January 28, 1979

"She [the Church] does not need to have recourse to ideological systems in order to love, defend, and collaborate in the liberation of man: at the center of the message of which she is the depositary and herald, she finds inspiration for acting in favor of brother-hood, justice, and peace, against all forms of domination, slavery, discrimination, violence, attacks on religious liberty, and aggression against man, and whatever attacks life."

—Address to the Latin American Episcopate (Puebla), January 28, 1979

"Human rights are being violated in various ways, if in practice we see before us concentration camps, violence, torture, terrorism, and discrimination in many forms.... The common good that authority in the State serves is brought to full realization only when all the citizens are sure of their rights. The lack of this leads to the dissolution of society, opposition by citizens to authority, or a situation of oppression, intimidation, violence and terrorism, of which many examples have been provided by the totalitarianisms of this century."

—Encyclical *Redemptor Hominis* March 4, 1979

"Before the phenomenon of blind violence and destructive ter-rorism which still troubles Italian society and spreads among its members agonizing alarm and paralyzing fear, the Catholic Church, while it turns minds away from the hallucinating temptation of an equally provoking and oppressive retaliation, is concerned to foster in hearts—of the young in the first place—openness to ide-als of freedom, justice, brotherly solidarity, love, and disinterested service of the common good."

—Audience to the Ambassador of Italy to the Holy See, June 25, 1979

"But Christianity does not command us to close our eyes to difficult human problems. It does not permit us to neglect and refuse to see unjust social or international situations. What Christianity does forbid is to seek solutions to these situations by the ways of hatred, by the murdering of defenseless people, by the methods of terrorism. Let me say more. Christianity understands and recognizes the noble and just struggle for justice, but Christianity is decisively opposed to fomenting hatred and to promoting or provoking violence or struggle for the sake of struggle. The command, 'Thou shalt not kill,' must be binding on the conscience of humanity, if the terrible tragedy and destiny of Cain is not to be repeated.... Secondly, peace cannot be established by violence, peace can never flourish in a climate of terror, intimidation, and death. It was Jesus himself who said so: 'All who take the sword will perish by the sword.' This is the word of God, and it commands this generation of violent men to desist from hatred and violence and to repent.... To all of you who are listening I say, do not believe in violence; do not support violence. It is not the Christian way. It is not the way of the Catholic Church. Believe in peace, and forgiveness, and love; for they are of Christ. Communities who stand together in their acceptance of Jesus' supreme message of love, expressed in peace and reconciliation, and in their rejection of all violence, constitute an irresistible force for achieving what many have come to accept as impossible and destined to remain so.

"Now I wish to speak to all men and women engaged in violence. I appeal to you, in language of passionate pleading. On my knees, I beg you to turn away from the paths of violence and to return to the ways of peace. You may claim to seek peace. I, too, believe in justice and seek justice. But violence only delays the day of justice. Violence destroys the work of justice. Further violence in Ireland will only drag down to ruin the land you claim to love and the values you claim to cherish. In the name of God I beg you, return to Christ, who died so that men might live in forgiveness and peace. He is waiting for you, longing for each one of you to come to him so that he may say to each of you, 'Your sins are forgiven; go in peace.'"

—Homily at Drogheda (Ireland), September 29, 1979

"Violence flourishes in lies and needs lies. It seeks to gain respectability in the eyes of the world by pretexts that have nothing to do with its reality and are often contradictory. What would one say of the practice of combatting or silencing those who do not share the same views by labeling them as enemies, attributing to them hostile intentions, and using skillful and constant propaganda to brand them as aggressors? Selective indignation, sly insinuations, the manipulation of information, the systematic discrediting of opponents—their persons, intentions, and actions—blackmail, and intimidation: these are forms of nontruth working to develop a climate of uncertainty aimed at forcing individuals, groups, governments, and even international organizations to keep silence in helplessness and complicity, to surrender their principles in part or to react in an irrational way. All these attitudes are equally capable of favoring the murderous game of violence and of attacking the cause of peace.... Restoring peace means, in the first place, calling by their proper names acts of violence in all their forms. Murder must be called by its proper name: murder is murder; political or ideological motives do not change its nature, but are, on the contrary, degraded by it. The massacre of men and women, whatever their race, age, or position, must be called by its proper name. Torture must be called by its proper name; and, with the appropriate qualifications, so must all forms of oppression and exploitation of man by man, of man by the State, of one people by another people.

The Roots of Violence

The purpose of doing so is not to give oneself a clear conscience by means of loud all-embracing denunciations—this would no longer be calling things by their proper names—not to brand and condemn individuals and peoples, but to help to change peoples' behavior and attitudes, in order to give peace a chance again.... The Gospel places in striking relief the bond between falsehood and murderous violence, in the words of Christ: 'As it is, you want to kill me when I tell you the truth as I have learned it from God.... What you are doing is what your father does.... The devil is your father, and you prefer to do what you father wants. He was a murderer from the start; he was never grounded in the truth; there is no truth in him at all; when he lies he is drawing on his own store, because he is a liar, and the father of lies.' This is why I was able to say with such conviction at Drogheda in Ireland and why I now repeat. 'Violence is a lie, for it goes against the truth of our faith, the truth of our humanity.... Do not believe in violence; do not support violence. It is not the Christian way. It is not the way of the Catholic Church. Believe in peace and forgiveness and love; for they are of Christ.'"

—Message for the World Day of Peace January 1, 1980: "Truth, the Power of Peace"

"I learned that a young Christian ceases to be young, and has no longer been a Christian for a long time, when he lets himself be won over by doctrines or ideologies that preach hatred and violence ... when he adopts the belief that the only hope of improving society is to promote struggle and hatred between social classes, that it is to be found in the utopia of a classless society, which very soon reveals itself as the creator of new classes."

—Homily at Belo Horizonte (Brazil), July 1, 1980

"The truth is that, in the general definition of violence, it is not possible to prescind from the idea of law, as that concrete system in which human values, including the supreme one, are ordered among themselves and with regard to the common end of the subjects. The true concept of law, the fundamental concept of all law, is that of an 'order of justice among men.' The first, most radical—even though embryonic—order of justice among men is natural law, which makes the human person the first foundation and the ultimate end of all human life associated politically. That law from which the various positive systems spring, in the variety and changeability of historical situations. That law which, before and even more than the police, ensures these systems their ethical validity, their continual perfectibility, and their growing communicability with regard to vaster and vaster civilizations up to the universal one. Well, violence in general cannot be defined otherwise than as the violation of such an order of justice."

—Address to the National Meeting of the Union of
Italian Catholic Jurists, December 6, 1980

"Unfortunately, in some nations such as Spain, Italy, Ireland, and elsewhere, there is still a very serious danger of terrorism and violence, this real war waged against defenseless people and institutions, moved by obscure centers of power, which do not realize that the order which they hope to reach through violence cannot but call further violence.... And an order that came into being on the ruins and killings of violence would be the peace of the cemetery."

—Address to the Sacred College of Cardinals, December 22, 1980

"Humanity is not destined to self-destruction. Clashes of ideologies, aspirations, and needs can and must be settled and resolved

The Roots of Violence

by means other than war and violence.... Let us not repeat the past, a past of violence and destruction.... Humanity owes it to itself to settle differences and conflicts by peaceful means."

—Address at the Peace Memorial in Hiroshima (Japan), February 26, 1981

"In this context, I feel it my duty to raise my voice against the serious and still unsolved phenomenon of international terrorism, which is a permanent threat to the internal and international peace of peoples. President Sadat, a courageous promoter of international understanding and of the advancement of his ancient, noble, and strong people, has fallen a victim to it. There have been innumerable other victims, all over the world, struck down when carrying out their duty and made the object of unspeakable, cowardly actions, which are really and truly acts of murderous war, covered by the tacit complicity of a few and by the anonymity of the cities which are becoming dehumanized and are disintegrating. Also the President of the United States escaped from one of these attacks. Nor can I forget my personal experience, on the afternoon of May 13 [1981] in St. Peter's Square, when I escaped death by the evident protection of the Lord, granted to me through the intercession of the Blessed Virgin, on the anniversary of her apparition at Fatima. *Misericordiae Domini quia non sumus consumpti* [By God's mercy, we are not consumed], I repeat also today. Reason is disturbed and dismayed when it seeks a motive for such acts, which spring from roots which are indeed unknown, but which can always be traced to hatred, ideological confusion, and the attempt to sow uncertainty and fear in international life."

—Address to the Sacred College of Cardinals, December 22, 1981

"In the first place, I recall the seriously tense situations in several Central American countries, in which the number of victims caused by actions of repression or guerrilla warfare continues to grow with a macabre monthly balance sheet, as if it were an uncontrollable epidemic of violence. I return to the situation in the Middle East in which an already fragile truce is continually threatened by constantly renewed acts of violence and by the rigidity of intransigent positions. I mention a wound still open of internal terrorism, which touches particularly, albeit in different contexts and for different reasons, regions which are so dear to us and which we love so much. I am thinking here of Northern Ireland; I am thinking also of what is happening in Italy."

—Address to the Diplomatic Corps to the Holy See, January 16, 1982

"Whatever the roots of terrorist action may be, whatever the attempts to justify it, we can only repeat once again and always: *'Terrorism is never justified in a civilized society.'* It is a sophisticated relapse into savagery, anarchy. It is always an expression of hate, of ideological confusion, with the aim of sowing uncertainty and fear in national and international life. It wishes to justify its ends, and at times poor ends, by means unworthy of man. It attacks property and a valuable patrimony without any regard for the rights that people or society legitimately have to them. Above all, and this cannot be accepted under any pretext, it attacks *in a cowardly way*—in the form of kidnapping, torture, or murder—the liberty and *the human life of defenseless people* who have nothing to do with the cause in question and who are simply a symbol of a responsibility or a power that they oppose" (emphases added).

—Message to the World Christian Democratic Union, February 19, 1982

"In view of the manipulation of which he may feel himself to be the object through drugs, exasperated sexuality, and violence, the young Christian will not seek methods of action that lead him to the spiral of terrorism. The latter would plunge him into the same evil he criticizes and rejects, or into a worse evil yet. He will not fall into insecurity and demoralization, he will not take refuge in the specious paradises of evasion or indifference. Neither drugs, nor alcohol, nor sex, nor a resigned passivity devoid of criticism—what you call 'addiction to the past'—are an answer to evil."

—Address to the Youth in Madrid (Spain), November 3, 1982

"Likewise the Church takes to heart the fate of those who are subjected to torture, whatever be the political regime, for nothing in its eyes can justify this degradation which unfortunately is often accompanied by barbaric and repulsive savagery. Likewise, it cannot remain silent over the criminal action that consists in making a certain number of persons disappear without trial, leaving their families in cruel uncertainty besides."

—Address to the Diplomatic Corps to the Holy See, February 15, 1983

"The ecclesiastical community is and should be leaven in the world. It is a most potent seed of unity and peace. There are, unfortunately, divisive forces that loom threateningly over your countries. Tensions abound, also clashes which forebode graver conflicts, the doors having been opened to a devastating torrent of violence in every form. How many lives have been mown down cruelly and pointlessly! People who have a right to peace and justice are terrorized by inhuman strife, hatred, and vengeance. Honest, hard-working people have lost their peace and safety."

—Address to the Bishops of the Episcopal Secretariat of Central America (SEDAC) in San Jose Costa Rica, March 2, 1983

"In the search for a greater justice and the elevation of your position, *you cannot let yourselves be carried away by the temptation to violence,* armed guerrilla warfare, or selfish class struggle, because this is not the path of Jesus Christ nor of the Church, nor of your Christian faith. These are those who are interested in making you abandon your work, to take up the arms of hatred and of struggle against your brothers. You must not follow them. To what does this path of violence lead? Undoubtedly, it will increase hatred and the distance between social groups; it will increase the social crisis of your people; it will increase tensions and conflicts, to the point of unacceptable bloodshed, as in fact has already occurred. With these methods, completely contrary to the love of God, to the teachings of the Gospel and of the Church, you will render impossible the achievement of your noble aspirations" (emphasis added).

—Address to the "Campesinos" of Central
America, Panama, March 3, 1983

"It is urgent to bury the violence that has claimed so many victims in this and in other nations. How? With a true conversion to Christ. With a reconciliation capable of bringing together those who are divided today by political, social, economic, and ideological fences. With mechanisms and instruments of authentic participation in the economic and social fields, with the possibility offered to everyone to have access to the goods of the earth, with the possibility to fulfill himself in work; in a word, with the application of the social doctrine of the Church. It is in all this that a valid and generous effort in favor of justice is inserted, a justice which can never be prescinded from. All this in a climate renouncing violence. The Sermon on the Mount is the 'Magna Carta' of Christianity."

—Homily at San Salvador (El Salvador), March 6, 1983

The Roots of Violence

"To this problem [outrageous injustice] is added another of equal gravity: recent history shows that frequently, whether through misguided idealism, or ideological pressure, or impelled by interests of a party, or of systems within the power struggle, many young people yield to the temptation of fighting injustice with violence. And by trying to suppress injustice with more violence, they unleash a process that saddens us all."

—Address to Assembly of CELAM, Port-au-Prince (Haiti), March 9, 1983

"The events of recent years prove, however, that solutions have been sought rather along the path of violence, by imposing guerrilla warfare which, in San Salvador alone, has already claimed tens of thousands of victims, including Archbishop Oscar Romero. Such warfare is carried on in large measure with the help of foreign forces and of arms supplied from abroad against the will of the vast majority of the society that desires, on the contrary, peace and democracy."

—General Audience, March 16, 1983

"Yes, for the entire world! May they find a place in our prayer those men and women, wherever they may be, who suffer from famine or other disasters, from the ravages of war, from the movement of populations; those who are the victims of terrorism, whether political or not, which strikes indiscriminately at the innocent; the victims of hatred, various forms of oppression, injustices of all kinds; those who are kidnapped, imprisoned illegally, tortured, condemned without recourse to justice; all those who suffer intolerable attacks on their human dignity and fundamental rights, who are prevented from expressing themselves freely in thought and in action, who are humiliated in their legitimate national aspirations."

—Address at Lourdes (France), August 14, 1983

"Yet another grave act of violence has struck public opinion this morning: Mrs. Indira Gandhi, the prime minister of India, fell victim to assassination. A new and very sad link is added to the chain of atrocities that stain the world with blood, arousing horror and dismay in everyone."

—General Audience, October 31, 1984

"I exhort you to offer a special heartfelt prayer to the Lord for all those who have died from violence. Unfortunately, they are many, and in many regions of the world! The heart is oppressed at the thought of so much human blood spilled, so much suffering, so many tears. Even these past days have been ruined by sad news. I am thinking of Mrs. Indira Gandhi, prime minister of India, who was assassinated yesterday in New Delhi; I am thinking of the Polish priest, Fr. Jerzy Popieluszko, whose tragic death has touched the world; I am thinking of the people who have met death in the recent uprisings in Chile, the victims of the repressions in South Africa, and all the numerous victims of violence in so many other countries in the world. May the great and merciful God give peace to their immortal souls and grant the living to understand that not with violence but with love will a future be built that is worthy of man."

—Angelus, November 1, 1984

"We like to affirm our solidarity ... with the widows and orphans who mourn their husbands and fathers, who were treacherously snatched from their affection and who never returned home ... with all the victims of violence, recalling especially the Italian families grieving over the tragic happening the day before yesterday on the Naples-Milan train and extending a word of comfort to the many who were injured ... with those struggling to escape from the toils of drugs, violence, and criminal organizations ... with those who are subjected to forms of psychological violence which profane the inner sanctuary of the conscience, ignobly attacking personal dignity."

—Christmas Message, December 25, 1984

"At the dawn of this new year, there unfortunately continue to arrive from various parts of the world echoes of wars and violence, in contrast with the aspirations and proposals we recently renewed on the World Day of Peace. At the very moment when it is raging against defenseless people who have consecrated their lives to the service of God in the most tried and needy brethren, violence manifests its blindness, its sterility, its foreignness to man."

—General Audience, January 9, 1985

"But we must also discourage violence under all its aspects, including that perpetrated against political prisoners, secretly and without restraint, as though it were a matter left to the arbitrary discretion of the powers, even under the pretext of security, in concentration camps, in prisons, in other places of confinement. There are cases where they are set upon in an ignoble way by those who are willing to go so far as the complete destruction of their personality. This is the disgrace of our humanity. There must be at least a denunciation of these deeds, a very clear condemnation on the part of international opinion, and visiting rights for humanitarian agencies legitimately recognized for this purpose."

—Address to the Diplomatic Corps to the Holy See, January 12, 1985

"You rightly feel—you must feel it always—the longing for a more just and firm society; but do not follow those who affirm that social injustices disappear only through class hatred or recourse to violence or other anti-Christian means. Only conversion of heart can assure a change of structures to lead to a new world, a better world. 'To put one's trust in violent means, in the hope of restoring more justice, is to become the victim of a fatal illusion: *violence begets violence and degrades man.* It mocks the dignity of man in the person of the victims and it debases that same dignity among those who practice it'" (emphasis original).

—Homily at Mass for Young People in Lima (Peru), February 2, 1985

"Painfully it must be recognized that there are still too many places —on the map of the world—where human rights are denied or violated under the form of the most stringent oppression; where places of torture, segregation camps, and camps of inhuman labor continue to reap innumerable victims, often silenced and forgotten; where ideologies that instill hatred, violence, and aggression do not cease to deceive or poison societies; where numerous wars of differing extension and duration, but with an ever greater force of destruction, continue to sow ruin and drench with blood various parts of the world."

—Easter Message, April 7, 1985

"I am following with concern the news of the liner *Achille Lauro*, hijacked the day before yesterday off the coast of Alexandria, Egypt. I cannot help but express my strongest, saddest criticism of this serious act of violence against innocent and defenseless persons. It is a deed that arouses dismay and condemnation in all right-thinking men; it is not by recourse to violence that one can find a just solution to the problems. Violence only generates violence."

—General Audience, October 9, 1985

The Roots of Violence

"The coming feast of Christmas makes ever more alive our attachment to that land where Jesus, the Prince of Peace and Love, was born. That land cannot continue to be a theater of violence, opposition, and injustice, with suffering for those peoples to whom I feel particularly close. Let us address our prayer to God Almighty that He may inspire all the parties involved, and those who are in a position to collaborate, to bring an end to this violence and to find peaceful solutions."

—Angelus, December 20, 1987

"At the same time, reason itself still pleads that violence not be accepted as the solution to violence. (Violence is not overcome by violence.) But that it must give way to reason, mutual trust, sincere negotiations, and fraternal love. In the present context of apartheid, a call to conversion becomes ever more relevant and necessary for your people. The only adequate solution to the problem is the conversion of hearts."

—Address to the Bishops of Southern Africa, November 27, 1987

SELECTED BIBLIOGRAPHY

Alexander, Yonah. *Terrorism in Italy*. New York: Crane, Russak, 1979.

Antonio, Gene. *The Aids Cover-Up*. San Francisco: Ignatius Press, 1986.

Aquinas, St. Thomas. *Summa Theologica*, Vol. II. New York: Benziger, 1948.

Arendt, Hannah. *Eichmann in Jerusalem*. Middlesex, England: Penguin, 1965.

——. *On Violence*. New York: Harcourt, Brace & World, 1970.

Becker, Jillian. *Hitler's Children*. London: Panther Books, 1987.

Bell, J. B. *Transnational Terror*. Palo Alto, CA: Hoover Institute, 1975.

Bell, J. Bowyer. *A Time of Terror*. New York: Basic Books, 1931.

Bindoff, S.T. *Tudor England*. London: Pelican, 1952.

Bocca, Giorgio. *Il Terrorismo Italiano 1970–1980*. Milan: Rizzoli, 1978.

Bolt, Robert. *A Man for All Seasons*. New York: Random House, 1962.

Caute, David. *Essential Writings of Karl Marx*. London: Panther, 1967.

Chaliand, Gerard. *The Palestinian Resistance*. London: Penguin, 1972.

Contemporary Terrorism: Selected Readings. Gaithersburg, MD: International Association of Chiefs of Police, 1978.

Cotta, Sergio. *Perche La Violenza?* L'Aquila, Italy: L.U. Japadre, 1978.

Davies, Michael. *Cranmer's Godly Order.* Devon, UK: Augustine Publishing, 1976.

De Jaegher, R. J. *The Enemy Within.* Bombay: Pandra, 1969.

De Jouvenel, Bertrand. *Power: The Natural History of Its Growth.* London: Hutchinson, 1952.

De Unamuno, Miguel. *The Tragic State of Life in Men and Nations.* Princeton, NJ: Princeton University Press, 1972.

Dobson, Christopher, and Payne, Ronald. *The Carlos Complex.* London: Coronet Books/Hodder & Stoughton, 1977.

——. *The Terrorists.* New York: Facts on File, 1979.

Fairlie, Henry. *The Seven Deadly Sins Today.* London: Notre Dame Press, 1979.

Fanon, Frantz. *The Wretched of the Earth.* New York: Grove Press, 1968.

Girard, René. *La Violenze E Il Sacro.* Milan: Adelphi, 1986.

Guiso, Giannino. *La Condanna Di Aldo Moro.* Milan: Sugar, 1979.

Halpern, Ernst. *Terrorism in Latin America.* London: Sage Publications, 1976.

Hart, B. H. Liddell. *The Revolution in Warfare,* London: Faber, 1946.

Heiden, Konrad. *Der Fuehrer.* Boston: Houghton, Mifflin, 1944.

Hughes, Philip. *The Reformation in England.* 3 vols. London, 1950.

Huxley, Francis. *Affable Savages.* New York: Capricorn, 1966.

Jaspers, Karl. *Nietzsche and Christianity.* Chicago: Regnery, 1961.

Jules, Henry. *Jungle People.* New York: Vintage Books, 1964.

Kaufmann, Jacques. *L'Internationale Terroriste.* Paris: Plon, 1976.

Kaufmann, Walter. *The Portable Nietzsche.* New York: Viking, 1967.

Labin, Suzanne. *La Violence Politique.* Paris: France-Empire, 1978.

Lean, Garth. *Brave Men Choose.* London: Blandford Press, 1961.

Lilienthal, Alfred M. *What Price Israel?* Chicago: Regnery, 1953.

——. *The Other Side of the Coin.* New York: DevinAdair, 1965.

Lipper, Elinor. *Eleven Years in Soviet Prison Camps.* Chicago: Regnery, 1951.

Lowrie, Robert. *Primitive Society.* New York: Liveright, 1970.

Lyons, Eugene. *Workers' Paradise Lost.* New York: Funk, 1967.

Mackiewicz, Joseph. *The Katyn Murders.* London: Hollis & Carter, 1951.

Malinowski, Bronislaw. *Crime and Custom in Savage Society.* New York: Harcourt, Brace, 1926.

——. *Sex and Repression in Savage Society,* New York: Meridian, 1955.

May, Rollo. *Power and Innocence.* New York: W.W. Norton, 1972.

Meese, Edwin. *Attorney General's Commission on Pornography: Final Report,* vols. I and II. Washington, DC: U.S. Department of Justice, 1986.

Merleau-Ponty, Maurice. *Humanism and Terror.* Boston: Beacon Press, 1969.

Miceli, Fr. Vincent P., *The Gods of Atheism.* New Rochelle, NY: Arlington, 1971.

Mills, C. Wright. *The Power Elite.* New York: Oxford University Press, 1956.

Netanyahu, Benjamin, ed. *Terrorism: How the West Can Win.* New York: Avon Books, 1986.

Nietzsche, Friedrich. *The Gay Science.* New York: Viking, 1954.

——. *Beyond Good and Evil.* Chicago: Regnery, 1966.

Nugent, Christopher. *Masks of Satan.* London: Sheed and Ward, 1983.

O'Ballance, Edgar. *Language of Violence.* San Rafael, CA: Presidio Press, 1979.

Ponsonby, Arthur. *Falsehood in Wartime.* London: Allen & Unwin, 1928.

Pope John Paul II. *The Theme of Violence*. Vatican City: Justitia and Pax, 1978.

Possony, Stefan, and Francis Bouchey. *International Terrorism: The Communist Connection*. Washington, DC: The American Council For World Freedom, 1978.

Rapoport, David C., and Yonah Alexander, eds. *The Morality of Terrorism*. New York: Pergamon Press, 1982.

Roberts, Arch E. *The Anatomy of Revolution*. New York: Harold Pratt, 1968.

Scott, David A. *Pornography: Its Effects on the Family, Community and Culture*. Washington, DC: Free Congress Foundation, 1985.

Shirer, William L. *The Rise and Fall of the Third Reich*. New York: Simon and Schuster, 1960.

Smith, Colin. *Carlos: Portrait of a Terrorist*. New York: Sphere, 1976.

Sorel, Georges. *Reflections on Violence*. New York: Collier, 1961.

Spaight, J. M. *Bombing Vindicated*. London: Bles, 1944.

Sterling, Claire. *The Terror Network*. New York: Holt, Rinehart, and Winston, 1981.

———. *The Time of the Assassins*. New York: Holt, Rinehart, and Winston, 1983.

Stevenson, William. *Ninety Minutes at Entebbe*. New York: Bantam, 1976.

Stoor, Anthony. *Human Aggression*. New York: Bantam, 1968.

Tinnen, David, and Dag Christensen. *The Hit Team*. New York: Deli, 1977.

Tournier, Paul. *The Violence Within*. San Francisco: Harper & Row, 1978.

Trevor-Roper, H. R. *The Last Days of Hitler*. New York: Macmillan, 1947.

Turner, Victor. *The Drums of Affection*. London: Oxford, 968.

Utley, Freda. *The High Cost of Vengeance*. Chicago: Regnery, 1949.

Vaillant, George. *The Aztecs of Mexico.* New York: Pelican, 1950.

Veale, F.J.P. *Advance to Barbarism.* Appleton, WI: C.C. Nelson, 1953.

Wardlaw, Grant. *Political Terrorism.* London: Cambridge, 1982.

Watson, Francis. *Wallenstein.* London: Chatto & Windus, 1938.

Weber, Max. *Politics as a Vocation.* 1921.

Whilhelmsen, Frederick, ed. *Seeds of Anarchy: A Study of Campus Revolution.* Dallas: Argus Academic Press, 1969.

Wilkinson, Paul. *Terrorism and the Liberal State.* London: Macmillan, 1977.

About the Author

Fr. Vincent P. Miceli, S.J. (1915–1991), earned his doctoral degree in contemporary philosophy from Fordham University while studying under Dietrich von Hildebrand. He taught at Loyola University, Pontifical Gregorian University, Pontifical University of St. Thomas, and Christendom, among other colleges. He is the author of several books and wrote extensively for journals and magazines such as *L'Osservatore Romano*, *Homiletic and Pastoral Review*, and *National Catholic Register*. Fr. Miceli made innumerable appearances on national TV and radio programs to promote the Faith and cohosted the syndicated radio program *Where Catholics Meet*.

Sophia Institute

Sophia Institute is a nonprofit institution that seeks to nurture the spiritual, moral, and cultural life of souls and to spread the gospel of Christ in conformity with the authentic teachings of the Roman Catholic Church.

Sophia Institute Press fulfills this mission by offering translations, reprints, and new publications that afford readers a rich source of the enduring wisdom of mankind.

Sophia Institute also operates the popular online resource CatholicExchange.com. *Catholic Exchange* provides world news from a Catholic perspective as well as daily devotionals and articles that will help readers to grow in holiness and live a life consistent with the teachings of the Church.

In 2013, Sophia Institute launched Sophia Institute for Teachers to renew and rebuild Catholic culture through service to Catholic education. With the goal of nurturing the spiritual, moral, and cultural life of souls, and an abiding respect for the role and work of teachers, we strive to provide materials and programs that are at once enlightening to the mind and ennobling to the heart; faithful and complete, as well as useful and practical.

Sophia Institute gratefully recognizes the Solidarity Association for preserving and encouraging the growth of our apostolate over the course of many years. Without their generous and timely support, this book would not be in your hands.

www.SophiaInstitute.com
www.CatholicExchange.com
www.SophiaInstituteforTeachers.org

Sophia Institute Press is a registered trademark of Sophia Institute.
Sophia Institute is a tax-exempt institution as defined by the
Internal Revenue Code, Section 501(c)(3). Tax ID 22-2548708.